GENDERING THE MIDDLE AGES

Gendering the Middle Ages

EDITED BY
Pauline Stafford and Anneke B. Mulder-Bakker

A *Gender and History* special issue

Copyright © Blackwell Publishers Ltd 2001

First published as a special issue of Gender and History Vol. 12, No. 3, 2000
Reprinted 2005

Blackwell Publishers Ltd
108 Cowley Road
Oxford OX4 1JF
UK

Blackwell Publishers Inc
350 Main Street
Malden, Massachusetts 02148
USA

British Library Cataloguing in Publication Data
A CIP catalogue record for this book is available from the British Library

Library of Congress Cataloging-in-Publication Data has been applied for

ISBN: 0-631-22651-6

Typeset in Great Britain
by Advance Typesetting
Printed in Great Britain by Athenaeum Press Ltd., Gateshead, Tyne & Wear

This book is printed on acid-free paper

Contents

Introduction

Pauline Stafford and Anneke B. Mulder-Bakker

The purpose of this Special Issue is twofold: to bring to the attention of a wider audience working on gender a cross-section of the excellent work being done by medieval historians, and – if that is necessary – to bring to the attention of those taking a gendered approach to medieval studies the importance of *Gender and History* in this field. As last year's Special Issue, Retrospect and Prospect, pointed out, *Gender and History* has, with some significant and important exceptions, attracted relatively few articles on the medieval period. This is in no way a reflection of the strength of interest in gender among medievalists. Sexuality, Gender and Women's Studies have, for example, consistently been among the larger index entries of the programme of the International Medieval Congress in Leeds, the largest gathering of European medieval scholars. Many of the papers and sessions have presented the work of young scholars and graduate students and it is a particular pleasure to be able to include here work by such young scholars as Katherine Lewis, and of graduate students in collaboration with more established authors. Gender has become a vital question, in every sense, in medieval studies; we hope that this Special Issue represents some of this vitality.

The Special Issue was edited from the European base of the Gender and History collective. As editors, we thus deliberately excluded the work of the multitude of those working in this field outside Europe, most notably in North America. (Rosalynn Voaden, who spent many years in York and Oxford, is in this company an honorary European.) This exclusion is no measure of the editors' esteem for this work. Many of those at the forefront of the field have worked and published there. But the European contribution has been equally significant, and a deliberate concentration on it has allowed us to bring to the attention of an Anglophone audience some authors and work which may be less accessible and familiar. If we have one regret, it is that men and masculinity are not as well represented as women and femininity. In this respect, medieval studies reflects the relatively early stage of development of this area in other historical periods. A number of recent collections of essays indicate growing interest. Unfortunately it proved impossible to find a suitable reviewer to do them justice, since almost everyone in the field had published in one or other volume. We did, however, manage to persuade one of those authors, Conrad Leyser, to write here. Given the importance of the middle ages in fashioning some of the fundamental models of western masculinity, most obviously the chivalric ideal, there is clearly much exciting work to come in this field.

'Gendering the middle ages' is no easy task, not least because the so-called middle ages embraced around a thousand years, a period which saw enormous changes over the wide area of western Europe to which this periodisation is normally applied. Two contributions tackle, directly or indirectly, this question of periodisation from a gendered perspective. 'When did the middle ages end' is a question to which there are many answers; but an economic and social historian would certainly point to the shifts and changes in the wake of the Black Death as central. Steve Rigby, reviewing recent work, indicates how far a gender-aware perspective is necessary. That work has questioned whether these fundamental demographic and economic changes affected men and women equally, and whether they can be understood without taking the activity of both genders into account. Julia Smith, a member of a large European Science Foundation-funded project on the 'Transformation of the Roman World', asks how far the critical transformation which occurred at the beginning of the middle ages can be understood if the work of such projects remains gender blind. Gender blindness is, of course, a feature of many of the older narratives of western history. Correcting it is a pressing need for the early middle ages. Their narratives and paradigms were largely created in the period of emerging nation states, which looked to these centuries of perceived origins for validation and naturalisation.

The middle ages in general, and the early middle ages in particular, saw the transmission and transformation of the Greco-Roman and Judaeo-Christian/Islamic inheritance of the Near East. Although this was a common European inheritance, these traditions were not necessarily appropriated everywhere in the same way. Several essays address questions arising from this appropriation and transformation in a Byzantine, or a comparative Byzantine/western European framework: those of Leslie Brubaker and Helen Tobler, Smith, and Eva Synek, who refuses to confine her gendered view of canon law to western authors. Jinty Nelson's call for more comparative work here must be taken seriously. It should be extended throughout eastern Europe. The new ideals of Christianity, not least asceticism, posed a challenge to Greco-Roman ideas, as Kate Cooper and Conrad Leyser argue in relation to ancient notions of masculinity. That potential was both realised and side-stepped in key debates among Christian leaders. Side-stepped, but not neutralised. As Synek's subtle reading of the development of early canon law makes clear, asceticism retained its ability to subvert simple gender divisions. It produced other categorisations which did not easily map on to those of gender. Synek's important chapter demonstrates the need to bring gender into the study of the most conservative of traditional areas, not least because the interpretation of canon law still has impact on the daily lives of so many.

Another common feature of the middle ages was the central role of dynastic, familial power, with all that means for public/private divisions and for women. Women's fertility was politically crucial, and along with its expression in motherhood, furnished potent imagery to be deployed in the struggles over inheritance and succession which were such a feature of politics. Using Byzantine coinage, Brubaker and Tobler show how this imagery functioned – usually in the interests of sons and husbands, but also in those of wives and mothers, most spectacularly in the case of the empress Eirene. It was in the context of such a politics of family and inheritance that Sikelgaita of Salerno operated. That context, however, included a strongly gendered language of power which could legitimise – and threaten – both men and women. This gendered world of family and dynasty spanned the medieval centuries, and Cordula Nolte explores its workings at the end of the middle ages in the German principalities. Courts, as households writ large and political, and nunneries, as households writ religious, share a common domesticity, which, as Felicity Riddy argues, is often – half consciously? – identified with women, and which demands revaluation. It also requires constant rethinking, along with all other aspects of that public/private division which medieval historians, like so many others, are concerned to nuance and contextualise.

Nolte draws attention to other hierarchies which worked in conjunction with gender, such as age. Age and lifecycle, like family and its politics, are fruitfully reviewed. Rosalynn Voaden and Stephanie Volf compare the gendered lifecycles of male and female saints, or rather of their biographies and personal narratives, highlighting the difference between male and female experience and perception. The value of their discussion reinforces Katherine Lewis's criticism that even now too much allegedly 'gender' history of sanctity concentrates on female saints alone. Anneke Mulder-Bakker is also attentive to the need to place female alongside male experience, and to deepen our understanding by considering age and authority, lay and professional status. The result is a rich, long overview of the transmission of knowledge in the medieval world. In providing it, she passes from the first truly autobiographical writings of the late eleventh century to the much fuller sources of the later medieval northern urban Rhineland.

One of the great problems for medievalists is their sources – usually their paucity. Rigby highlights this even for the relatively well-documented later middle ages: it is a perennial limitation for those working in the earlier centuries. Sources attributable to women themselves, either written by them directly or through a secretary or confessor (a significant difference), or produced under their patronage, have survived in greater numbers from the later period. This almost certainly reflects a real growth rather than accidents of survival, a product of increasing literacy. Nolte's family letters have few parallels for the early period. Early medievalists have combed their sources for evidence of female involvement in the production, commissioning and shaping of the surviving texts. Elisabeth van Houts's book, reviewed here by Jinty Nelson, is concerned with the study of medieval memory. Women were oral witnesses, for example in cases concerning inheritance, and active in the keeping and transmission of the family past. Where politics were family politics, historical writing and family memory intertwined. Inheritance and succession, and the related issues of legitimisation and validation, central issues of such politics, could be major stimuli to the written preservation of memory, and to its construction. This insight allows Patricia Skinner to speculate productively on Sikelgaita's possible involvement in fashioning contemporary historical writing, and her own identity.

Some of the source problems faced by medievalists are peculiar to their period, but those faced by medieval gender historians are shared by anyone interested in the history of women in other times and places. It is well to be reminded that there are rich seams waiting to be mined, and in what may appear the most unpromising places. Ludwig Schmugge's work on the records of the papal Penitentiary reveals something of their treasures. Where sources are scarce and at first sight recalcitrant, we must, of course, learn to question and read them in new ways. To a greater or lesser extent all the chapters in this volume are engaged with this and with the methodologies which have proved so productive in unlocking meanings. It is perhaps significant that the clearest engagement with post-Foucauldian approaches comes in Cooper and Leyser's chapter which straddles the study of antiquity and the middle ages. Medieval studies have been far from immune to such approaches, but they have had less influence here than in the study of classical antiquity. Foucault's own interest in the latter period 'gave classics a significant purchase on the historiography of gender and sexuality'[1] which has been less marked in study of the centuries which followed. Medieval historical studies, as opposed to literary, are characterised by an eclectic approach to theoretical and methodological questions in which a modified empiricism is still respected. Medieval gender studies, perhaps especially in Europe, share much of this eclecticism. The papers gathered here mix their theoretical ingredients in different quantities. The results are, we hope, a tribute to the value of such culinary variety as well as an indication of the wealth and diversity of the results it has produced.

Note

1. See Maria Wyke, Introduction, *Gender and the Body in Mediterranean Antiquity*, Special Issue, *Gender and History*, 9 (1997), p. 425.

1

The Gender of Grace: Impotence, Servitude, and Manliness in the Fifth-Century West

Kate Cooper and Conrad Leyser

> To talk about grace properly is to adduce the dependence of the slave on his master, or the way the footman clings inseparably to his patron or lord. ... Just as it is unfitting for a helmsman's rower to fail him, or a bishop's attendant, or a commander's soldier, so it is fitting that grace and its foster child, obedience, should be linked inseparably together through servitude.
>
> (Faustus of Riez, *De gratia*, prologue, pp. 3–4)

> [T]he pusillanimous youth preferred the penance of the monastic to the dangers of a military life; ... whole legions were buried in these religious sanctuaries; and the same cause, which relieved the distress of individuals, impaired the strength and fortitude of the empire.
>
> (Edward Gibbon, *History of the Decline and Fall of the Roman Empire*, III, pp. 62–4)

Modern images of ancient man and the process by which he became 'medieval' still owe much to Gibbon. In his *History of the Decline and Fall of the Roman Empire*, the great historian left readers in no doubt that Roman manliness had been fatally compromised by the rise of ascetic Christianity. Christian superstition had sapped the civic spirit of the empire, argued Gibbon, and of this superstition, there was no more deadly version than the monastic life. The modern historian of gender may be tempted to agree, given that the late Roman period witnesses the consolidation of a polarised vision of manhood and masculine authority: on the one hand, that of the married Christian layman, sexually and financially active, prepared to use violence if need be; on the other, that of the ascetic, a celibate man who has foresworn all personal possessions and the bearing of arms. It is not hard to see here the lineaments of the medieval world, with its *bellatores* and *oratores*, a division of labour unknown to the ancient Romans.[1]

It has often been assumed that Roman men (and the barbarian warriors who came to occupy the western empire, and subsequently to convert to Christianity) must have had their propensity to violence stemmed by the Gospel's injunction to turn the other cheek.[2] But the story is more complicated: if we turn to the writings of 'those who prayed', we see that for a figure such as Faustus, bishop of Riez (*c.* 408 – *c.* 490), it was precisely the language of ancient social relations which served as a template, rather than an antithesis, for describing the Christian's relations with God. It is the austere power of the *patronus*, with its implicit threat of violence, which best serves to delineate the Deity's ultimately benevolent, yet awesome and inescapable authority, while the cowering uncertainty of the *servus* embodies the Christian's existential condition. Where social relations were concerned, the Christianisation of language did not imply a whole-hearted departure from the ancient paradigm of masculinity.

Where sexual relations were concerned, the continuity among Roman, late Roman, and early medieval visions of masculinity is more elusive, but equally significant. Approaches to late antiquity from Gibbon to Foucault have held in common an assumption that asceticism was at the centre of the changing construction of masculinity, or the changing subjectivity of men. It is this widespread assumption that the present essay seeks to challenge. Read in light of the language of male power and dependence at the end of antiquity, central ascetic writers such as Faustus, it will be argued, are noticeable not for any escalation of the sexual discourse of masculine identity, but rather for their increasing emphasis on social (rather than sexual) relations as the crucial discursive element – a stress especially pronounced in the writings of Augustine of Hippo. This reading sits uneasily with a widely held view of the role played by Augustine in the development of the western idea of (male) sexuality, a view put forward most influentially by Michel Foucault.[3]

Such a critique, however, emerges precisely from a post-Foucauldian vein of work on masculinity in the Roman world, work which shifted attention away from repression and towards the representation of sexual desire. While the Victorians imagined ancient men as unrepentant libertines, whose prodigious sexual energies were then condemned and repressed by the monastic movement,[4] for Foucault and his school 'repression was only a subordinate mechanism in a more fundamental historical development: the creation of that thing we call sexuality as the centre of the Western idea of the self'.[5] In the pages of Foucault's *History of Sexuality*, the male elite 'subjects of Rome' emerge – in contrast to Gibbon's reading – as a group highly concerned to regulate their violent rage and their sexual passion. The contrast presumed between pagan licentiousness and Christian puritanism largely disappears. Already in ancient Greece, argues Foucault, the crucial association was forged between sexuality and male subjectivity. (Although Foucault's title implies a discussion of female sexuality, this is not a promise on which his work delivers.) On this view, ancient man saw his identity as a man to reside in his capacity to avoid being ruled by the passions. The degree of excess or moderation in his sexual behaviour told him and his peers the truth about who he really was. In this culture of self-control, a man at the mercy of his lust risked, literally, losing his very claim to be male.[6]

The volatility of gender was directly linked to the instability of biological sex.[7] Ancient physiology was predicated on the understanding that the human body, like all matter in the cosmos, was composed of a delicate mixture of the four elements: earth, water, air, and fire. This elemental balance was easily upset: merely through eating, a person could alter their physical makeup with immediate consequences for their health and character. It was the task of doctors to monitor and to correct for excess, bearing in mind that different people had slightly different constitutions. A person's sex, in this scheme of things, was a function of their elemental makeup: the male body was understood to have a higher proportion of air and fire than the female, which was wetter and colder. Notoriously, the conclusion was drawn that men were better balanced than women, less prone to engulfment in labile passions. By the same token, however, no man could rest complacent. If he had too much sex, if he spent too much semen, he risked degeneration to the point where he became indistinguishable from a menstruating woman. Gender, then even more than now, was regarded as a provisional marker of social identity – always under contest, always in need of affirmation.

Intersecting with this biological paradigm was a keen sense of the self as a product of social theatre. Ancient and late ancient writers showed an interest in the representation and competitive self-fashioning of the public man which has been the subject of vivid interest across the last two decades of the twentieth century. Ancient masculinity therefore was constituted across a matrix of malleable social and biological elements. Self-control was its hallmark; this meant that not only austerity but also moderation was prized. Perceived virtue was the prerequisite to power, yet on this model even self-control ceased to seem virtuous if it was practised in a spirit of excess.[8] If the discourse of ancient masculinity was agonistic, its terms favoured the *status quo*. While the competition was, for those involved, a very high-stakes game of reputations won and lost, its overall function was conservative and reassuring: the audience knew that the skills showcased by each of the players were a mark of elite cultural hegemony. At one extreme stood the man whose power over others was justified by his control of himself; at the other, the man without control, the so-called *kinaedos*, who had surrendered all attempt to remain master of his passions to the point where he was ready to be penetrated by other men simply in order to satisfy his lust.[9] This was the world-view shared by philosophers and statesmen. It was, on the face of it, a moral universe in which there was not much to be gained by standing on pillars or other feats of ascetic heroism: the more radical ascetics, however, would prove that there was.

This reading of the parameters of ancient masculinity has led to a changed perception of gender and sexuality in the writings of the Church Fathers. Ascetic masculinity can no longer be understood, in Gibbon's terms, as 'fanaticism' degenerating into 'hypocrisy'. The shrill asceticism of a man like Jerome now appears as an attempt to participate in, while altering the rules of, the ancient game of masculinity. Jerome took to extreme lengths the public performance of sexual austerity, and managed to persuade at least some of his audience that this was not dangerous extremism, but in fact a more trustworthy course than that of the married man. Whether a majority of his audience was convinced is a point for debate, but what is certain is that the late fourth century inaugurates a period when men went to extraordinary lengths in discussing sexual purity.[10]

Ascetics did not necessarily agree with one another. It is now possible to see the constellation of ascetic writers at the turn of the fourth to fifth century as characterised not by unity of vision but rather as themselves engaged in a risky game of competitive self-fashioning,

each attempting to constitute and win currency for his own new
language of masculine self-control. Jerome was only one of many
who thought that self-control should no longer, in itself, be understood as something to be practised in moderation. While the quasi-
pornographic and distinctly hallucinatory qualities of his letter 22
To Eustochium have brought it as wide an audience as anything
produced by this school of thought, its most cogent expositor is
not Jerome, but his younger contemporary John Cassian. Cassian's
Conferences, for example, take the problem of a man's nocturnal
emissions as the occasion for developing a fine science of the fully
controlled body, where the ideal of balance has given way to a vision
of desire eradicated, of the body finally freed from its power.[11]

Augustine, by contrast, was uncomfortable with the ascetic movement's more exaggerated claims. At the level of the individual, he
believed the ascetic claim to purity to be illusory. Indeed, his suspicion
of any discourse which lionised the achievements of one class of individuals at the expense of another has been shown by Robert Markus
to be at the core of his approach to Christian community.[12] We will
see below that his keen sense of irony left him particularly ill-suited
to the kind of ascetic triumphalism espoused by Jerome and, in a
modified form, by Cassian. Augustine was certainly an ascetic and a
proponent of asceticism, but it was an asceticism which was suspicious
of the exaltation of the individual. What was important to Augustine
about asceticism was its ability, when understood correctly, to foster
the communion of hearts.

The repercussions of Augustine's debate with Pelagius on grace
and free will for the study of gender are much contested. In the work
of writers like Elaine Pagels and Kim Power, Augustine appears as the
man who gave definitive form to Christian fear of sex and of women.[13]
Emerging as victor over Pelagius, Augustine is seen by Pagels in
particular to have brought an end to the ancient tradition of moral
freedom, and to have inaugurated a dark medieval authoritarianism,
emphasising human helplessness before God and the powers that be.[14]
Power, by contrast, offers an independent but complementary psycho-
sexual reading of 'woman's symbolic status as dangerous desire'[15] in
Augustine's thought. It can be argued that neither approach takes
fully into account the work of Markus, with its insight into the social
basis of Augustine's repudiation of ideologies of human perfectibility:
the result of Markus's work is to indicate that Augustine was in fact
attacking the very positions he is so often presumed to have espoused.

If he was not prepared to stake all on a performance of sexual and moral purity, this was because it threatened to open up a rift between radical ascetics and the less fiercely committed Christian majority. Our view of Augustine's authoritarianism thus needs to be balanced against a recognition of his commitment to an ideal of community where the relationship between the religious specialist and the non-specialist would not be poisoned by quarrelling over status.

Augustine's contribution to the late Roman discussion of civic masculinity has yet accurately to be differentiated from that of his interlocutors – we will see below, for example, that Foucault went so far as to conflate the views of Augustine with the very different position of Cassian. Precision is of fundamental importance here. It is widely and erroneously assumed that Augustine regarded sexual desire as fundamentally excessive and dangerous. But this was not how Augustine himself posed the problem of masculinity. In a context where ancient writers had for millennia discussed male desire in terms of controlling excess, Augustine set out to explain, in his discussion of grace and free will in Book Fourteen of the *City of God*, that the real problem lay not in the force of desire, but rather in its unpredictability. Lust was not everywhere: it required mobilisation, and, when summoned, it might not appear, without any explanation for its absence. The most profound challenge for men was not to bridle their lust, but to face the humiliation of impotence. More emphatically even than the involuntary erection, sexual failure spoke to the true condition of humanity after the Fall.

Most ancient authors who opined on the subject of impotence regarded it as an embarrassment, to be sure, but as a relatively minor medical condition for which there were a number of tried and tested remedies. Unlike the problem of excess, impotence was certainly not a problem of ethical or philosophical dimensions. Augustine, however, departed from conventional wisdom by introducing impotence into the philosophical discourse of excess and self-control.[16] Augustine pointed out that men were at the mercy not only of the force but also of the hollowness of their desires. 'Sometimes, the [sexual] impulse is an unwanted intruder', he admits but, he continued:

> Sometimes, it abandons the eager lover, and desire cools off in the body while it is at boiling heat in the mind. Thus strangely does lust refuse to be a servant not only to the will to procreate, but even also to the lust for lascivious indulgence; and although on the whole it is totally opposed to the mind's control, it is quite often divided against itself. It arouses the mind, but does not follow its own lead by arousing the body.[17]

This was not a temporary embarrassment. As Augustine saw it, impotence pointed to the fundamental and humiliating inability of the mind to control the body, a rift deep in the psyche itself between will and desire, or even within desire itself. Male subordination to lust did not only, or primarily, involve passion-crazed transgression: it connoted an unbearable fear of failure.

> The genital organs have become as it were the private property of lust, which has brought them so completely under its sway that they have no power of movement if this passion fails ... It is this that arouses shame; it is this that makes us shun the eyes of beholders in embarrassment. A man would be less put out by a crowd of spectators watching him visiting his anger unjustly upon another man than by one person observing him when he is having lawful intercourse with his wife.[18]

All of this was a sign that the original perfection of Paradise had been lost, and that humans suffered under dire punishment.

Although many commentators would have it otherwise, Augustine was adamant that the body and its desires were not to blame for the expulsion from Paradise. The original sin had nothing to do with sex: it was the sin of pride. When Adam and Eve took the apple, it was not because they were gluttons; nor was it a series of sexual seductions – the serpent of Eve, Eve of Adam. The problem was that they thought they live independently of God who had created them. Sex in Paradise, Augustine believed, would have been unimaginably exquisite. Humans would have known no frustration or interruption of desire: men would have been spared the embarrassment of impotence, women the pain of the breaking of the hymen (and later, the pains of labour). The body was a site of punishment: it was not the cause of the problem.[19]

Sex was, however, where men came face to face with Original Sin – that is to say, with the disjunction of the human will, that fact that outside of Paradise even desire could only be, irredeemably, 'divided against itself'. To the degree that he acknowledged sex as a central site for the human experience of this dislocation, Augustine was attempting to situate his theory of the will in terms of the ancient discourse which had linked masculine authority to sexual morality. But Augustine was not, after his ascetic conversion, himself deeply interested in sex. What did interest him, what his mind returned to again and again, was the problem of human weakness. When he watched babies (most likely, his own son, born before he had reached the age of twenty), he saw their vulnerability to their own needs and desires, their powerlessness to control, or even to understand, the currents of volition pulsing through them. This profound human help-lessness was visible in sex, but only because its signs were everywhere.

Unlike many of his ascetic contemporaries, Augustine viewed the ancient discourse of self-control through a lens of irony. Some lines below the passage on Adam and Eve cited above, Augustine turned his critique of ascetic triumphalism into parody. The only humans who seemed to be capable of exerting serene control over themselves, to have never to experience the dissonance of mind and body – or, worse, the dissonance internal to mind – were circus artists, 'freaks' who did tricks in the town squares:

> Some can swallow an incredible number of various articles and then with a slight contraction of the diaphragm, can produce, as if out of a bag, any article they please, in perfect condition. There are others who imitate the cries of birds and beasts and the voices of any other people, reproducing them so accurately as to be quite indistinguishable from the originals, unless they are seen. A number of people produce at will such musical sounds from their behind (without any stink) that they seem to be singing in that region.[20]

The scatological *chutzpah* of this argument has gone largely unremarked. In his survey of ancient attitudes towards the body, Augustine parades a solemn regiment of world philosophers – Cicero, the Platonists, the Cynics, the gymnosophists of India – only to bring before his readers the street performers of provincial North Africa. He reasons, with impeccable tabloid logic, 'I know from my own experience of a man who used to sweat whenever he chose; and it is a well-known fact that some people can weep at will and shed floods of tears' – but not so with the flow of semen.[21] Book Fourteen of the *City of God* may be 'a story of human bondage':[22] it is also a lowbrow satire of ancient phallocentric pretensions.

It is tempting to imagine that Augustine's critique of the ancient paradigm of masculinity could be summarised thus: if so earnest a com-petition for moral authority could be won by the self-promotionalism of radical ascetics – monks no better than charlatans bent on short-circuiting the system to their own advantage by a calculated claim of eradicating what others had merely held in check – surely such a system for establishing the *bona fides* of an elite male leadership was at worst fundamentally flawed, and at best a matter for black humour? By satirising the ancient discourse of sexual self-control, Augustine collapsed the polarity defining ancient manhood, and so removed the conventional basis for claims to moral authority. No man could claim with any security that he was morally entitled to rule another; no man could know whether he numbered among the saved or the damned. Augustine's point was that the ancient 'hard man' who thought he was dominant was mistaken. Conversely, the soft man, the *kinaedos*, was not merely the archetypal figure of masculine powerlessness: he was everyman.

Augustine's debate on grace, free will, and predestination with Pelagius and his followers was to influence and be influenced by his thinking about masculinity. For Augustine, the Pelagian vision of human responsibility untrammelled by the disjunction of the will was untenable, since it depended on an inherited language for calculating human *virtus* which radical ascetics had now shown to be untenable. (The very word *virtus* – connoting both virtue and manliness – reflects the intrinsic link that had long been assumed to obtain between the two.) Augustine's views, which hardened rather than softened as he continued the polemic well into his seventies, caused a degree of consternation around the Mediterranean, even among those who were not inclined to sympathise with Pelagius. We can track their reception in southern Gaul in particular. According to one of Augustine's disciples, there was a group of ascetics in Marseilles who balked at Augustine's late views on grace and predestination. The leader of these 'new Pelagians' (known somewhat misleadingly since the seventeenth century as 'semi-Pelagians') was John Cassian, whose view of asceticism was very different from that of Augustine.[23] It was Cassian above all who made clear that the ancient language of male authority could be turned to the advantage of the ascetic speaker.[24]

After years of travel in the deserts of Egypt and Syria, Cassian had settled in Provence to offer ascetic instruction to local enthusiasts. Over a decade or so, he had articulated a view of ascetic masculinity that extended, rather than broke with, the traditional moral discourse. His goal was to find a middle way. We find little of the stridency of Jerome about ascetic purity – far more on the difficulty of the ascetic art. On the other hand, its goals remain within reach. Cassian did not follow Augustine into a consideration of male impotence. He endorsed the traditional premise that the problem of sexual desire was one of excess and its regulation. In dealing, for example, with the question of nocturnal emission and its reduction, Cassian invoked for reference the standard procedures adopted by ancient athletes looking to maximise their sporting performance by minimising the loss of vital fluid.[25] Christian ascetics, Cassian effectively suggested, combined the physical rigour of athletics with the moral stringency of philosophy. They were at the pinnacle of what ethical manhood could achieve.

By the death of Augustine in 430, literate Christian men were left in something of a dilemma. The reconciliation of the views of Augustine and Cassian was a difficult task, all too easily reduced to polemic, as shown by the flurry of prose and verse argument and counter-argument in the early 430s. The subsequent decades saw no real consensus emerge: in addition to the complexity of the issues, the times themselves were hardly conducive to leisured reflection. In 451, Pope Leo the Great met Attila the Hun in an instantly iconic encounter: this was a season for authority in action, not for Augustine's fine sarcasm about impotence, or Cassian's careful monitoring of nocturnal emissions.

In the search for moral authority, Augustine's was a name to conjure with, so long as one could steer clear of the emasculating content of what he had said. This balancing act is what we find in the writings of Faustus of Riez.[26] After nearly thirty years as abbot of Lérins, Faustus had moved *c.* 462 to take up the see of Riez. A decade later, Faustus was recognised by his episcopal colleagues in the Gallic church as their pre-eminent spokesman, and it was he who was delegated to handle the delicate matter, in the early 470s, of the priest Lucidus, whose intemperate predestinarian views resulted in a formal recantation at the synod of Arles in 473. Afterwards, Faustus undertook to compose a treatise expounding the full logic of the synodal position: the result was the two books *De gratia*.

Faustus couched his argument as a refutation of two extremes – Pelagianism on the one hand, and, on the other, the error of Lucidus. Faustus was at pains to make clear that 'predestinarianism' was based on a misreading of Augustine. Although Faustus has generally been understood as Cassian's successor in taking up the legacy of Pelagius, it was to Augustine that Faustus appealed in articulating his own, centrist position, by name and through tacit citation.[27] At the same time, however, his treatise advanced positions that were far from the letter or the spirit of what Augustine had written. He was unrestrained in his affirmation that human beings were powerless to choose the good without the support of divine grace – but he drew a distinction (alien to Augustine) between divine foreknowledge and predestination. Even as he quoted Augustine on the punishment of Adam and Eve, Faustus offered a view of the capacities of the fallen human will that was some way from Augustine's sense of the helplessness of the post-lapsarian condition.[28]

Crucial is the distinction between Faustus and Augustine when it comes to their engagement with the ancient discourse of masculine authority and power. Where Augustine had exposed the vanity of competitive display, Faustus saw meaningful reciprocity: this allowed him to annex the ancient discourse for theological use. The dominant metaphor of *De gratia* is that of the *patronus* and his man. In their relationship, the *gratia* extended by the master requires an active response from the recipient, namely a labour of obedience. The *gratia* involved here is the 'first grace' of creation: the created being can hardly refuse the duty of obedience, but having, in the garden of Eden, done just this, humans on earth are now constrained by still stronger duty. What Faustus insists upon is the dynamic of reciprocity at work even in relations of abject dependence. Weak and infirm as he is,

> The slave extends the hand of faith by which he may be drawn to the master who assists and calls ... So these two are joined together: the power of one who draws in (*adtrahit*), and the disposition of the one who obeys.[29]

Even in the post-lapsarian condition, then, Faustus attempts to find grounds for mutuality in social relations. This language of the civic sphere is assimilated to his language of male spiritual authority:

> What is it to draw in (*adtrahere*) but to preach? To excite with the consolations of the Scriptures, to deter with rebukes, to set forth what must be desired, to draw attention to what must be feared, to threaten judgement and to promise a reward.

The connection envisaged here between society and the holy was no mere metaphor. Relations between masters and slaves, bishops and their attendants were not simply an echo of the relation between God and humanity: rather, they served as instruments through which that relation was embodied. It was precisely God's *gratia* which a bishop was to dispense in his preaching.

It can hardly fail to strike the modern reader that the gender of grace, here as elsewhere, was overwhelmingly male. Yet it is important to observe the way in which the body, sexuality, and semen have been dropped from the discussion. Faustus drew his metaphors from the scene of politics, warfare, the ecclesiastical hierarchy – anywhere but the bedroom in which Augustine had so mischievously lingered. This, more then any single argument, is what signals Faustus's determination to reassert traditional norms of civic masculinity, but to side-step the sexual code on which it had traditionally been based. The subversion of this code by Augustine could not be reversed.

Thus the message of the tradition of civic masculinity was Christianised at the same time as its essential social conservatism was reasserted. Faustus turned a blind eye to Augustine's irony: the language of *De gratia* locates religious community squarely within the frame of a traditional idea of civic masculinity. The rise of asceticism had not, for Faustus, irredeemably ruptured the model of male ethical conduct inherited from the ancients. Rather, he saw the valour of the soldier and the subservience of a priestly acolyte as equally relevant parallels for human obligation to God. Seen as a form of 'male bonding', the relationship between humans and the Godhead was to be defeated neither by differentials of status, nor by the troubling implications of changing sexual *mores*. This analysis of salvation served not to sunder men from the world, nor the medieval from the classical epoch, but rather to uphold and extend an ancient model of manhood based on reciprocity.

To understand Augustine and Faustus along the lines indicated above is to open the way for a re-evaluation of the accounts of the end of antiquity posed by both Gibbon and Foucault. While it would fall far beyond the scope of an essay such as this to offer substantial proposals, it may be worth initiating a discussion here about the shape such a re-evaluation might take. To begin with, as might have been suspected, one cannot accept categorically Gibbon's proposal that the net effect of asceticism was to emasculate Roman men. On this point, the ascetic movement was characterised by diversity rather than unity; we have seen a full spectrum of opinions in play, from Jerome's triumphalism to Augustine's irony to Faustus's desire to side-step the sexual discourse altogether. Though less well documented and certainly less well studied, the married laity must equally have numbered among its members proponents of a variety of strategies for resolving the tensions created by radical asceticism. At the very least, however, we can imagine that the ascetic Faustus's willingness to avoid the issue of sexual deportment as an ethical marker was welcome to that element of the married laity who were moving toward a model of masculinity pieced together from elements of classical philosophy, the Hebrew Bible, and the ethos of the warlord.

Where Foucault and his heirs are concerned, the salient issue to emerge from the above is Augustine's supposed role in the sexualisation of human identity. Two points bear emphasis. The first is that, within the diversity of ascetic readings of the discourse of masculinity, Augustine stood precisely at the opposite end of the spectrum from those who took sexual behaviour in earnest as the summary of a man's moral standing. Foucault's reading of Book Fourteen of the *City of God* apprehended Augustine's main point as being about erection, rather than impotence:

> The famous gesture of Adam covering his genitals with a fig leaf is, according to Augustine, due not to the simple fact that Adam was ashamed of their presence but to the fact that his sexual organs were moving by themselves without his consent. Sex in erection is the image of man revolted against God.[30]

It is Foucault's easy equation here between 'moving by themselves without his consent' and 'sex in erection' which we have sought to undo.[31] Our second, and connected, point is that Foucault was wrong to suggest that Augustine can be read as characteristic of 'the ascetic and monastic literature of the fourth and fifth centuries':[32] in that highly contested milieu, Augustine's was a minority position. This holds true equally for the subsequent intellectual history of the Church: his was a name to contend with but his vision was never dominant.[33] To conflate Augustine with the ascetic triumphalism he critiqued is to misunderstand him. The lively and ongoing debate among ascetics ensured that no single voice emerged to speak for moral masculinity in the late Roman west.

Much remains to be done if the implications of systematic attention to masculinity for the study of the fifth century are to be realised concretely and fully. In plotting a course for future work, we might return attention to the scholarship of an earlier generation. Some four decades ago, scholars in the newly forming field of late antiquity, eager to move away from Gibbon's narrative of decline and fall, began to ask afresh how ascetic theory might have jostled against the harsh social realities of the end of an empire. Specifically, in 1960 J. N. L. Myres, an authority on Roman Britain, offered to account for British support for Pelagius in terms of a connection between religious and political dissent. Struck by the fact that early fifth-century Britain was in revolt against Rome, and that it was also seen to be a hotbed for followers of Pelagius, Myres suggested that *gratia*, the key term in the Pelagian controversy, did not only connote God's saving power. In the later Roman empire, it meant 'not so much "grace" as "favour", and not so much "favour" as "favouritism" '. Pelagius, in other words, had protested against the association of God with political corruption, and his followers in Roman Britain had actually led a revolt against what they perceived to be the corrupt regime of the empire itself. 'Behind the whole Pelagian movement lay a simple, rather pathetic, claim to elementary social justice', argued Myres.[34]

Myres's critics have not been few, and his thesis is now rarely discussed.[35] But the time may be ripe to reopen his inquiry into *gratia* and its social meanings. As we have seen, *gratia* was wider in its connotations than political corruption, but, equally significantly, recent work on 'corruption' itself indicates that it was a far from simple target for the social philosopher. In a face-to-face society such as the Roman empire, governed by an impossibly thin administrative staff, it served a more complex function than Myres's analysis would allow. Put simply, corruption and *gratia* were – in tandem – what allowed imperial autocracy and imperial bureaucracy to coexist.[36] On this model, it would have been eminently reasonable for a Faustus – or indeed for an Augustine or a Pelagius – to see *gratia* as the vehicle through which a language of moral authority, and moral responsibility, should be contested.

Far from fatally compromising the ancient tradition of civic masculinity, as Gibbon argued, the rise of ascetic Christianity led to its reconstitution and renewal in a form which would prove enduring through the instability of a devolving empire. Like asceticism itself, Augustine's challenge had posed a real threat to the social conservatism of ancient definitions of masculinity. But by disengaging sexual self-control from the exercise of *gratia*, writers such as Faustus were able to re-establish the language of male authority in terms perhaps even more public and even more firmly based in male social relationships than the language inherited from antiquity. If a man could no longer be judged by his ability to resist the lure of women, what remained was how he would relate to other men. Of course, the moral language of self-control and resistance to womanly influence was never entirely to lose its currency among the laity in the early middle ages, as a case such as the divorce of Lothar II makes all too clear.[37] But the negotiation of ascetic claims to this aspect of the male code was peculiarly suited as a vehicle for the problem of how the new ascetic class would relate to the secular men of authority. The division of the male polity into these two complementary classes of men – the *oratores* and the *bellatores* – may still, as Gibbon suggested, turn out to have been the defining factor at stake in the end of an age.

Notes

1. For a recent discussion of 'men who fought' and 'men who prayed', see J. L. Nelson, 'Monks, Secular Men and Masculinity', *Masculinity in Medieval Europe*, ed. D. M. Hadley (Longman, London and New York, 1999), pp. 121–42.
2. P. Wormald, 'Bede, "Beowulf" and the Conversion of the Anglo-Saxon Aristocracy', in *Bede and Anglo-Saxon England*, ed. R. T. Farrell (British Archaeological Reports, British Series 46, Oxford, 1978), pp. 32–95.
3. See below nn. 30, 31.
4. See P. R. L. Brown, *The Body and Society: Men, Women, and Sexual Renunciation in Early Christianity* (Columbia University Press, New York, 1988), on William Lecky, pp. xvi–xvii.
5. Danny Praet, in 'Hagiography and Biography as Prescriptive Sources for Late Antique Sexual Morals', *Litterae Hagiologicae*, 5 (1999), pp. 2–13, at p. 3.
6. M. Foucault, *The Care of the Self*, trans. R. Hurley (Pantheon Books, New York, 1985), and *The Use of Pleasures*, trans. R. Hurley (Pantheon Books, New York, 1985).
7. See, with a measure of caution, A. Rousselle, *Porneia: On Desire and the Body in Late Antiquity*, trans. F. Pheasant (Blackwell, Oxford, 1988).
8. J. Francis, *Subversive Virtue: Asceticism and Authority in the Second-Century Pagan World* (Pennsylvania State University Press, University Park, 1995).
9. J. J. Winkler, *The Constraints of Desire: The Anthropology of Sex and Gender in Ancient Greece* (Routledge, New York and London, 1990); D. M. Halperin, J. J. Winkler, and F. Zeitlin (eds), *Before Sexuality: The Construction of Erotic Experience in the Ancient Greek World* (Princeton University Press, Princeton, NJ, 1990); M. W. Gleason, *Making Men: Sophists and Self-Presentation in Ancient Rome* (Princeton University Press, Princeton, NJ, 1995); see also K. Cooper, 'Insinuations of Womanly Influence: An Aspect of the Christianization of the Roman Aristocracy', *Journal of Roman Studies*, 82 (1992), pp. 150–64, and K. Cooper, *The Virgin and the Bride: Idealized Womanhood in Late Antiquity* (Harvard University Press, Cambridge, MA, 1996), esp. ch. 1, 'Private Lives, Public Meanings', pp. 1–19.
10. On Jerome and his critics, see Cooper, *Virgin and Bride*, pp. 92–115.
11. C. Leyser, 'Masculinity in Flux: Nocturnal Emission and the Limits of Celibacy in the Early Middle Ages', in Hadley, *Masculinity*, pp. 103–20.
12. Crucial here is Robert Markus, *Saeculum: History and Society in the Theology of Saint Augustine* (Cambridge University Press, Cambridge, 1970); Markus's reading is made more accessible in his *The End of Ancient Christianity* (Cambridge University Press, Cambridge, 1990), esp. ch. 4, 'Augustine: A Defence of Christian Mediocrity', pp. 45–62. See also Brown, *Body and Society*, ch. 19, pp. 387–427.
13. E. Pagels, *Adam, Eve, and the Serpent* (Random House, New York, 1988); K. Power, *Veiled Desire: Augustine's Writing on Women* (Darton, Longman and Todd, London, 1995).
14. Pagels, *Adam, Eve and the Serpent*, pp. 96–126, esp. p. 118.
15. Power, *Veiled Desire*, p. 4.
16. P. R. L. Brown, 'Sexuality and Society in the Fifth Century A.D.: Augustine and Julian of Eclanum', in *Tria Corda: Scritti in onore di Arnaldo Momigliano*, ed. E. Gabba (Como, New Press, 1983), pp. 49–70.
17. Augustine, *De Civitate Dei* XIV.16, ed. L. Verheijen, *Corpus Christianorum, Series Latina* (2 vols, Brepols, Turnhout, 1955), vol. 2, p. 439; *St Augustine, City of God*, trans. H. Bettenson (Penguin, Harmondsworth, 1972), p. 577. All subsequent page references refer to this edition and this translation.
18. Augustine, *Civ. Dei* XIV. 19, p. 442, trans. p. 581.
19. Augustine, *Civ. Dei* XIV. 26, pp. 449–50.
20. Augustine, *Civ. Dei* XIV. 24, p. 447, trans. p. 588.
21. 'Far more incredible is the case of Restitutus of Calama …' continues the passage in mock sensationalism: Augustine, *Civ. Dei* XIV. 24, p. 447, trans. p. 588.

22. Pagels, *Adam, Eve, and the Serpent*, p. 105.

23. For an introduction, see C. Leyser, 'Semi-Pelagianism', in *Augustine Through the Ages: An Encyclopedia*, ed. A. Fitzgerald (Eerdmanns, Grand Rapids, MI, 1999), pp. 761–6.

24. C. Leyser, '*Lectio divina, oratio pura*: Rhetoric and the techniques of asceticism in the *Conferences* of John Cassian', in *Modelli di santità e modelli di comportamento*, ed. G. Barone et al. (Rosenberg and Sellier, Turin, 1994), 79–105.

25. The most reliable guide is C. Stewart, *Cassian the Monk* (Oxford University Press, New York, 1998), pp. 62–84; see also the debate between D. Brakke, 'The Problematization of Nocturnal Emissions in Early Christian Syria, Egypt and Gaul', *Journal of Early Christian Studies*, 3 (1995), pp. 419–60, and Leyser, 'Masculinity in Flux'.

26. On Faustus, see in particular T. A. Smith, *'De Gratia': Faustus of Riez's Treatise on Grace and its Place in the History of Theology* (University of Notre Dame Press, Notre Dame, 1990).

27. See Smith, '*De Gratia*', pp. 126–40.

28. *De gratia* I.1–2, *Patrologia Latina* 58, 785–9, citing, for example, Augustine's *De nuptiis et concupiscnetia*, I.6.7.

29. *De gratia* I.17, *PL* 58, 810. The following citation is the continuation of the passage.

30. M. Foucault, 'Sexuality and Solitude', in *Religion and Culture by Michel Foucault*, ed. J. R. Carrette (Manchester University Press, Manchester, 1999), pp. 182–7 at p. 186.

31. Foucault's repeated use of the word 'technique' with regard to Augustine (p. 186 as n. 30) and his invocation of Cassian without preamble in his conclusion (p. 187), lend substance to the suspicion that Foucault has assimilated Augustine to Cassian.

32. Foucault, 'Sexuality and Solitude', p. 187.

33. In the fifth and sixth centuries, Augustine was a figure of controversy and not without a readership, but his writings were often condemned and his thought not necessarily a predominant influence even on those who invoked his authority: see C. Leyser, *Authority and Asceticism from Augustine to Gregory the Great* (Oxford University Press, Oxford, 2000).

34. J. N. L. Myres, 'Pelagius and the End of Roman Rule in Britain', *Journal of Roman Studies*, 50 (1960), pp. 21–36, esp. pp. 24–5.

35. See W. Liebeschuetz, 'Did the Pelagian Movement have Social Aims?', *Historia*, 12 (1963), pp. 227–41; P. R. L. Brown, 'Pelagius and his Supporters: Aims and Environment', *Journal of Theological Studies*, n.s., 21 (1968), pp. 93–114; repr. in his *Religion and Society in the Age of Saint Augustine* (Faber and Faber, London, 1972), pp. 183–207.

36. See C. M. Kelly, 'Later Roman Bureaucracy: Going through the Files', in *Literacy and Power in the Ancient World*, ed. K. Bowman and G. D. Woolf (Cambridge University Press, Cambridge, 1994), pp. 161–76; the same author's 'Emperors, Government, and Bureaucracy', in *The Cambridge Ancient History*, vol. 13, *The Late Empire, A.D. 337–425*, ed. A. Cameron and P. Garnsey (Cambridge University Press, Cambridge, 1998), pp. 138–83; and J. D. Harries, *Law and Empire in Late Antiquity* (Cambridge University Press, Cambridge, 1999), esp. pp. 153–71.

37. S. Airlie, 'Private Bodies and the Body Politic in the Divorce Case of Lothar II', *Past & Present*, 161 (1998), pp. 3–38.

2

Did Women Have a Transformation of the Roman World?

Julia M. H. Smith

The transition from the Roman empire to the middle ages is surely one of the major landmarks in the history of world civilisation. Reasons for this profound shift have been debated ever since Edward Gibbon published his *Decline and Fall of the Roman Empire* two centuries ago, and whatever methodology, frame of reference or ideological starting point is adopted, the centuries from *c*. 300 to *c*. 800 pose a persistent historiographical challenge. Indeed, scholarly attention has never been greater than at present, as the spate of recent international conferences, monographs and new journals dedicated to the period indicate. Most voluminous and longest running has been a five-year project under the auspices of the European Science Foundation, involving scholars representing many countries and an equally wide range of academic disciplines. Although simply entitled 'The Transformation of the Roman World', the project has in fact focused most of its attention on the European provinces of the Roman empire and their hinterland, with more limited consideration of the eastern Mediterranean, north African and Near Eastern provinces of the empire. The issues and geographical scope addressed in this particular scholarly enterprise form the immediate historical context for my remarks. Their political context stems from the fact that, despite its conceptual breadth, one notable omission from the project's remit was attention to women and gender.[1] My purpose here is to open a debate about ways in which attention to women and gender has the potential to deepen and enhance understanding of the transition from antiquity to the middle ages, and to argue that the continuing marginalisation of gender from the historical mainstream is to the general detriment of studies of this period.

First, however, it is necessary to sketch – in extreme brevity – some of the main themes in current understanding of the period *c.* 300 to *c.* 800. 'Transformation' is indeed central to recent ways of thinking, not least because it shifts attention away from models of decline, decay and collapse. Used as a shorthand term to refer to complex, multi-causal and evolutionary changes in all aspects of human society, 'transformation' obviates the implicit value-judgements of older historiography. Instead of finding the post-Roman world underdeveloped, unsophisticated and uncivilised or, in Byzantium, simply decadent in comparison to the heydays of empire, 'transformation' finds it different but also pays attention to aspects of continuity and to the reception of the Roman cultural inheritance.

Several themes are central.[2] In political terms, the interaction between Rome and the 'barbarian' peoples fringing its north-western frontiers is seen as creative not destructive, and indeed, 'the Germanic world was perhaps the greatest and most enduring creation of Roman political and military genius'.[3] Out of this, there emerged new dominant groups with collective identities and political aspirations, which came to form the successor kingdoms that replaced imperial hegemony in Europe. These groups coalesced around ethnic identities but, in a process historians now refer to as 'ethnogenesis', these ethnicities were new allegiances emerging out of temporally and culturally specific circumstances.[4] In the eastern Mediterranean, the continuity of an unbroken tradition of imperial government encouraged perceptions of east–west divergence, but the reception and reuse of the cultural building blocks of *Romanitas* marked all these polities in one way or another, whether in the western successor kingdoms' gradual adoption of the Roman state religion, Christianity, and their deployment of Roman trappings and ideologies of power, or in the Byzantine empire's self-conscious restatements of Roman ideologies and imperatives.

In socio-economic terms, the demise of taxation and military provisioning in the west and then in the east the loss of the most prosperous provinces to Islam disrupted the nature and rhythms of material and economic life by gradually severing long-distance networks of exchange, altering patterns of production and opportunities for material displays of rank and status. As the Mediterranean was reorganised into local or regional networks of production and exchange, new emporia developed around the North Sea and southern Baltic, and came to complement and extend the Mediterranean economies. Cities had been the key political, ideological and economic focuses of the ancient Mediterranean: the transformation of the Roman world was perhaps most dramatically witnessed in the reordering of urban space, the changed use (practical and symbolic) of buildings, shrinking urban populations and declining standards of material life. Yet in rural areas and north of the former Roman frontier, the adoption of aspects of Roman urban terminology and deference to Roman ways of organising space demonstrated the adaptability of Roman civic ideology even in rural or non-Roman settings, whilst city life remained vigorous in parts of the Byzantine east as well as in some of the provinces taken over by the Arabs. In both east and west, patterns of rural settlement altered, in part reflecting economic and demographic changes. In the west, from the fifth century the ruralisation and militarisation of elites further contributed to new ways of legitimating power and authority, whilst a similar but more gradual process affected the sociopolitical organisation of outlying regions of the Byzantine empire from the seventh century onwards.

In brief, in place of traditional narratives of Roman decay and barbarian vigour, of the sundering of the socio-economic unity of the Mediterranean basin, of an identification of stable states and imperial hegemonies as the normative forms of political organisation, 'transformation' emphasises that 'Rome changed, evolved, [and] transformed slowly, at different momentums in different places, and with widely different results', results which were 'local and plural' not uniform and generalised.[5] Over the centuries from *c.* 300 to *c.* 800, the Roman world disaggregated into different regions, different polities, different economic networks, different religions (including different forms of Christianity), but also partially reintegrated as new links and identities emerged in altered geographical frameworks. No single explanatory factor, no single narrative can encapsulate this transformation: it is essential to focus on multiple perspectives, causes and chronologies.

Such are the preoccupations of contemporary scholars. In recent years, none of these discussions has paid more than glancing attention to the ordering of social life, and even less attention has been paid to a gendered approach to social, political, economic or religious change.[6] Women and eunuchs remain marginal, as do peasants and slaves. Yet a parallel historiographical development has been the emergence over the past three decades of women's history and, more recently, of gender as a powerful tool for investigating both the interrelationships of men with women and more generally the organisation and cultural expression of power relationships within a given society.[7] Scholarship on the ancient world, early Christianity and the middle ages has benefited from this.[8] And yet the Roman world which contemporary historiography has transformed remains largely gender-blind: women's history and gender history remain apart from the revisionist establishment.

This essay is then an exercise in historiographical *rapprochement*. It consists of two sections: first, a brief assessment of the ways in which the work of scholars who do pay attention to women's lives or to gender points to the inadequacies of contemporary thinking about the transition from late antiquity to the middle ages, and then some indications of ways in which a different perspective can develop this summary analysis. Too many questions remain unasked and unanswered to be able to offer a systematic gendered critique of the 'Transformation of the Roman World' project or other recent work on the period. My purpose can only be to draw attention to the work that has been done, to suggest larger issues deserving of attention and to posit that gender should be complementary not alternative to other questions and methodologies.

I turn first to the theme of political transformation. If 'ethnogenesis' is central to understanding the political transformation of the western provinces of the empire, we should nevertheless acknowledge that population displacement and military conflict were aspects of it.[9] In second- and first-century BC Rome, the strain which war placed on society had a very considerable impact on the position and legal status of women, offering them opportunities to renegotiate their lives and resources. This had implications for all social groups, male and female, elite and low status.[10] Can similar changes be detected in the early medieval west? The evidence of law codes and charters may help here.[11]

Moreover, although historians' discussions of 'ethnogenesis' have raised the question of whether the key markers of political and cultural identity were shared by, or were significant for, more than a fairly narrow political elite, they have not asked whether they were also significant for women. Burial archaeology can take these discussions forward. It suggests, first, that other identities were often more important than commonly realised in fifth- and sixth-century communities, notably distinctions based on age or gender.[12] Focus on 'ethnogenesis' as the transformative paradigm in political change may thus perpetuate the perspective of the warrior elite and thereby exaggerate its importance. Secondly, burial archaeology invites reconsideration of the association between men and weapons. Some recent studies suggest that this was not always normal or normative.[13] But in a more militarised society than the Roman empire, the association of men and weapons in many early medieval burial grounds also raises questions about the level and nature of the physical violence to which women and children were exposed. To what extent was enhanced domestic violence the invisible concomitant of ethnogenesis?

Inasmuch as 'ethnogenesis' involved the establishment of new identities, the transmission of those identities from one generation to the next ought to raise the issue of their cultural reproduction within the family and household. Marriages between Roman men and 'barbarian' women and between 'barbarian' men and Roman women were not uncommon in the fourth and fifth centuries.[14] In the post-Roman west, most notably in Visigothic Spain, legislation was nevertheless issued which prohibited mixed marriages.[15] But the legal apparatus of 'ethnogenesis' should not be confused with its social reality, and the presumption of mixed marriages in Visigothic Spain and elsewhere remains strong. Attention to marriage as an institution where ethnicity was renegotiated and transmitted within an inherently gendered context is a desideratum.

In the Mediterranean areas of the sixth-century successor kingdoms, the women of old senatorial aristocratic families can be found taking an active part in shaping the education and careers of their sons. Thus women's role not only in 'ethnogenesis' but also in the transmission and reception of ideas of *Romanitas* needs to be stressed. Furthermore, archaeological evidence suggests that women may have been particularly sensitive agents for the expression of a Romanising identity. Funerary archaeology reveals that Visigothic women abandoned their traditional forms of personal adornment and adopted Roman-inspired styles of jewellery in the late sixth century, and that Anglo-Saxon women did likewise in the course of the seventh century.[16] In both cases, women's jewellery was part of a wider re-evaluation of *Romanitas*. This suggests also that, in periods of cultural reorientation, women perhaps carried some social meanings whilst men adopted others.

In the construction and reception of *Romanitas* in the east, women were not merely prominent within early Byzantine dynastic memory and commemoration, they often actively constructed it themselves.[17] And if Byzantine law was one of the main expressions of an unbroken *Romanitas*, the frequent reorganisations or reissues of Justinian's sixth-century codification have to be set alongside the evidence within that legal corpus for shifts in the legal status of women. Although these shifts tended to restrict women's legal capacities, their consequences for the regulation of marriage and the transmission of property cannot have been without impact on men's lives too.[18] The Roman legal and cultural legacy was transmitted and interpreted within gendered environments in many different ways.

The late antique cultural legacy included Christianity. Least needs to be said here, since studies of patristic Christianity do now have a well-established and sophisticated tradition of attention to women, sexuality and gender.[19] Despite this, however, debates on Christianisation and acculturation have yet to pay full attention either to women's religious experience, or to the reorganisation of gender relationships as an integral part of the complex process of religious change. For example, it would be worth asking what the implications for women may have been of the gradual shift from the religious pluralism of the fourth and fifth centuries to the compulsory Christianity of the early middle ages. One obvious aspect is that, unlike pagan religions, Christianity certainly offered women some scope for involvement in the life of their community. In particular, they found a role in the ascetic life.[20] In the early days of the women's history movement, it was proposed that 'Christianity became a liberating force in the lives of women' via the search for God through renunciation.[21] Yet ideas of an essentialised female spirituality need to be tested not assumed.[22] In addition, it now seems appropriate to ask to what extent a masculine definition of ascetic Christianity provided the norms, supplied the vocabulary, restricted the social space for and regulated the content of women's religious experience, and to what extent women were able to negotiate within, or resist entirely, this pressure.[23] In other words, although Christianity did provide alternatives to marriage and child-raising, how far was this on men's terms?

Of all debates about the transformation of the Roman world, discussions of its economic transformation are the most solidly gender-blind. Yet, here too, questions need to be raised. Was the reorganisation of networks of production and exchange accompanied by a redefinition of the gender specificity of artisanal or agricultural labour? Early medieval textual evidence points to the overwhelmingly gendered nature of rural production, with women producing cloth and men working the land: to what extent did this pattern emerge in concert with the establishment of new regional or local economies?[24] Likewise, did the demise of cities as centres of large-scale production and consumption affect women's participation in the marketplace as both producers and consumers? Where urban economies persisted in the eastern Mediterranean, specifically urban forms of female employment are found, for example in the production and sale of cloth and foodstuffs, or as bath-house attendants and prostitutes.[25] By contrast, the under-representation of women in the graveyards of the new trading emporia of north-western Europe in the early middle ages suggests that these communities may have been occupied primarily by seasonally migrant male craftsmen and traders.[26] And since the reordering of urban space in the post-Roman cities of the Mediterranean was accompanied by new forms of elite residential building which lacked the huge scale and complexity of the late antique aristocratic housing stock, how did this affect the gendering of domestic space?[27] In all such respects, the economic transformation of the Roman world may not have been gender-neutral.

If we wish to establish a gendered perspective on late antiquity and the early middle ages, we have to start from a point of view which is not one of empire-wide grand narratives but one that is domestic and, by virtue of the poverty of documentation, often fragmented. Throughout antiquity and the middle ages, women are most consistently recognised in familial settings, although of course they were not the only inhabitants of domestic space.[28] But that domestic space was not unrelated to the public sphere, for the deportment and physical appearance of the Roman male elite began with the training and bodily moulding boys received in early childhood, and continued in adult public life to be intimately associated with both their reputation for sexual self-control and their wives' reputation for honourable conduct.[29] By turning our gaze within the household, we may simultaneously ask questions about the continuities and discontinuities of women's lives in the period *c.* 300 to *c.* 800, examine the ways in which women were able to influence the political arena and attend to the formation and transformation of gender identities in this period.

The late Roman household focused complex ideas and images about women which pertain directly to these questions. The explicit superiority of men, always a mainstay of ancient society, underlay the legal and cultural notions of women's weakness, their *imbecillitas sexus*.[30] In law, women's weakness not only was the doctrine that allowed special legal protection of women and their property, but also limited their legal capacities, restricted their access to the law courts and disqualified them from holding public office.[31] In social terms, the weakness of her sex gave a woman a special claim to be protected, but equally exposed her to the risk of violence and oppression, not least within the home.[32] Yet at the same time as men underscored women's inferiority, they also valued and appreciated them greatly as wives and mothers.[33] During the late fourth and fifth centuries, however, the powerful rhetoric of Christian asceticism tended to ignore more traditional voices. Christian authors emphasised the ideal of virginity or, failing that, chastity within marriage, and also made a wife's sexual conduct into a powerful metaphor for defining male secular and religious authority.[34] Despite this, the social blessings of motherhood nevertheless remained unstintingly accepted, particularly in the eastern Mediterranean.[35] In the post-Roman west, the ascetic vision of womanhood tended to predominate, and it was not until the ninth century that motherhood was once more affirmed in the Latin west as strongly as it had been in late antiquity.[36]

As much as motherhood is about biological reproduction, it is even more about social and cultural reproduction, and thus must be understood in quite culturally specific ways. One reminder of this is motherhood as a legal construct. Distinguishing between a *genetrix* and a *mater*, Roman law did not define a mother as one who had given birth, but rather as the legal wife of a *paterfamilias* whether or not she had borne children.[37] As the male head of a family group and its household, the *paterfamilias* mediated power between the domestic and the political life. His household authority was formally rooted in law, but the conduct of his wife and daughters in turn influenced his own public reputation. In this way, gender relations that were constructed around marriage, its expectations and responsibilities spilled over into wider social and political relationships. The organisation of power within Roman society at large was thus grounded in the gender relationships which marriage enabled.

Marriage, then, should be at the heart of an analysis which takes gender and the household as its point of departure. The formal legal distinction between *mater* and *genetrix* nevertheless became blurred in the early medieval Latin west as definitions of marriage themselves shifted, and here we can locate some of the discontinuities of women's experience. Consent of both parties lay at the heart of the Roman definition of marriage and, subject to growing ecclesiastical influence, remained so in Byzantium.[38] In the west, however, Roman law continued to be employed in an unbroken tradition only in Mediterranean regions and by the church; elsewhere 'barbarian' (that is, non-Roman) customs popularised a range of forms of sexual partnership from the more to the less formal, and stressed the importance of sexual intercourse and property transfers in determining the nature of a relationship.[39] In the west as in the east, growing ecclesiastical influence had a major impact by the ninth century, stressing for the first time the indissolubility of marriage and regulating incest taboos in such a way as to define and control the range of marriageable partners.[40]

Ecclesiastical influence on the social customs surrounding sexual practices and on the definition of marriage together with the spread of non-Roman traditions in the Latin west undoubtedly fundamentally reshaped marriage. Women's personal experience of these changes is an issue which the evidence is scarcely capable of answering, although we may nevertheless monitor the extent to which men's ideas about gender relations were reshaped.[41] As for men's experience, this has proven slightly easier to access. That acute anxiety over ideas and ideals of masculinity and sexual self-control might stem from boyhood conflict between ecclesiastical and secular values suggests that the reshaping of gender norms within marriage may have been fundamental.[42]

Marriage is also about the transmission of property from one generation to the next, and the divergence of the west from late antique ideas about marriage was paralleled by changes in inheritance traditions which profoundly affected women's access to landed wealth. Roman law had from the earliest times given daughters an entitlement to inherit part of their father's property.[43] Under Roman testamentary law, a parent was not obliged to give equal shares to all offspring, but neither could a parent easily disinherit a child altogether.[44] Although absence of systematic documentary evidence makes it impossible to offer anything more than an impressionistic statement, it is nevertheless clear that in late antiquity, women's access to property was commonplace, whether in full ownership or in more conditional forms of control such as dowry. It also spanned the entire social spectrum from female owners of vast urban palaces to the modest inheritances of the women of the villages of upper Egypt.[45] This pattern of female

inheritance persisted wherever Roman law persisted, in the Mediterranean regions of the west and in Byzantium.[46]

The transmission of property through the family is one subject
where the influence of 'barbarian' conventions in the early medieval
west is particularly clear. At the risk of doing scant justice to the
complexity and variety of post-Roman inheritance customs, it may
be said that all 'barbarian' legal sources evince a clear preference for
the inheritance of landed property (as distinct from moveable wealth)
by men rather than by women and that they acknowledge the interest
of collateral relatives in any individual's land. In both respects,
'barbarian' practice diverged from Roman law. Nevertheless, both the
law codes and the rather sparse documentary evidence for individual
land transactions point to the gradually growing influence of Roman
notions, not least in the relationship of women to land. In Frankish
Gaul, Lombard Italy, Visigothic Spain and, later, Anglo-Saxon England,
women could and did have access to land, sometimes in full ownership, more often held on the condition that it be passed on to sons or
to an external beneficiary, usually a church.

Despite the general proposition that in *c.* 800 women in the early
medieval west had somewhat greater chances of access to landed wealth
than in *c.* 500, their position as property holders was never protected
in the ways in which late Roman and Byzantine law claimed to secure
women's title. Indeed, western women's control of land remained
insecure throughout the early middle ages, and long thereafter.[47] Nor,
it seems, was the scale of their land holding remotely comparable to
that in the late Roman and early Byzantine worlds, in which women
are unlikely to have owned less than about 25 per cent of all land,
quite possibly rather more.[48] Any legal changes in the early Byzantine
period only confirmed women's access to land, and at no point did
Byzantine law discriminate against women's inheritance rights.[49]

Only by the eleventh century are very tentative east–west com-
parisons possible. In the Byzantine regions of southern Italy, approxi-
mately one quarter of all land transfers were effected by women,
whereas in eleventh-century England, the Domesday Book records
no more than one in seven landholders as women in any one section;
the total proportion of land under their control may have been little
more than 5 per cent.[50] Limited tenure of land designated as dower
or usufruct of land destined for a religious beneficiary may make
this an underestimate of women's overall access to land; but the point
remains that Anglo-Saxon women's full title remained extremely limited

in contrast to areas with a surviving Roman law tradition. In the face of continuing familial interest in relatives' land, a traditional preference for passing land among the males of a family and the absence of strong legal sanctions to enforce such titles and rights as they did have, early medieval women in the west generally only had access to land when it suited family strategy or in default of male heirs or collaterals.

The implications of this are more than simply legal. They concern women's ability to live independently and with a degree of economic security, and they affect directly their fate in widowhood. They touch intra-familial dynamics and hence gender relations within the household, but also the politics of religious benefaction and the economic motivations which might underlie churches' traditional care for widows. Further, early medieval inheritance strategies were fluid, negotiable, and frequently also of political import. Thus the politics of the western successor kingdoms cannot be divorced from the integral link between land, gender and power.

Marriage and motherhood focus attention not only on the transfer of property and wealth but also on the transmission of cultural norms. Roman tradition had stressed the role of the ideal wife as her husband's moral mentor, one who not merely managed the house and raised the children, but could also influence his behaviour for the better. As Augustine stressed, order in the social polity was grounded within the household: wives were central to the maintenance of a well-ordered state.[51] In the early middle ages, the clergy adhered to the same view in both east and west. By the ninth century, both Byzantine and western wives were explicitly expected to ensure the piety, rectitude and Christian conduct of all members of the household, and indeed might be called upon to assert moral leadership over their husbands.[52]

That this influence was indeed exercised is easier to document for mothers than for wives, and in practice is often associated with a mother's role in the education of her children.[53] Daughters are rarely as visible as sons in this context; but through the eyes of famous sons or of those who wrote about them, maternal influence in moulding the character of the male elite is acknowledged. Only occasionally can mothers' own voices be heard, as in the letters sent by Erchanfreda to her son Desiderius, bishop of Cahors (633–55), or in the extended handbook of moral and spiritual advice which Dhuoda wrote for her son William in 841–3.[54] What is clear, however, is that no matter how consistent maternal training of sons was, its sociopolitical context and cultural content changed over time. In the urban environment of the fourth-century empire, mothers such as Monica, mother of Augustine, or Nonna, mother of Gregory Nazianzus, did their best to raise their sons according to Christian norms in a world of civic education in the liberal arts and of religious pluralism; by the sixth century, Armentaria raised her son Gregory (future bishop of Tours, 573–94) in an environment where there was no longer any alternative to Christianity and where clerical relatives were on hand to educate the boy. The mothers of the male secular elite faced different tasks again. In the turmoil of mid fifth-century northern Gaul, the unnamed mother of Arbogast, count of Trier, raised her son in such a way that he was 'overflowing with abilities and ... adorned with accomplishments';[55] in the seventh century, Begga trained her son Pippin in the exercise of secular power (he became the most powerful man in late seventh-century court politics) in a world of bitter aristocratic rivalries,[56] whilst in the ninth, Dhuoda offered William an image of aristocratic conduct which balanced power with self-restraint and tempered lordship with humility. These brief examples suggest that, however constant the ideology and tasks of motherhood remained, their social expression nevertheless changed radically.

In the early middle ages as in late antiquity, women's presence at court and participation in court politics need to be taken into consideration. Debarred in the early middle ages, as in the ancient world, from holding public office, women nevertheless might wield considerable political influence. That they were able to do so in part reflected the ways in which formerly appointed public offices increasingly passed from generation to generation within one family, blurring the distinction between public and domestic power and influence.[57] But it also reflected their essential existence as wives and mothers, whether of fourth- and fifth-century emperors or eighth- and ninth-century 'barbarian' kings. Royal women's individual activities have for some time been the focus of attention of women's historians who have stressed the ways in which court politics were often an aspect of intra-familial relationships.[58]

Less attention has been paid to a complementary aspect of elite women's political actions which emerged in the west by the ninth century: their moral influence. This derived directly from the revived ideology of motherhood. In a culture where honour was one of the mainsprings of political action, women had responsibility for upholding of the honourableness of court and politics.[59] The *honestas palatii* was its moral tone, but also much more: its right ordering, decorum, and dignified conduct. This takes us to the heart of early medieval court culture: women and (sexual) morality were thus integral to effective political life. (By the same token, women might also be deemed to subvert it.)

Finally, we should acknowledge that female roles and ideologies of femininity do not exist in a social vacuum. In another grand imperial culture, the Victorian, masculinity was 'everywhere but nowhere' in the historical record, so normative as to be nearly invisible but nevertheless central to women's experience.[60] Similarly in the Roman empire and its successor cultures east and west: women and ideas about women's roles coexisted and interacted with male roles and notions of masculinity. Moreover, sociologists have taught us that in any one society, masculinities are multiple and susceptible to re-definition in the course of broader cultural changes, but that, within any one culture, one version is commonly dominant. Two implications are immediately evident for late antiquity and the early middle ages: and return us directly to my theme of women's role in cultural reproduction. The first concerns the transmission from one generation to the next of 'hegemonic masculinity'.[61] That, surely, is where mothers are crucial. Dhuoda's *Liber Manualis* is a mother's effort to inculcate in her son the norms of elite, secular, masculinity of the ninth century, and, as such, is a precious guide to what that ideal masculinity was. The second concerns the changes in those norms in the course of the period under discussion. In the immense political flux of late republican Rome, definitions of masculinity were contested and reassessed;[62] so too in late antiquity. The cultured self-control and educated self-presentation of the Roman senatorial elite is worlds apart from the valour, violence and vengeance normative for the aristocracy of the seventh–eighth century west, and from the martial but Christian ethos in which young William was trained. The transformation of elite masculinity is an aspect of the transition from antiquity to the middle ages which has yet to be broached, but it immediately raises the question as to what extent wives and mothers were responsible for shaping as well as reproducing those changes.

Attention to women in the context of ideologies of masculinity has a further aspect. Classical masculinities were multiple, and of differing status. In late antiquity, only one is well studied: that touching eunuchs. Politically central but rhetorically marginalised in late antiquity, eunuchs were present in late antique imperial palaces and aristocratic households in both the eastern and western parts of the empire, and a continuing presence in the Byzantine world. They were often perceived to have feminine moral attributes to match their altered physical being.[63] They stand as the antithesis to elite masculinity, and as a reminder that gender organises relationships of power among men as much as between men and women.

Both the very presence of eunuchs themselves and the textual rhetoric about them are powerful reminders of the immense subtlety of late antique and early medieval ideas of gender. In the early Byzantine east for example, eunuchs were sometimes deemed incapable of achieving true sanctity, yet women sometimes sought the religious life by cross-dressing, acquiring a eunuch-like appearance.[64] The absence of eunuchs from the early medieval west suggests, however, that we must also pay attention to both chronological and geographical variations in notions of gender. Unknown in the west except as passing cattle in the slave trade, eunuchs were textual constructs only, and then only occasionally. As a result, western discourses about gender acquired a polarity much simpler and sharper than in the east. Focus on late antique and early medieval discourses of femininity is inadequate without attention to the much wider mesh of ideas about gender within society as a whole.[65]

We still await an exploration of the full richness of the tapestry of gendered behaviour and discourse in late antiquity and the early middle ages. When we have it, it will, I predict, indicate that part of the Transformation of the Roman World was a transformation of the rhetoric and reality of gender as complex, as rich and as integral to the overall pattern of social change as the transformations of urban life which are now so clearly mapped. It will be a transformation which tells a story of changing political cultures and familial life, changing religiosity and material culture. Above all, it will be a historiographical transformation.

And so, finally, to answer the question: did women have a Transformation of the Roman World? The question is, of course, a borrowed one.[66] In lifting it from Joan Kelly's famous 1976 article on the Renaissance, my intent is to do as she did: to unsettle and disquiet by challenging accepted perspectives. But my argument differs from hers. Whereas Kelly found that the Renaissance was bad for women, and went on to simply reverse the conventional polarity of medieval primitivism and Renaissance achievement, my conclusions cannot take such a simplistic form. In the first place, four fundamental aspects of women's lives remained unaltered: their relative historical invisibility in the sources; the constancy of marriage and motherhood as the central facts of almost all women's lives; their place in a gender hierarchy predicated upon male superiority and the explicit weakness of the female sex; and their vulnerability to violence and/or exploitation. Yet women's lives nevertheless changed. Standards of living, access to property, the expectations and constraints of marriage, and the increasing availability of a religious alternative to marriage, all underwent significant shifts in the period *c.* 300 to *c.* 800. That these changes were often greater in western Europe than in Byzantium suggests we should acknowledge, too, the diversity of women's experience of the transformation of the Roman world. At the core of my argument, though, is a stress on the constant centrality of women to the reproduction and transformation of cultural systems east and west, despite the changing content of those systems themselves. Like elite masculinity, wife- and motherhood are 'everywhere but nowhere' in the historical record, only occasionally visible in the sources, but not thereby irrelevant.

Finally, women's lives were not insulated from other social transformations. All these changes – marriage, property law, gender discourses, the ordering of domestic space – affected men too. The conclusion is inevitable: we ought not to continue to treat women in late antiquity and the early middle ages in isolation. To that extent, to ask whether women had a Transformation of the Roman World is indeed a misplaced question. But, provided we situate women in a world of men – rulers, aristocrats, clergy, eunuchs, peasants, even slaves – we are talking about the transformation of social relationships of immense complexity and far-reaching historical impact. The transformation which has not yet taken place is the methodological and historiographical reorientation necessary to appreciate this fully.

Notes

Versions of this chapter were read to the Medieval Academy of America, the Medieval History Seminar, University of Oxford and the Women's History Seminar, University of London, and I acknowledge the comments of all those who participated in the ensuing discussions. For help with drafts of this chapter, I am immensely grateful to Leslie Brubaker, Jinty Nelson, Tom Noble, Peter Rietbergen, Barbara Rosenwein, Trish Skinner and Pauline Stafford; all opinions and errors remain my own. The final version of this chapter was written at the Netherlands Institute for Advanced Study whose support and tranquillity it is a great pleasure to acknowledge.

1. Ian Wood, 'The European Science Foundation's Programme on the Transformation of the Roman World and the Emergence of Early Medieval Europe', *Early Medieval Europe*, 6 (1997), pp. 219–27. I am grateful to the project's leaders, Ian Wood, Javier Arce and

Evangelos Chrysos for inviting me to participate. For the closing review of the project, see Thomas F. X. Noble, '*The Transformation of the Roman World*: Reflections on Five Years of Work', in *East and West: Modes of Communication*, ed. Evangelos Chrysos and Ian Wood (Brill, Leiden, 1999), pp. 259–77, esp. comments at p. 269.

2. A massive bibliography could be appended; the best introduction to the subject is *The Transformation of the Roman World, AD 400–900*, ed. Leslie Webster and Michelle Brown (British Museum Press, London, 1997). For overviews of the results of the 'Transformation of the Roman World' project see, in addition to Noble, 'Transformation', Paolo Delogu, '*Transformation of the Roman World*: Reflections on Current Research', in *East and West*, ed. Chrysos and Wood, pp. 243–57, and on the eastern Mediterranean, Averil Cameron, 'The Perception of Crisis', *Morfologie sociale e culturali in Europa fra tarda antichità e alto medioevo*, Settimane di studio del centro italiano di studi sull'alto medioevo, 45 (1998), pp. 9–31.

3. Patrick Geary, *Before France and Germany: The Creation and Transformation of the Merovingian World* (Oxford, 1988), p. vi.

4. Patrick Geary, 'Ethnic Identity as a Situational Construct in the Early Middle Ages', *Mitteilungen der anthropologischen Gesellschaft in Wien*, 113 (1983), pp. 15–26; Walter Pohl, 'Conceptions of Ethnicity in Early Medieval Studies', *Archeologia Polona*, 29 (1991), pp. 39–49.

5. Noble, 'Transformation', pp. 259, 276.

6. The same is true for the conference published as *Morfologie sociale* and for the international colloquium on 'The World of Late Antiquity: The Challenge of New Historiographies', Smith College, MA, 15–17 October 1999.

7. Cf. the overview of Olwen Hufton, 'Women, Gender and the *Fin de siècle*', in *Companion to Historiography*, ed. Michael Bentley (Routledge, London, 1997), pp. 929–40.

8. For recent surveys see, for the ancient world, the thematic reviews in *Gender and the Body in the Ancient Mediterranean*, ed. Maria Wyke (Blackwell, Oxford, 1998), pp. 173–213. For the middle ages see Elisabeth Van Houts, 'The State of Research: Women in Medieval History and Literature', *Journal of Medieval History*, 20 (1994), pp. 277–92; Miri Rubin, 'A Decade of Studying Medieval Women', *History Workshop Journal*, 46 (1998), 213–39; Janet Nelson, 'Gender, Family and Sexuality in the Middle Ages', in *Companion to Historiography*, ed. Bentley, pp. 153–76.

9. Although to what extent is hotly disputed. Guy Halsall, 'Movers and Shakers: Barbarians and the Fall of Rome', *Early Medieval Europe*, 8 (1999), pp. 131–45.

10. John Evans, *Women, War and Children in Ancient Rome* (Routledge, London, 1991).

11. For example Brigitte Pohl-Resl, '"Quod me legibus contanget auere": Rechtsfähigkeit und Landbesitz langobardischer Frauen', *Mitteilungen des Instituts für Österreichischen Geschichtsforschung*, 101 (1993), pp. 201–27; Cristina La Rocca, 'Pouvoirs des femmes, pouvoirs de la loi dans l'Italie lombarde', in *Femmes et pouvoirs des femmes à Byzance et en Occident (VIe–XIe siècles)*, ed. Stéphane Lebecq, Alian Dierkens, Régine Le Jan and Jean-Marie Sansterre (Centre de Recherche sur l'Histoire de l'Europe de Nord-Ouest, Lille, 1999), pp. 37–50.

12. Guy Halsall, 'Female Status and Power in Early Merovingian Central Austrasia: The Burial Evidence', *Early Medieval Europe*, 5 (1996), pp. 1–24; Guy Halsall, 'Social Identities and Social Relationships in Early Merovingian Gaul', in *Franks and Alamanni in the Merovingian Period: An Ethnographic Perspective*, ed. Ian Wood (Boydell Press, Woodbridge, 1998), pp. 141–75.

13. S. J. Lucy, 'Housewives, Warriors and Slaves? Sex and Gender in Anglo-Saxon Burials', in *Invisible People and Processes: Writing Gender and Childhood into European Archaeology*, ed. Jenny Moore and Eleanor Scott (Leicester University Press, London, 1997), pp. 150–68.

14. Alexander Demandt, 'The Osmosis of Late Roman and Germanic Aristocracies', in *Das Reich und die Barbaren*, ed. Evangelos Chrysos and Andreas Schwarcz (Böhlau, Vienna, 1989), pp. 75–86 with examples pp. 78–9.

15. Hagith Sivan, 'Why Not Marry a Barbarian? Marital Frontiers in Late Antiquity (the example of CTh. 3.14.1)', in *Shifting Frontiers in Late Antiquity*, ed. Ralph Mathisen and Hagith Sivan (Variorum, London, 1996), pp. 136–45; Peter Heather, *The Goths* (Blackwell, Oxford, 1996), pp. 289–90.

16. Heather, *Goths*, pp. 305–6; Nicholas Brooks, 'Canterbury, Rome and the Construction of English Identity', in *Early Medieval Rome and the Christian West*, ed. Julia Smith (Brill, Leiden, 2000), pp. 221–46.

17. Leslie Brubaker, 'Memories of Helena: Patterns of Imperial Female Matronage in the Fourth and Fifth Centuries', in *Women, Men and Eunuchs: Gender in Byzantium*, ed. Liz James (Routledge, London, 1997), pp. 52–75; Dorothy Abrahamse, 'Women's Monasticism in the Middle Byzantine Period: Problems and Prospects', *Byzantinische Forschung*, 9 (1985), pp. 35–58 at pp. 38–9. An analogous point has frequently been made about the role of royal women in shaping political memory, especially dynastic memory, in the successor kingdoms of the early medieval west: Karl Leyser, *Rule and Conflict in an Early Medieval Society: Ottonian Saxony* (Edward Arnold, London, 1979), pt II; Janet Nelson, 'Gender and Genre in Women Historians of the Early Middle Ages', in Nelson, *The Frankish World, 750–900* (Hambledon, London, 1996), pp. 183–97.

18. Joëlle Beaucamp, 'La Situation juridique de la femme à Byzance', *Cahiers de Civilisation Médiévale*, 20 (1977), pp. 145–76; Karsten Fledelius, 'Women's Position and Possibilities in Byzantine Society With Particular Reference to the Novels of Leo VI', *Jahrbuch der Österreichischen Byzantinistik*, 32 (1982), pp. 425–32.

19. A few examples among many: Peter Brown, *The Body and Society: Men, Women and Sexual Renunciation in Early Christianity* (Columbia University Press, New York, 1988); Lynda Coon, *Sacred Fictions: Holy Women and Hagiography in Late Antiquity* (University of Pennsylvania Press, Philadelphia, 1997); Elizabeth Clark, *Reading Renunciation: Asceticism and Scripture in Early Christianity*, (Princeton University Press, Princeton, 1999) and items in notes 20–21.

20. Susanna Elm, *Virgins of God: the Making of Asceticism in Late Antiquity* (Oxford University Press, Oxford, 1994).

21. Suzanne Wemple, *Women in Frankish Society: Marriage and the Cloister, 500–900* (University of Pennsylvania Press, Philadelphia, 1981), p. 191.

22. Suzanne Wemple, 'Female Spirituality and Mysticism in Frankish Monasteries: Radegund, Balthild and Aldegund', in *Medieval Religious Women: Peaceweavers*, ed. John Nichols and Lillian Shank (Cistercian Publications, Kalamazoo, 1987), pp. 39–53; cf. Simon Coates, 'Regendering Radegund? Fortunatus, Baudonivia and the Problem of Female Sanctity in Merovingian Gaul', *Gender and Christian Religion*, ed. Robert Swanson, Studies in Church History, 34 (Boydell Press, Woodbridge, 1998), pp. 37–50; John Kitchen, *Saints' Lives and the Rhetoric of Gender: Male and Female in Merovingian Hagiography* (Oxford University Press, New York, 1998).

23. Susan Ashbrook Harvey, 'Women in Early Byzantine Hagiography: Reversing the Story', in *That Gentle Strength: Historical Perspectives on Women in Christianity*, ed. Lynda Coon, Katharine Haldane and Elisabeth Sommer (University Press of Virginia, Charlottesville, VA, 1990), pp. 37–59; Judith Herrin, 'Public and Private Forms of Religious Commitment Among Byzantine Women', in *Women in Ancient Societies: an Illusion of the Night*, ed. Léonie Archer, Susan Fischler and Maria Wyke (Macmillan, London, 1994), pp. 181–203; Marie-France Aupézy, 'La Sainteté et le couvent: libération ou normalisation des femmes?', in *Femmes et Pouvoirs des Femmes*, ed. Lebecq et al., pp. 175–88; Julia Smith, 'The Problem of Female Sanctity in Carolingian Europe, *c*. 780–920', *Past and Present*, 146 (1995), pp. 3–37; Pauline Stafford, 'Queens, Nunneries and Reforming Churchmen: Gender, Religious Status and Reform in Tenth- and Eleventh-Century England', *Past and Present*, 163 (1999), pp. 3–35.

24. Ludolf Kuchenbuch, '*Opus feminile*: Das Geschlechtverhältnis im Spiegel von Frauenarbeiten im früheren Mittelalter', in *Weibliche Lebensgestaltung im frühen Mittelalter*, ed. Hans-Werner Goetz (Cologne, 1991), pp. 139–75.

25. Angeliki Laiou, 'The Role of Women in Byzantine Society', *Jahrbuch für Österreichischen Byzantinistik*, 31, pt 1 (1981), pp. 233–60; Judith Herrin, 'In Search of Byzantine Women: Three Avenues of Approach', in *Images of Women in Antiquity*, ed. Averil Cameron and Amélie Kuhrt (Croom Helm, London, 1983), pp. 167–89, esp. pp. 168–71.

26. Roberta Gilchrist, 'Ambivalent Bodies: Gender and Medieval Archaeology', in *Invisible People and Processes*, ed. Moore and Scott, pp. 42–58 at p. 45 and references there cited.

27. For changes in housing styles, see Riccardo Santangeli Valenzani, 'Residential Building in Early Medieval Rome', in *Early Medieval Rome*, ed. Smith, pp. 101–12. For the gendering of domestic space during the Roman republic and principate, see Andrew Wallace-Hadrill, 'The Social Structure of the Roman House in the Late Republic and Early Empire', *Paperss of the British School at Rome*, 56 (1988), pp. 43–97, and, for late antiquity, the cautious comments of Gillian Clark, *Women in Late Antiquity: Pagan and Christian Lifestyles* (Oxford University Press, Oxford, 1993), pp. 97–8.

28. Suzanne Dixon, *The Roman Family* (London, 1992); André Burguière (ed.), *Histoire de la famille*, vol. I, *Mondes lointains, mondes anciens* (Armand Colin, Paris, 1986); David Herlihy, *Medieval Households* (Harvard University Press, Cambridge, MA, 1985); Wemple, *Women in Frankish Society*.

29. Peter Brown, 'Late Antiquity', in *A History of Private Life, I: From Pagan Rome to Byzantium*, ed. Paul Veyne (Harvard University Press, Cambridge, MA, 1987), pp. 235–311. For shaping boys' bodies, see Maud Gleason, 'The Semiotics of Gender: Physiognomy and Self-Fashioning in the Second Century C.E.', in *Before Sexuality: The Construction of Erotic Experience in the Ancient Greek World*, ed. David Halperin, John Winkler and Froma Zeitlin (Princeton University Press, Princeton, 1990), pp. 391–415 at pp. 402–3.

30. Helen Saradi-Mendelovici, 'A Contribution to the Study of the Byzantine Notarial Formulas: The *Infirmitas Sexus* of Women and the *SC Velleianum*', *Byzantinische Forschung*, 83 (1990), pp. 72–90.

31. Antti Arjava, *Women and Law in Late Antiquity* (Oxford University Press, Oxford, 1996), pp. 230–56; Joëlle Beaucamp, 'Le Vocabulaire de la faiblesse féminine dans les textes Juridiques Romains du IIIe au VIe siècle', *Revue d'Histoire du Droit Français et Étranger*, 54 (1986), pp. 485–508; Joëlle Beaucamp, *Le Statut de la femme à Byzance, IVe–VIIe siècle*, 2 vols (Paris, 1990–92), esp. vol. I, pp. 11–16.

32. Brent Shaw, 'The Family in Late Antiquity: The Experience of Augustine', *Past and Present*, 115 (1987), pp. 3–51 at pp. 31–2.

33. Suzanne Dixon, *The Roman Mother*, 2nd edn (Routledge, London, 1990).

34. Averil Cameron, 'Virginity as Metaphor: Women and the Rhetoric of Early Christianity', in *History as Text: The Writing of Ancient History*, ed. Cameron (Duckworth, London, 1989), pp. 184–205; Kate Cooper, 'Insinuations of Womanly Influence: An Aspect of the Christianisation of the Roman Aristocracy', *Journal of Roman Studies*, 82 (1992), 150–64; Kate Cooper, *The Virgin and the Bride: Idealized Womanhood in Late Antiquity* (Harvard University Press, Cambridge, MA, 1996).

35. Evelyne Patlagean, 'Famille et parentèle à Byzance', in *Histoire de la famille*, vol. I, ed. Burguière, pp. 421–41; Jean Gouillard, 'La Femme de qualité dans les lettres de Théodore Stoudite', *Jahrbuch der Österreichischen Byzantinistik*, 32, pt 2 (1982), pp. 445–52; Patricia Skinner, '"The light of my eyes": Medieval Motherhood in the Mediterranean', *Women's History Review*, 6 (1997), pp. 391–410.

36. Katrien Heene, *The Legacy of Paradise: Marriage, Motherhood and Women in Carolingian Edifying Literature* (Peter Lang, Frankfurt, 1997).

37. Yan Thomas, 'The Division of the Sexes in Roman Law', in *A History of Women in the West, I: From Ancient Goddesses to Christian Saints*, ed. Pauline Schmitt Pantel (Harvard University Press, Cambridge, MA., 1992), pp. 83–138.

38. Angeliki Laiou, 'Consensus Facit Nuptias – et Non: Pope Nicholas I's *Responsa* to the Bulgarians as a Source for Byzantine Marriage Customs', *Rechtshistorisches Journal*, 4 (1985), pp. 189–201.

39. On Roman and 'barbarian' law in the early medieval west, see the succinct and exemplary summary of Patrick Wormald, *The Making of English Law: King Alfred to the Twelfth Century*, vol. I, *Legislation and its Limits* (Blackwell, Oxford, 1999), pp. 36–44.

40. Wemple, *Marriage and the Cloister*; James Brundage, *Law, Sex and Society in Medieval Europe* (University of Chicago Press, Chicago, 1987); Raymund Kottje, 'Eherechtliche Bestimmungen der germanischen Volksrechte (5.–8. Jh.)', in *Frauen in Spätantike und Frühmittelalter: Lebensbedingungen, Lebensnormen, Lebensformen*, ed. Werner Affeldt (Thorbecke, Sigmaringen, 1990), pp. 211–20; Pierre Toubert, 'L'Institution du mariage chrétien, de l'antiquité à l'an mil', *Morfologie*, pp. 503–49; Mayke de Jong, 'To the Limits of Kinship: Anti-Incest Legislation in the Early Medieval West 500–900', in *From Sappho to de Sade: Moments in the History of Sexuality*, ed. J. Bremmer (Routledge, London, 1989), pp. 36–59; Mayke de Jong, 'An Unsolved Riddle: Early Medieval Incest Legislation', in *Franks and Alamanni*, ed. Wood, pp. 107–40.

41. Julia Smith, 'Gender and Ideology in the Early Middle Ages', in *Gender and Christian Religion*, ed. Swanson, pp. 51–73.

42. Janet Nelson, 'Monks, Secular Men and Masculinity, *c.* 900', in *Masculinity in Medieval Europe*, ed. Dawn Hadley (Longman, Harlow, 1999), pp. 121–42.

43. Arjava, *Women and Law*, p. 65.

44. Arjava, *Women and Law*, pp. 46–7, 63.

45. Clark, *Women*, p. 97; cf. Roger Bagnall, *Egypt in Late Antiquity* (Princeton University Press, Princeton, 1993), pp. 92–9, 130–33; Arjava, *Women and Law*, p. 69.

46. For example, Patricia Skinner, 'Women, Wills and Wealth in Medieval Southern Italy', *Early Medieval Europe*, 2 (1993), pp. 133–52.

47. Janet Nelson, 'The Wary Widow', in *Property and Power in the Early Middle Ages*, ed. Wendy Davies and Paul Fouracre (Cambridge University Press, Cambridge, 1995), pp. 82–113; Julia Crick, 'Women, Posthumous Benefaction and Family Strategy in Pre-Conquest England', *Journal of British Studies*, 38 (1999), pp. 399–422.

48. Arjava, *Women and Law*, p. 71; Bagnall, *Egypt*, p. 130.

49. Stressed by Beaucamp, 'Situation juridique', p. 176.

50. Judith Herrin, 'In Search of Byzantine Women', pp. 177–8; cf. Pauline Stafford, 'Women in Domesday Book', *Reading Medieval Studies*, 15 (1989), pp. 75–94 at pp. 81–2; Marc Meyer, 'Women's Estates in Later Anglo-Saxon England: The Politics of Possession', *Haskins Society Journal*, 3 (1991), pp. 111–29 at p. 113.

51. Cooper, *The Virgin and the Bride*, *passim*.

52. Gouillard, 'Femme de qualité', p. 450; Smith, 'Gender and Ideology', pp. 54–8.

53. Janet Nelson, 'Women and the Word in the Earlier Middle Ages', *Studies in Church History*, 27 (1990), pp. 53–78; Herrin, 'Public and Private', p. 187.

54. *Vita Desiderii Cadurcensis*, chs 9–11, ed. Dag Norberg, CCSL 117, pp. 352–6; Dhuoda, *Liber Manualis*, ed. Pierre Riché, Sources Chrétiennes 225b, 2nd edn (Paris, 1991).

55. Auspicius of Toul, panegyric on Arbogast, in *Epistulae Austrasicae*, 23, *MGH Epp.* III, pp. 135–6, lines 21–3. I am grateful to Ralph Mathisen for the reference and for supplying me with a copy of his translation, which I have chosen not to use here.

56. *Annales Mettenses Priores*, a. 678, ed. B de Simson, MGH SSRG (Hanover, 1905), p. 3.

57. Janet Nelson, 'The Problematic in the Private', *Social History*, 15 (1990), pp. 355–64; Régine Le Jan, *Famille et pouvoir dans le monde franc, VIIe–Xe siècle* (Publications de la Sorbonne, Paris, 1995).

58. Kenneth Holum, *The Theodosian Empresses* (University of California Press, Berkeley, 1982); Pauline Stafford, *Queens, Concubines and Dowagers: The King's Wife in the Early Middle Ages* (Batsford, London, 1983); Lynda Garland, *Byzantine Empresses: Women and Power in Byzantium, 527–1081* (Routledge, London, 1999); Anne Duggan (ed.), *Queens and Queenship in Medieval Europe* (Boydell Press, Woodbridge, 1997).

59. *Vita Balthildis*, 4, *MGH SSRM*, II, pp. 485–6; Hincmar, *De Ordine Palatii*, ed. T. Gross and R. Schieffer, *MGH Fontes Iuris Germanici*, 145 (Hahn, Hanover, 1990), ch. 5, lines 360–62, p. 72; Smith, 'Gender and Ideology', pp. 70–71.

60. John Tosh, 'What Should Historians Do With Masculinity? Reflections on Nineteenth-Century Britain', *History Workshop Journal*, 38 (1994), pp.179–202, quotation from p. 180. Similarly, Charles Barber, 'Homo Byzantinus?', *Women, Men and Eunuchs*, ed. James, pp. 185–99.

61. Cf. R. W. Connell, *Masculinities* (Polity Press, Cambridge, 1995), esp. p. 77.

62. Richard Alston, 'Arms and the Man: Soldiers, Masculinity and Power in Republican and Imperial Rome', in *When Men were Men: Masculinity, Power and Identity in Classical Antiquity*, ed. Lin Foxhall and John Salmon (Routledge, London, 1998), pp. 205–23.

63. Keith Hopkins, *Conquerors and Slaves* (Cambridge University Press, Cambridge, 1978), pp. 172–96; Shaun Tougher, 'Byzantine Eunuchs: An Overview With Special Reference to their Creation and Origin', *Women, Men and Eunuchs*, ed. James, pp. 168–84; Shaun Tougher, 'Images of Effeminate Men: The Case of Byzantine Eunuchs', *Masculinity in Medieval Europe*, ed. Hadley, pp. 89–100; Kathryn Ringrose, 'Living in the Shadows: Eunuchs and Gender in Byzantium', in *Third Sex, Third Gender: Beyond Sexual Dimorphism in Culture and History*, ed. Gilbert Herdt (Zone, New York, 1996), pp. 85–109.

64. Kathryn Ringrose, 'Passing the Test of Sanctity: Denial of Sexuality and Involuntary Castration', in *Desire and Denial in Byzantium*, ed. Liz James (Ashgate, Aldershot, 1999), pp. 123–37; Evelyne Patlagean, 'L'Histoire de la femme déguisée en moine et l'évolution de la sainteté féminine à Byzance', *Studi Medievali*, 3rd ser., 17 (1976), pp. 597–623; N. Delierneux, 'Virilité physique et sainteté féminine dans l'hagiographie orientale du IVe au VIIe siècle', *Byzantion*, 67 (1997), pp. 179–243, esp. pp. 199–200.

65. Cf. Allen Frantzen, 'When Women Aren't Enough', in *Studying Medieval Women*, ed. Nancy Partner (Medieval Academy of America, Cambridge, MA, 1993), pp. 143–69.

66. Joan Kelly-Gadol, 'Did Women have a Renaissance?', in *Becoming Visible: Women in European History*, ed. Renate Bridenthal, Claudia Coonz and Susan Stuard (Houghton Mifflin, Boston, 1976), pp. 139–64.

3

The Gender of Money: Byzantine Empresses on Coins (324–802)

Leslie Brubaker and Helen Tobler

Coins played different roles in the ancient and medieval worlds from those that they play in the economy today. In the late antique and early Byzantine world – that is, roughly between 300 and 800 – there were in a sense two currencies: gold coins and base metal (copper) coins. Both were minted and distributed by the state, but the gold *solidi* (in Latin) or *nomismata* (in Greek), introduced in 309, were by the end of the fifth century in practice used above all for the payment of tax and for major transactions such as land sales, while the copper coins (*nummi*, replaced in 498 by *folles*) were broadly the currency of market transactions.[1] Another striking difference is that late antique and Byzantine coin types changed with great frequency: as an extreme example, Maria Alföldi catalogued over seven hundred different types for a single emperor, Constantine I the Great (306–37, sole ruler from 324).[2] There are many reasons for this, but one of the most important has to do with communication: centuries before the advent of the press, images on coins were a means to circulate information about the state. This is particularly true of the first three and a half centuries covered by this chapter. While the extent to which coins were used in daily exchange transactions is still uncertain, and was very variable, the frequency with which they appear in archaeological excavations of urban sites throughout the former eastern Roman empire until 658 indicates their wide diffusion. After this, gold coinage continues in the east, albeit on a reduced scale, but copper coins become very rare until the ninth century.[3] Until the 650s, then, copper coins may be seen as a vehicle for the dissemination of ideas and ideals approved by the state to a reasonably wide popular base.[4] Gold coins had a more restricted audience, the precise configuration of which remains unclear, but one that spans the entire period covered here.

Little attention has been paid to the ways coins communicated in the late antique and early Byzantine world,[5] or to the gender strategies that played themselves out at the mints.[6] In particular, while various aspects of the role of the Byzantine empress have been studied in recent years,[7] little attention has been paid to the portraits of empresses on Byzantine coinage. These portraits are, however, important witnesses to how imperial women were presented to the collective gaze. We use the passive tense intentionally, for on the whole the coins do not show us how empresses represented themselves, but rather how their images were constructed by others to convey a series of messages for public consumption.[8] Byzantine mints were at least nominally controlled by the state,[9] and the decoration stamped on coins normally promoted state interests. Generally, Byzantine coins communicated aspects of imperial ideology, and the coins portraying empresses were no exception. The coin messages were conveyed through a combination of words and images, and usually the images were imperial portraits.

Underpinning the numismatic iconography of individual rulers is an assumption that, so far as we are aware, was never articulated: the importance of expressing hierarchical structure. Coins make hierarchy explicit through a series of carefully calibrated details, the meaning of which remained remarkably stable throughout the period covered by this chapter.[10] The most significant indicator was the position of a figure (or figures) on the coin, with the obverse (front) being more important than the reverse (back).

A second index of importance applied only to group portraits. These replicated actual imperial protocol, where the more important figure always stood or sat to the right of the less important figure; on coins, this means that from the viewer's perspective the more important figure is always on the left. When the emperor and empress are shown together (Figures 6, 7, 8, 9), the emperor is always on (our) left. In three-figure compositions, the most important figure was placed in the centre, the second ranking figure was located to the central figure's right (the viewer's left) and the least important figure was set on the central figure's left (the viewer's right). When the imperial couple flanks Christ (Figures 4–5), the emperor is thus on (our) left, the empress on (our) right; and when an empress and a junior emperor appear together with the senior emperor (Figure 8), the empress takes the tertiary position on (our) right.

A final expression of hierarchy on Byzantine numismatic portraiture is defined by absence. Imperial control of the mints allowed the senior ruler considerable control over numismatic content, and no emperor was obliged to include portraits of his junior co-rulers or of his wife. In other words, Herakleios did not have to include his wife Martina and his son Herakleios Constantine on the coin illustrated in Figure 8, but elected to do so. To a certain extent, the decision to include or omit additional figures on coinage was conditioned by recent convention: if the previous emperor had struck coins without additional figures, the current emperor was likely to follow suit. Changes in practice are therefore particularly noteworthy, and sometimes occasioned comment at the time.[11] While an emperor might deny association for a variety of personal or political reasons,[12] the abrupt addition of another figure, or figures, was almost always politically motivated. The role of gender in the visual rhetoric of politics is thus especially well revealed on coins.

For all of these reasons, it is legitimate to look to coin imagery as a barometer of imperial status and authority, as a rich source of information on the officially promoted position of the empress in Byzantium, and as an index of how perceptions of her role changed over time.

One final introductory excursus is necessary, on the ideological and legal relationship between an emperor and an empress in Byzantium. To put it crudely, the Byzantine state system was structured around the belief that the emperor was God's chosen representative on earth. In theory, his authority was unlimited and he was enveloped in an aura of holiness and unapproachability, created and maintained through a complicated tapestry of ceremonial and ritual, that served to emphasise his role as the link between the terrestrial and celestial spheres.[13] Especially in the early Byzantine years, the emperor's close association with God sometimes slipped into the older Roman notion of the *divus augustus*: in the early fifth century, for example, Priskos was sent by the emperor Theodosios II on an embassy to the Huns, along with the interpreter Vigilas, and 'the barbarians toasted Attila and we Theodosios. But Vigilas said that it was not proper to compare a god and a man, meaning Attila by a man and Theodosios by a god. This annoyed the Huns'.[14] The association did not extend to the empress. If the emperor was chosen by God, the empress was chosen by the emperor. She was not usually crowned by the archbishop of Constantinople (the patriarch), but by the emperor himself in a ceremony that could take place following their marriage (if he was already an emperor) or at some point after his coronation (if they were already married). It could even not take place at all, should the emperor decide, for whatever reason, not to crown his wife.[15] The significant distinction here is that the empress did not receive her authority from God, but from the emperor; in legal terms, the empress was subject to the law, the emperor was above it.[16]

The emperor Constantine I the Great (sole rule 324–37), regarded as a saint soon after his death, was revered by later Byzantines for two reasons. First, he was credited with converting the Roman empire to Christianity, and was thus hailed as the first Christian emperor. Second, he refounded the old city of Byzantium and renamed it Constantinople ('Constantine's city'). Called Istanbul since its conquest in 1453 by the Ottoman Turks, it was the major city of the Byzantine empire from the fourth to the fifteenth century; until at least the twelfth, it was the largest and richest city in the Christian world.[17] Coins minted during the reign of Constantine did not demonstrate any particular break from earlier Roman patterns. It is nonetheless important to introduce them here, because the coin types became important touchstones for later generations of Byzantine rulers who wished to associate themselves with the Constantinian house.

Constantinian coinage includes portraits of his wife Fausta (minted in the brief interlude between 324 and her disgrace and murder in 326), his mother Helena, and his stepmother Theodora. In all cases, the women are depicted alone on the obverse (front) of the coin in the contemporary Roman style of the profile bust; all are identified by name and title. The title, *augusta*, was conceived as a female form of the Roman emperor Augustus's name (which he assumed in 27 BC, before which he was known as Octavian), and willed to Augustus's wife Livia after his death in AD 14; imperial women are so designated on Roman coinage from the reign of Claudius (41–54).[18] In the Greek east, it was regularly – though not inevitably – used as a title for imperial wives until the thirteenth century, and it was also bestowed on other female family members such as Helena (mother of Constantine I) and Pulcheria (sister of Theodosios II).[19] The designation *basilissa* also appears in the sources but is not found on coins until 797.[20]

The reverse of the Constantinian empress coins always depicts a personification. Fausta's are identified either as *salus reipublicae* (well-being or health of the republic) or as *spes reipublicae* (hope of the republic) (Figure 1), each holding two children; both appear on *nummi* and, occasionally, on *nomismata*.[21] These personifications had appeared on Roman coins: *salus* since the republic, *spes* since the first century AD.[22] While they had not normally appeared with children, the constellation of messages now conveyed by Fausta's coins – fertility, security and dynastic stability – continued associations between imperial women and the well-being of the state that had long been a commonplace of Roman imperial imagery.[23] The same emphases are repeated time and again in later empress coins, and, though they certainly perpetuated earlier Roman patterns, their constant reiteration suggests that they struck chords with contemporary Byzantine beliefs as well. In fact, they correspond exactly with one of the crucial roles of imperial women: ideologically, and also practically, speaking, the primary duty of the empress was to provide heirs to the throne, thereby guaranteeing the succession and, by implication, the stability and security of the state. Normally, this was achieved biologically, but the empress could also secure a stable succession in other ways: for example, she could legitimise a potential male ruler through adoption or marriage. Fausta followed the normal course of events, and in 317 gave birth to the future Constantius II, Constantine's successor. This was not necessarily a foregone conclusion, and subsequent coin issues would respond to the crisis in Constantinian succession.

Figure 1: *Nomisma*: Fausta (obverse); *spes reipublicae* (reverse) (325–6).

Long before this, however, coins were minted in honour of Constantine's mother Helena. These are very similar to Fausta's, save that the personification is differently identified (Figure 2). In coins issued between 324 and 329/30, Helena is accompanied by *securitas reipublice* (security of the republic): Helena has provided for the security of the republic by providing her son as its ruler.[24]

Helena died in 329 or 330. About seven years later, in mid 337, a *nummus* was struck with a profile portrait of Helena on the obverse, and a personification identified as *pax publica* (public peace) on the reverse.[25] Like the *salus*, *spes* and *securitas* coins, the posthumous association of Helena with public peace inscribed a message of state well-being on a portrait of an imperial woman, but the nuances of that message were changed by the use of a different personification. The *pax* coins appeared only after Constantine's death in May of 337, and they were matched by the issue of a *nummus* that promoted Constantine's stepmother, Theodora, in the same year. The latter shows Theodora on the obverse, with a personification of *pietas romana* (Roman piety), infant at her breast, on the reverse.[26] Both series were minted in response to the struggle for succession after Constantine's death, which pitted Constantine's own sons against the sons of his father's second wife, Theodora: the posthumous Helena/*pax* coins promoted the interests of Constantine's sons and Helena's grand-sons, while the Theodora/*pietas* coins championed the interests of her sons, Constantine's half-brothers.

Figure 2: *Nomisma* (double weight): Helena (obverse); *securitas reipublicae* (reverse) (324–30).

In this context, the Helena and Theodora *nummi* are interesting
for a number of reasons. First, it is clear that both sides considered
coins to be useful and suitable ammunition in the contest for supporters. Second, both sides evidently believed that the virtues attached
to women, and conveyed through images of women, were appropriate buttresses for their own positions. Third, the women selected
to carry these virtues were mothers rather than wives. This was no
doubt due to the particular circumstances of the struggle to which
the coins respond, the contest between the grandson of Constantius
Chlorus's first partner, Helena, and the offspring of his second,
Theodora. As Jan Drijvers has already noticed, the two women are
presented 'as the ancestresses of the respective branches of the Constantinian family'.[27] The messages carried by the personifications are
also important, and they hint at the issues involved in dynastic politics
in the second quarter of the fourth century. Both personifications
salute old Roman values – *pax* and *pietas* – that had long been associated with women, and both stress their 'roman-ness' in the legends
attached to the image: *pax publica*, *pietas romana*. But the juxta-
position also seems to imply a choice between the peaceful continuation of the new order and the return to Roman (non-Christian)
piety, a contest between new and old values – a contest that would be
brought to a head when Theodora's grandson Julian (the Apostate)
finally achieved the throne in 360/1.[28] This is a lot of weight for a
small coin to bear, but the issues make no sense otherwise; and one
suspects that inexpensive *nummi* were chosen for this visual contest
because they enjoyed a wider circulation and reached a wider audience
than high denomination gold coinage.

In the aftermath of this high-profile use of empress coins in a
political contest, after 340 there are no more empress coins for over
forty years; nor did the emperors who followed Constantine name
their wives or mothers *augustae* until 383, when Theodosios I revived
both the title and the coin type.[29] In a series of high-value *nomismata*
and low-value *nummi* issued by the eastern mints, Theodosios's wife,
the *augusta* Flacilla, appeared on coins from 383 until her death four
years later (Figure 3).[30] The coinage shows the same type of profile
bust portrait on the obverse as had the Helena and the Fausta coins,
and the legend on the reverse, *salus reipublicae*, repeats the words
found on an earlier Fausta coin as well. The personification, however,
is now victory, and Christian victory of a very imperial and Constantinian sort, as indicated by the *chi-rho* – a reference to Constantine's

Figure 3: *Nomisma*: Flacilla (obverse); *salus reipublicae* (reverse) (383–7).

adoption of the first two letters of Christ's name, *chi* (X) and *rho* (P) in Greek, as insignia on shields and on his standard during battle – on victory's shield. Here, then, the imperial female portrait participated in a campaign to align Theodosios and his family with the old and already-by-then venerable Constantinian house:[31] the numismatic Flacilla not only guaranteed the safety and victory of the republic but also – backed by the Constantinian *chi-rho* and cast as the visual successor to Helena and as the continuator of her title – assured all those who handled the coins that with her family the prestige of the Constantinian house had been restored.

The use of Flacilla on coins to cement dynastic links continues the pattern seen already in the Constantinian coinage, which itself perpetuated older Roman practice. It is also true, however, that in the fourth and early fifth centuries images meant to evoke associations with the Constantinian house virtually always involved women. Either the links were made through images of women, as on the Flacilla coin, or they were expressed in imperial female building commissions.[32] Both of these roles pay tribute to Helena's lasting (and, indeed, growing) prestige, which itself inspired, and was significantly augmented by, the legend of her discovery of the True Cross that surfaced in the 390s.[33]

Allusions to Constantinian symbolism were continued in later empress coins issued for various female members of the Theodosian house, most notably Pulcheria, sister of Theodosios II and *augusta* from 414 until her death in 453, who took particular care to associate herself with Helena.[34] Pulcheria's campaign is evident in many media, one of which is the coinage minted in her name.[35] The early *nomismata* (414–19) continue the formula favoured by Flacilla,[36] but from 420 the reverse shows either a personification of victory holding a long cross or, in 430 and 442/3, a personification of Constantinople holding an orb surmounted by a cross (the *globus cruciger*), a motif for which Philip Grierson and Melinda Mays believe that Pulcheria may have been responsible.[37] Victory holding a long cross appears as well on the coins of Pulcheria's brother, and on one level certainly refers to the cross that Theodosios II erected (according to the contemporary historian Sokrates, at Pulcheria's instigation) on Golgotha, in exchange for which the bishop of Jerusalem is said to have sent him relics of the right arm of St Stephen the protomartyr.[38] On another and more important level, both of these crosses allude to the True Cross – which Helena was by then believed to have discovered in Jerusalem.[39] The latter association was certainly appreciated by Pulcheria's contemporaries, and the *augusta* was duly christened the 'new Helena' by the Council of Chalcedon in 451; she was the first woman to achieve this title, which henceforth became a commonplace in Byzantine imperial rhetoric.[40] The coinage suggests (and this suggestion is corroborated by various other sources) that the Council did not dream up the epithet without help; instead, Pulcheria's designation as the 'new Helena' seems to have been the result of a concerted effort on the *augusta*'s part to attain such recognition.[41] The *nomismata* that show Pulcheria with the cross-bearing victory or Constantinople holding the *globus cruciger* are rare examples of coin formulas that may actually have been inspired by the *augusta* herself.

As the mid fifth-century Pulcheria coins suggest, once reintroduced in 383 for Flacilla, empress coinage continued. In fact, it continued for over a century: with few exceptions, between 383 and 491 most imperial wives were given the title *augusta* and were commemorated on the coinage. The coin types continued to portray the empress in profile on the obverse, while the reverses repeated the range of inscriptions and personifications already described, with the notable addition of a cross in a wreath – a clear indication of the lasting association of imperial women with the cross[42] – that first appeared under Eudoxia (400–404).[43] There are, however, two significant deviations from this pattern, both of which tie into issues of succession. They are provided by the gold *nomismata* commissioned to celebrate or commemorate the marriages of Marcian and Pulcheria in 450 (Figure 4), and of Anastasios and Ariadne in 491(Figure 5), both of which show the emperor in military costume on the obverse and the imperial couple flanking Christ on the reverse.[44]

Figure 4: *Nomisma*: Marcian (obverse); Marcian and Pulcheria blessed by Christ (reverse) (450).

The marriage *nomismata* present the emperor as the most important figure: his portrait alone occupied the obverse (and was thus allowed to take precedence over the image of Christ on the reverse) and the emperor also took precedence over the empress in the triple portrait, where he was portrayed standing at the right hand of Christ. The reverse composition was apparently modelled on an earlier *nomisma* struck to celebrate the marriage of Valentinian III and Licinia Eudoxia in 437; here, however, the central figure was not Christ but rather Licinia Eudoxia's father, the senior, eastern emperor Theodosios II.[45] The substitution is remarkable: despite the imposition of standard imperial protocol, both Marcian and Pulcheria (later followed by Anastasios and Ariadne) share a groundline with and are blessed by Christ, a configuration that does not appear in other media until the late ninth century.[46] The near-equity between emperor and empress, and their association with Christ, needs to be seen in the context of the marriage coins themselves, which are exceptional commemorative issues: that depicting Marcian and Pulcheria, for example, survives in only one copy.

It is surely no coincidence that these *nomismata* commemorated marriages whereby the empress legitimised the emperor. When Theodosios II died without issue in 450, his sister Pulcheria (an *augusta* since 414, as we have seen) selected and married Marcian and thereby legitimised his succession to the throne. When Leo II died at the age of seven in 474, only shortly after the death of his grandfather Leo I earlier that year, the throne passed to his father Zeno, and his mother Ariadne (who was Leo I's daughter) was named *augusta*. On Zeno's death in 491, Ariadne married Anastasios, and it was her status

Figure 5: *Nomisma*: Anastasios (obverse); Anastasios and Ariadne blessed by Christ (reverse) (491).

as *augusta* – triply confirmed by her status as the daughter of one emperor, mother of another, and wife of a third – that legitimised the succession of her second husband Anastasios. Both Pulcheria and Ariadne were, in other words, *augustae* in their own rights and daughters of a previous emperor; in each case, the *augusta* legitimised the *augustus* through marriage rather than the reverse. The selection of Christ to sanction the process must be credited to Pulcheria and Marcian, and seems likely to reflect Pulcheria's early pledge of virginity and claim to be a 'bride of Christ';[47] parallels with the earlier Licinia Eudoxia marriage coins suggest, at any rate, that Christ's role here is as a familial marriage sponsor as well as a guarantor of its success.

The Theodosian house, which ended in 518 with the accession of Justin I, had been able (admittedly tenuously) to claim continuity with the Constantinian dynasty, and this claim was important to the legitimacy of the house: it was one reason, as we have seen, for the revival of the empress coins under Theodosios I. The often-fragile links between the imperial family and the old Roman senatorial aristocracy that had been sustained for nearly two centuries were, however, broken once and for all with the advent of Justin I.[48] This break is marked not just by a change in the ruling family's genealogical background, but also by the total absence of empress coins during the reigns of Justin I (518–27) and Justinian I (527–65).

While it might be tempting to interpret this hiatus as a visual signal meant to differentiate the new rulers, with their roots in the military elite of the provinces, from the old urban aristocratic families, the evidence simply does not support this opposition. Anastasios had not in fact minted coins that portrayed the *augusta* Ariadne (who died only in 515) since 491, the year of their marriage: by the time Justin

I came to the throne, empress coins had not been struck for nearly thirty years. In addition, an entirely new form of low-denomination coinage had been introduced in 498. Throughout the remainder of Anastasios's reign, this invariably portrayed the emperor on the obverse, and an indication of the coin's worth on the reverse: E, the Greek number five, on the *pentanummium*, with a value five times that of the old *nummus*; I, the Greek number ten, on the *decanummium*, with a value ten times that of the old *nummus*; K, the Greek number twenty, on the half-*follis*, with a value twenty times that of the old *nummus*; and M, the Greek number forty, on the *follis* itself (Figures 6–8), with a value forty times that of the old *nummus*.[49] Perhaps to accustom its public to the new coinage, the sequence shows little variation; it never incorporates an image of the empress, and neither do the higher denomination coins. Rather than marking change, then, the omission of the *augustae* Euphemia and Theodora on the coinage of Justin I and Justinian I seems to continue the pattern instigated with the reorganisation of the mints in 498 under Anastasios.

It is the rejuvenation of empress coins in 565, rather than the absence of them earlier in the century, that is striking, as is their new form: when empress coins begin again to be minted after the death of Justinian in 565, they look quite different from the earlier versions. Between 565 and 641, a period that encompasses the reigns of five imperial couples, the empress no longer appears alone on coins at all; instead, when she appears she is joined by her husband: either the imperial couple are shown together on the obverse of the coin (Figure 6), or the emperor appears on the obverse and the empress on the reverse. With only one exception (a *follis* and half-*follis* struck in Carthage in 572/3 for Justin II and Sophia),[50] the emperor is named but the empress remains anonymous.

This phase represents a new departure, which has been interpreted as representing the shared nature of imperial prestige and authority under Justin II and Sophia,[51] during whose reign the type was instigated,[52] although it might also be read as a sign that the empress was no longer important in her own right at all. At least one of the messages that these coins were apparently intended to convey, however, continued a familiar pattern. As under the Theodosians, the reintroduction of empress coinage runs parallel to the association of the imperial family with Constantine and Helena: in response to a gift sent to the pope by Justin II and Sophia, they were dubbed the new Constantine and the new Helena by Venantius Fortunatus.[53] The new

Figure 6: *Follis.* Justin II and Sophia (obverse); M with year 574/5 (reverse).

portrait type itself, with the imperial couple together, may in fact represent an attempt to invoke Constantine-and-Helena, whose symbolic resonance was by now usually as a pair rather than as individuals. Be that as it may, once the coin type was re-established, the practice and the evocation of Constantine were sustained by Justin's successor, Tiberius Constantine, given his second name by Justin II in 574 when he was declared Caesar, and his wife Ino-Anastasia (578–82), who apparently re-named one of their daughters Constantina.[54] Coins with the double portrait are, however, preserved only from the mint at Thessalonike in 579,[55] and seem to have commemorated the beginning of their rule, after which the portraiture is limited to Tiberius. Maurice (582–602), who married the daughter Constantina, also continued the double enthroned portrait on his coins. Here too the datable examples appear only at the beginning of the reign, and were minted in Thessalonike.[56]

This practice contrasts sharply with the Justin II/Sophia issues, which were numerous and continued to be minted throughout Justin II's reign.[57] The consistent use of the joint portrait between 565 and 578 evidently impressed the pattern on subsequent rulers, and it may be recalled that the two *augusti* who followed Justin II were in the way of being family members – Tiberius was Justin II's adopted son, while Maurice was both married to Tiberius's daughter and, perhaps, favoured by Sophia herself[58] – who may have continued the coin type as a visible means of promoting familial continuity. That the frequency of issue was not maintained suggests, however, a re-evaluation of the double portrait under Tiberius and Maurice. It now seems to have been considered appropriate as an inauguration image, in at least some parts of the empire, but not as a normal issue. The *augusta* has been subsumed into an expression of imperial unity, necessary only at the beginning of a reign; she is not, on the Tiberius and Maurice coins, an essential component of, or even a participant in, the empire's day-to-day ideological programme. In their restricted use as, apparently, commemorative issues, the Tiberius/Anastasia and Maurice/Constantina coins recall the marriage *nomisma* of Anastasios/Ariadne, but subsequent events make it clear that, however rarely they were struck in the last two decades of the sixth century, the significance of the double portrait was not forgotten.

Phokas, who usurped the throne in 602, crowned his wife Leontia immediately and promptly issued copper coins bearing their joint portrait (Figure 7). These were struck in all of the mints then operating in the eastern empire, some of which continued to issue them until the final year of Phokas's reign.[59] The decision to mint coins portraying the imperial couple throughout the east and for virtually

Figure 7: *Follis:* Phokas and Leontia (obverse); M with year 602/3 (reverse).

all of the reign was certainly intentional, and fits into the larger picture of Phokas's numismatic patronage, which included the revival of individualised portraiture.[60] At least in part, Phokas presumably returned to coin types sanctified by tradition in an attempt to legitimise his abrupt and irregular rise to power by associating himself with the authority of the past. This is the context for the coins that portray the imperial couple together, which demonstrate that the *augusta* continued to play an important role in expressions of imperial unity, but also suggest that when issues of dynastic continuity, well-being and stability were at stake, the role of the empress increased correspondingly. On the Phokas/Leontia coins, the *augusta* was, once again, used to reinforce imperial authority and dynastic pretensions.

The use of coins to promote dynasty continued under Herakleios (610–41), who himself usurped the throne in 610, which suggests that it was viewed as a successful ploy. Herakleios's son, born in 612 and called Herakleios the new Constantine, was crowned in 613 and appeared immediately on coins; Herakleios's first wife Eudokia died shortly after the boy's birth. At some point thereafter, the emperor married his niece, Martina, who was named *augusta* and appeared on coins from 616 to 629 (Figure 8); a second son, designated Caesar in 632 and *augustus* in 638, appears on coins of the last decade of the

Figure 8: *Follis*. Herakleios Constantine, Herakleios, Martina (obverse); M (reverse) (615–24).

reign.[61] Martina's omission after 629 corresponds with a change in type that, in Grierson's words, 'marks a major attempt at monetary reform';[62] it also followed Herakleios's triumphal return from Jerusalem after his defeat of the Persians, and the emperor now appears in military costume.

The unnamed empresses on this group of late sixth- and early seventh-century coins served almost exclusively as symbols of continuity and stability for the state, and it is significant that *augustae* who were not imperial wives do not appear on coins of this period at all.[63] To an extent, their anonymity serves to downplay their potential roles as actual mothers; the anonymous empress-as-symbol on the coins, standing by her man, can have stamped upon her whatever messages seem appropriate: she is, for example, perfectly suited to be cast as an imperial attribute that allows the portrait to evoke the idealised rule of Constantine-and-Helena. The empress portraits had always conveyed abstract and ideological messages – Helena was not just mother of Constantine, she was also the security of the republic – but it is important to signal that, in the years around 600, the abstract ideological messages subsumed whatever personal underpinning they had had in late antiquity.

After 629, there are no empress coins of any description for a century and a half. Neither the immediate followers of Herakleios nor any of the Isaurians who instigated Iconoclasm issued coins portraying women. Though dynastic continuity was promoted through coins, the message was no longer carried by the empress but rather by portrayals of the heir apparent, the reigning emperor's son, a process that had already begun under Herakleios.[64]

The next empress coins do not appear, in fact, until 780, with the empress Eirene. No coins with her portrait were struck during the lifetime of her husband Leo IV, but after his death in 780 – when Eirene began to act as regent for her nine-year-old son Constantine VI – coins bearing her effigy, along with that of her son, immediately appeared.[65] For ten years (780–90), Constantine VI and Eirene appear together as bust portraits on the obverse of coins, both holding the *globus cruciger* (Figure 9); the reverse normally celebrates familial ancestors. Constantine VI takes precedence over his mother, but even in the coins struck in 790, by which point he was nineteen years old, he is shown beardless to signal his relative immaturity. The inscriptions, which designate Constantine VI as *caesar*, *basileus* and *despotes*, then Eirene as *augusta*, unusually begin on the reverse and

Figure 9: *Nomisma*: Constantine VI and Eirene (obverse); Constantine V, Leo III and Leo IV (reverse) (780–90).

conclude on the obverse, so that Eirene's name appears on the front of the coin. This oddity aside, the coins return to one version of the numismatic iconography of the last series of empress coins. The major differences are the appearance of frontal bust portraits in place of standing or enthroned figures and the placement of ancestors on the reverse; but neither of these features is an innovation: both derived from numismatic practices during Iconoclasm.[66]

Things changed slightly between 790 and 792 when Constantine attempted to assert his authority. It is an indication of how important small changes on coins can be that this turning point is marked not by the removal of Eirene from coins – she remains – but by a shift in her attributes: between 790 and 792 Eirene is simply no longer given

Figure 10: *Nomisma*: Constantine VI and Eirene (obverse); Constantine V, Leo III and Leo IV (reverse) (790–2).

the sign of highest authority, the *globus cruciger* (Figure 10).[67] Roles
reversed again between 792 and 797. Coins now show Eirene, labelled
augusta, on the obverse and relegate Constantine (labelled *basileus*)
to the reverse (Figure 11). Despite his age (twenty-one in 792, twenty-
six by 797), he is still shown beardless, with the implication that he is
too young to rule. Again, a small detail on a small coin; but again,
one with large implications.[68] Finally, in 797, Constantine VI was
blinded and deposed; after this, Eirene ruled alone until her own de-
position in 802. This change of status, as is widely known, was commemorated by a series of coins, minted in Constantinople between
797 and 802, that show Eirene on both sides (Figure 12).[69] She is

Figure 11: *Nomisma*: Eirene (obverse); Constantine VI (reverse)
(792–7).

Figure 12: *Nomisma*: Eirene (obverse); Eirene (reverse) (797–802).

now labelled *basilissa*, the first time that this designation appears on coins.

The double portrait has occasioned considerable comment, sometimes suggesting that it demonstrates Eirene's over-ambitious and power-hungry nature. Yet the new numismatic formula went unremarked at the time, and, more important, was copied by three subsequent emperors, Michael I in 811, Leo V in 813 and Michael II in 821, none of whom have been characterised as overly ambitious or power-hungry.[70] To its Byzantine audience, the double portrait was accepted, and found to provide a useful new pattern. Taken together, Eirene's coins show how precise the messages carried by coins could be, and they are also informative about the construction of gender in modern scholarship.

The empress coins minted between 324 and 802 consistently stress the role of the *augusta* in promoting messages of security, well-being, stability and harmony; she embodies domestic virtues applied to the state. In the early issues, the women appear alone, backed by a personification or, later, a cross that explicitly supported these roles. The marriage *nomismata* of 437, 450 and 491 then introduce the double imperial portrait, which was adopted as the standard formula from 565 until 629. With this, the empress loses her identity: both her name and her personal attributes disappear, as indeed do any individualising characteristics in the portraiture itself. She has been modelled into an implicit rather than an explicit sign of concord and continuity. Eirene's coins restore a measure of balance, and one that will have repercussions in coins minted throughout the ninth century, when not only does the duplicated portrait continue, but imperial women return again to coins.[71]

Confining ourselves to the coinage considered here, however, it is clear that even beyond the consistent messages of state well-being carried by all of the empress coins, certain other structural features remain constant. Imperial women were always available as an ideological resource, and the mints keep coming back to them. Concomitantly, when empresses appear on coins, they are always meaningful, and they often appear at points of fracture or transition. Images of imperial women seem somehow to have bestowed legitimacy on husbands, sons or, in the isolated case of Eirene, themselves. Symbols of legitimisation are always important, and particularly so during crises of succession, which, as we have seen, regularly called forth imperial female images on coins. That this was at least sometimes recognised by the *augustae* themselves is suggested by the cases of Pulcheria and Eirene, who used coins minted in their names to precise ends: Pulcheria valorised her association with Helena and the cross; Eirene, more traditionally, legitimised her claim to the throne.

....

Notes

The genesis of this study was Helen Tobler's BA dissertation, 'Images of Empresses on Byzantine Coins' (University of Birmingham, 1997); a revised version was presented at Leeds in 1998 by Leslie Brubaker. The authors thank Ruth Macrides and Paul Magdalino, in whose house that version was written, for stimulating discussions of coin imagery, and Chris Wickham, for perceptive comments on the text.

1. M. Hendy, *Studies in the Byzantine Monetary Economy c. 300–1450* (Cambridge University Press, Cambridge, 1985), pp. 284–5, 294–6, 466. For convenience, we use 'copper' to cover the various types of base-metal coins. Silver coins were less common, particularly in the fifth and sixth centuries, and will not be considered here.

2. M. Alföldi, *Die constantinische Goldprägung: Untersuchungen zu ihrer Bedeutung für Kaiserpolitik und Hofkunst* (Römisch-Germanischen Zantralmuseums, Mainz, 1963).

3. See J. F. Haldon, *Byzantium in the Seventh Century: The Transformation of a Culture* (Cambridge University Press, Cambridge, 1990), pp. 117–20, 447–9, and 'Production, Distribution and Demand in the Byzantine World, c. 660–840', in *The Long Eighth Century*, ed. I. L. Hansen and C. J. Wickham (Brill, Leiden, 2000).

4. On coins as publicity, see further M. Grant, *Roman Imperial Money* (Thomas Nelson and Sons, London, 1954), pp. 7–8.

5. J. D. Breckenridge, *The Numismatic Iconography of Justinian II* (Numismatic Notes and Monographs 144, New York, 1959), and D. Wright, 'The True Face of Constantine the Great', *Dumbarton Oaks Papers*, 41 (1987), pp. 493–507, are exceptions.

6. G. Zacos and A. Veglery, 'Marriage Solidi of the Fifth Century', *Numismatic Circular* 68 (1960), pp. 73–4; K. Holum, *Theodosian Empresses: Women and Imperial Dominion in Late Antiquity* (University of California Press, Berkeley, 1982), pp. 32–4, 65–7, 110, 123, 129–30, 209, 221; L. Garland, *Byzantine Empresses, Women and Power in Byzantium AD 527–1204* (Routledge, London, 1999), pp. 50–51, 62, 83, 99, 102.

7. For example, Holum, *Theodosian Empresses*; Garland, *Byzantine Empresses*; B. Hill, *Imperial Women in Byzantium, 1025–1204: Power, Patronage and Ideology* (Longman, Harlow, 1999). More generally, on the use of the visual to tell us about the voiceless, see R. Gilchrist, *Gender and Material Culture: The Archaeology of Religious Women* (Routledge, London, 1994), and, for the period under consideration here, L. Brubaker, 'Memories of Helena: Patterns in Imperial Female Matronage in the Fourth and Fifth Centuries', in *Women, Men and Eunuchs: Gender in Byzantium*, ed. L. James (Routledge, London, 1997), pp. 52–75.

8. R. J. A. Talbert, *The Senate of Imperial Rome* (Princeton University Press, Princeton, 1984), p. 379, notes that in republican Rome the senate had been responsible for coin design but that this responsibility had been passed to the emperor at the beginning of the principate. Imperial responsibility, perhaps mediated through the state bureaucracy, continued in Byzantium.

9. In practice, regional mints apparently had some latitude in the selection of coin types to stamp: see below.

10. See P. Grierson and M. Mays, *Catalogue of Late Roman Coins in the Dumbarton Oaks Collection and in the Whittemore Collection* (Dumbarton Oaks Research Library and Collection, Washington DC, 1992), pp. 73–8, for coins minted between 393 and 491; P. Grierson, *Catalogue of the Byzantine Coins in the Dumbarton Oaks Collection and in the Whittemore Collection II,1–2* (Dumbarton Oaks Research Library and Collection,

Washington DC, 1968), pp. 68–70, for coins minted between 602 and 717; P. Grierson, *Catalogue of the Byzantine Coins in the Dumbarton Oaks Collection and in the Whittemore Collection III, 1–2* (Dumbarton Oaks Research Library and Collection, Washington DC, 1973), pp. 106–16, for the period between 717 and 1081.

11. See Holum, *Theodosian Empresses*, pp. 127–30.

12. Discussion in Grierson, *Catalogue III*, p. 9.

13. See A. Cameron, 'The Construction of Court Ritual: The Byzantine *Book of Ceremonies*', in *Rituals of Royalty: Power and Ceremonial in Traditional Societies*, ed. D. Cannadine and S. R. F. Price (Cambridge University Press, Cambridge, 1987), pp. 106–36; G. Dagron, *Empereur et prêtre: Étude sur le 'césaropapisme' byzantin* (Gallimard, Paris, 1996).

14. R. C. Blockley (ed.), *The Fragmentary Classicising Historians of the Later Roman Empire II: Eunapius, Olympiodorus, Priscus and Malchus: Text, Translation and Historiographical Notes* (Francis Cairns, Liverpool, 1983), pp. 246–7.

15. See S. Runciman, 'Some Notes on the Role of the Empress', *Eastern Churches Review*, 4 (1972), pp. 119–24.

16. S. Maslev, 'Die Staatsrechliche Stellung der byzantinischen Kaiserinnen', *Byzantinoslavica*, 27 (1966), pp. 308–43, esp. p. 308; J. Beaucamp, *Le Statut de la femme à Byzance 1* (De Boccard, Paris, 1990), p. 274.

17. The bibliographies on Constantine and on Constantinople are vast; for convenient surveys, see A. Kazhdan (ed.), *The Oxford Dictionary of Byzantium I* (Oxford University Press, Oxford, 1991), pp. 498–500, 508–12.

18. See Grant, *Roman Imperial Money*, pp. 133–48, esp. p. 142.

19. See Maslev, 'Staatsrechliche Stellung', p. 309; and Runciman, 'Some Notes', p. 119. D. Missiou, 'Über die Institutionelle Rolle der byzantinischen Kaiserin', *Jahrbuch der Österreichischen Byzantinistik*, 32 (1982), pp. 489–97, argued (incorrectly) that the title was only conferred to imperial wives who bore heirs. By the middle Byzantine period, an *augusta* was necessary for certain court ceremonies (for which reason, after the death of his second wife, Leo VI (886–912) elevated his daughter Anna to the rank) but it is unclear when this system originated: see E. Bensammer, 'La Titulature de l'Impératrice et sa Signification', *Byzantion*, 46 (1976), pp. 243–91, esp. p. 276.

20. See Bensammer, 'Titulature de l'Impératrice', p. 270, and p. 589 above.

21. P. Bruun (ed.), *The Roman Imperial Coinage VII: Constantine and Licinius AD 313–337* (Spink and Son, London, 1966), pp. 53, 116, 137, 205, 209, 263, 266, 475, 519, 571, 615, 621, 624, 690, 709 (copper coins), 383, 613 (*nomismata*), pl. 18 (no. 12). Sometimes both *salus* and *spes* are invoked: Alföldi, *Die constantinische Goldprägung*, p. 194 (nos 441–2), fig. 157.

22. Grant, *Roman Imperial Money*, pp. 125, 141, 162, pls I,6; XIII,3.

23. See M. B. Flory, 'Livia's shrine to Concordia and the Porticus Liviae', *Historia*, 33 (1984), pp. 309–30; K. Cooper, 'Insinuations of Womanly Influence: An Aspect of the Christianization of the Roman Aristocracy', *Journal of Roman Studies*, 82 (1992), pp. 150–64; S. Fischler, 'Social Stereotypes and Historical Analysis: The Case of the Imperial Women at Rome', in *Women in Ancient Societies, An Illusion of the Night* , ed. L. J. Archer, S. Fischler and M. Wyke (Macmillan Press, Houndmills, 1994), pp. 115–33, esp. p. 129.

24. Bruun (ed.), *Roman Imperial Coinage VII*, pp. 53, 116, 137, 205–6, 209, 212–13, 264, 266–70, 325, 330, 385, 387, 447–8, 450, 453, 475, 519, 551–4, 557, 571, 615, 621, 624, 626, 647, 649–51, 689–91, 709–11 (copper coins), 383, 476, 514, 517, 613 (*nomismata*), pls 16 (no. 149), 17 (no. 110).

25. J. Kent (ed.), *The Roman Imperial Coinage VIII, The Family of Constantine I AD 337–364* (Spink and Son, London, 1981), pp. 143, 250–51, 449–50, pl. 21 (no. 33); the coins were struck in Constantinople, Rome and Trier.

26. Kent (ed.), *Roman Imperial Coinage VIII*, pp. 142, 250–51, 449–50, pls 1, 21 (nos 43, 51); minted at Constantinople, Rome, and Trier.

27. J. W. Drijvers, *Helena Augusta: The Mother of Constantine the Great and the Legend of her Finding of the True Cross* (E. J. Brill, Leiden, 1992), pp. 43–4.

28. Julian was the son of Iulius Constantius (second son of Theodora) and his second wife Basilina: A. M. H. Jones, J. R. Martindale and J. Morris, *Prosopography of the Later Roman Empire 1: AD 260–395* (Cambridge University Press, 1971), pp. 477–8.

29. See, in general, Grierson and Mays, *Late Roman Coins*, pp. 6–8.

30. J. W. E. Pearce, *The Roman Imperial Coinage IX: Valentian I – Theodosius I* (Spink and Son, London, 1968), pp. 153, 184, 195–6, 226, 229, 233, 257, 259, 261, 284, 289, 291 (copper coins), struck at Antioch, Constantinople, Heraklea, Nikomedia, Siscia and Thessalonike; pp. 225, 231 (*nomismata*), struck at Constantinople. A gold and a silver coin with Flacilla on the obverse, the *chi-rho* in a wreath on the reverse were also minted in Constantinople (Pearce, *Roman Imperial Coinage IX*, 232). A few of the copper coins replace victory with a standing portrait of the empress: Pearce, *Roman Imperial Coinage IX*, pp. 197, 245, 261, 302 (from Alexandria, Cyzicus, Heraklea, Nikomedia).

31. See Brubaker, 'Memories', esp. p. 60, and Holum, *Theodosian Empresses*, pp. 31–3, who, however, finds the *chi-rho* imagery 'trivial' (p. 32).

32. Brubaker, 'Memories'.

33. Drijvers, *Helena*, pp. 79–180, esp. p. 95; L. Coon, *Sacred Fictions: Holy Women and Hagiography in Late Antiquity* (University of Pennsylvania Press, Philadelphia, 1997), pp. 95–103.

34. See A. Williams, 'The Roles and Functions of Early Byzantine Imperial Women in the Succession to the Throne' (MPhil dissertation, University of Birmingham, 1998).

35. Grierson and Mays, *Late Roman Coins*, pp. 152–4, pls 18–19.

36. One critical distinguishing feature is the hand that emerges from the top of the coin and holds a diadem over the *augusta*'s head, a motif that had appeared on coins minted by Pulcheria's father Arcadius (emperor 395–408) in his youth and on the coins of her mother Eudoxia (*augusta* 400–404). On its significance, see I. Kalavrezou, 'Helping Hands for the Empire: Imperial Ceremonies and the Cult of Relics at the Byzantine Court', in *Byzantine Court Culture from 829 to 1204*, ed. H. Maguire (Dumbarton Oaks, Washington DC, 1997), pp. 63–4.

37. Grierson and Mays, *Late Roman Coins*, p. 152.

38. See K. Holum, 'Pulcheria's Crusade and the Ideology of Imperial Victory', *Greek, Roman and Byzantine Studies*, 18 (1977), pp. 153–72, esp. pp. 162–3; Holum, *Theodosian Empresses*, pp. 109–10.

39. Brubaker, 'Memories', p. 62.

40. See Holum, *Theodosian Empresses*, p. 216.

41. See note 34 above.

42. The cross is not regularly associated with emperors on coins until the reign of Tiberius II (578–82).

43. Grierson and Mays, *Late Roman Coins*, pp. 133–5, pl. 11. On the other empress coins of the period, Grierson and Mays, *Late Roman Coins*, pp. 6–9, 155–6, 165–6, 170–71, 176, pls 18, 23.

44. Zacos and Veglery, 'Marriage solidi of the fifth century', pp. 73–4; A. Bellinger, *Catalogue of the Byzantine Coins in the Dumbarton Oaks Collection and in the Whittemore Collection I: Anastasius I to Maurice 491–602* (Dumbarton Oaks, Washington DC, 1966), p. 4, pl. 1; Grierson and Mays, *Late Roman Coins*, p. 158.

45. Grierson and Mays, *Later Roman Coins*, pp. 145, 158, pl. 15. Four examples survive.

46. See L. Brubaker, *Vision and Meaning in Ninth-Century Byzantium: Image as Exegesis in the Homilies of Gregory of Nazianzus* (Cambridge University Press, Cambridge, 1999), pp. 158–9.

47. Holum, *Theodosian Empresses*, p. 209; and on Pulcheria's relation to Christ, K. Cooper, 'Contesting the Nativity: Wives, Virgins, and Pulcheria's *Imitatio Mariae*', *Scottish Journal of Religious Studies*, 19 (1998), pp. 31–43.

48. The forced retirement of the last western emperor (Romulus Augustus) in 476 had already shattered imperial continuity in the west.

49. See, for example, Bellinger, *Catalogue I*, p. 2.

50. Bellinger, *Catalogue I*, pp. 254–5.

51. A. Cameron, 'The Empress Sophia', *Byzantion*, 45 (1975), pp. 5–21, esp. p. 11; closely followed by Garland, *Byzantine Empresses*, pp. 40–57.

52. Bellinger, *Catalogue I*, pp. 204 (silver half *siliqua*, minted in Constantinople); 204–14, 226–31, 234–7, 243–5, 254–6 (*folles*, minted in Constantinople, Nicomedia, Cyzicus, Antioch, Carthage); 214–17, 221–5, 231–3, 238–9, 245–7, 255, 257–8 (half-*folles*, minted in Constantinople, Thessalonike, Nicomedia, Cyzicus, Antioch, Carthage, Constantine in Numidia, Rome); 248–9, 255–6 (*decanummium*, minted in Antioch, Carthage).

53. Discussion in A. Cameron, 'The Early Religious Policies of Justin II', in *The Orthodox Churches and the West*, ed. D. Baker, *Studies in Church History*, 13 (1976), pp. 57–9; M. Whitby, 'Images for Emperors in Late Antiquity: A Search for New Constantine', in *New Constantines: the Rhythm of Imperial Renewal in Byzantium, 4th–13th Centuries*, ed. P. Magdalino (Variorum, Aldershot, 1994), p. 89.

54. Whitby, 'Images for Emperors', pp. 83–93. Helena was, however, rejected as the new name of Tiberius's wife in favour of Anastasia.

55. Bellinger, *Catalogue I*, p. 277 (half-*follis*).

56. Bellinger, *Catalogue I*, pp. 373–4 (*folles*, minted in Cherson); 320, 373 (half-*folles*, minted in Thessalonike, Cherson); 374–5 (*pentanummia*, minted in Cherson). The Thessalonikan coins were minted in 582/3; those from Cherson cannot be precisely dated.

57. See note 52 above.

58. The latter point is controversial: see M. Whitby, *The Emperor Maurice and his Historian. Theophylact Simocatta on Persian and Balkan Warfare* (Clarendon Press, Oxford, 1988), pp. 7–8.

59. Grierson, *Catalogue II,1*, pp. 147, 162–3, 176, 180, 186–8 (*folles* struck in Constantinople and Nicomedia 602–4; in Cyzicus 602–3; in Antioch 602–9); 166–7, 174–5, 179, 184, 189–90 (half-*folles* struck in Constantinople, Nicomedia and Cyzicus 602–3; in Thessalonike 603–5; in Antioch 602–8); 190–91 (*decanummium* struck in Antioch 602–9).

60. See Grierson, *Catalogue II,1*, pp. 89–90.

61. Grierson, *Catalogue II,1*, pp. 216–383, with a chart on p. 226 setting out the range of the empress *folles* clearly.

62. Grierson, *Catalogue II,1*, p. 228. Garland, *Byzantine Empresses*, p. 63, believes that Martina's omission was due to her unpopularity in Constantinople. There is no evidence for this.

63. For example, Epiphania-Eudokia, born in 611 to Herakleios and his first wife, crowned *augusta* in 612: J. R. Martindale, *The Prosopography of the Later Roman Empire III: AD 527–641* (Cambridge University Press, Cambridge, 1992), pp. 445–6. C. Zuckerman, 'La Petit Augusta et le Turc: Epiphania-Eudocie sur les Monnaies d'Héraclius', *Revue Numismatique*, 150 (1995), pp. 113–26, has been countered by Garland, *Byzantine Empresses*, p. 255, note 10. The practice was revived under Theophilos (829–42): see Grierson, *Catalogue III,1*, pp. 407–8, 415–16.

64. For Herakleios, see above; for the Iconoclast emperors, see, for example, Grierson, *Catalogue III,1*, pp. 226–30, 232–4, 291–2, 294–5, 325–6.

65. Grierson, *Catalogue III,1*, pp. 337–8.

66. References in the preceding two notes.

67. Grierson, *Catalogue III,1*, p. 338.

68. Grierson, *Catalogue III,1*, pp. 338–9.

69. Grierson, *Catalogue III,1*, pp. 181, 327–48; Garland, *Byzantine Empresses*, p. 87.

70. Grierson, *Catalogue III,1*, pp. 367, 375, 394.

71. For *augustae* on the coins of Theophilos, see note 63 above; for Theodora (mother of Michael III) and Eudokia (wife of Basil I) see Grierson, *Catalogue III,1*, pp. 461–5 and *III,2*, pp. 489–90.

4

'Ex utroque sexu fidelium tres ordines' – The Status of Women in Early Medieval Canon Law

Eva M. Synek

From both sexes of the faithful, we know that there are three orders (*ordines*), as if three classes (*gradus*), in the holy and universal Church; of which, although none is without sin, the first is nevertheless good; the second better; and the third is the best. The first order (*ordo*) exists in both sexes of married people; the second in the continent and widows; the third in virgins and nuns. Likewise, there are three grades or orders (*gradus vel ordines*) of men: the first is that of the lay, the second that of the clerics and the third that of the monks.[1]

The work of Abbo, an abbot of Fleury (d. 1004), and an adherent of the tenth-century Cluniac reform movement, is of particular interest for our topic: first, because it explicitly refers to women; second, as the status classification he provides is highly ambiguous in several respects; and third, because it is evidence of an alternative model to Gratian's system of two ecclesiastical orders – cleric and lay (*clerici et laici*).[2] This latter 'bi-partite division of the entire Christian world: namely, lay/cleric', which was fostered by the western canonists of the second millennium, 'had a lengthy and at times violent pre-history'.[3] It is a model rooted in late antique canon law, and a very successful one. But, as Abbo's formulation demonstrates, it is insufficient and inadequate as a description of the early medieval situation. During the first millennium[4] we have not only to deal with ambiguous formulations concerning women, we also have to be aware of a variety of status definitions. Canon law provided for various categorisations among Christians. Often it is not clear (at least at first glance) whether a category is only for men or for women as well. Taking as its starting point the question of lay status, this chapter intends to clarify the terminological difficulties (without claiming to provide a full systematic survey of the multifold problems of women's status in the medieval world). It will touch upon the question of female clergy and address the comparatively greater equality of men and women within the important ascetic tradition of the church, as well as commenting briefly on the *status sui generis* of queens and empresses.

According to current Roman Catholic canon law, women in general are defined as lay Christians. It has often been assumed that this has been the case for the whole history of canon law, at least since the division of the Christian community into two categories – *clergy* and *laity* – became a characteristic feature of the late antique church order. However, since the appearance of Alexandre Faivre's book, *Les Laïcs aux origines de l'église* (Paris, 1984), women's general classification as lay has been challenged by the idea of a general exclusion of women from both lay and clerical status in formative Christianity. Faivre's thesis of women as outcasts of the general ecclesiastical system was popularised and extended to medieval and modern canon law by Marie Zimmermann.[5] Yet Faivre's argument (and, even more, its superficial adaptation to later times by Zimmermann) is highly problematical as I have argued elsewhere.[6] It is true, there are no female forms of '*laikos/laicus*'. But on the other hand, the lay status of women is already explicitly stated in the nineteenth canon of the First Council of Nicaea (325). The Nicaean canons are part of the universally adopted legal inheritance of the ancient church. They are reproduced in both eastern and western canon law collections. This alone might serve as a strong argument against women's specific exclusion from lay status in canon law. Neither androcentric speech nor differences in the rights and duties ascribed to men and women respectively are sufficient evidence for Zimmermann's theory. *Mutatis mutandis*, as far as the more ambiguous medieval canon law texts are concerned, the arguments against women's exclusion from the early Christian perception of lay have to be reconsidered.

A major argument is the predominant tradition of inclusive language in Roman law. Roman jurists argued that in legal texts male forms of generic terms are to be interpreted inclusively in principle even if a specific feminine form existed 'because the masculine always includes the feminine sex'.[7] In so far as Roman law was continuously preserved not only in the east but at least to some extent also by the western church until its great renaissance in the twelfth century, this is an important key to ambiguous formulations.

But to some extent, such ambiguous texts as the above-quoted *Apologeticus* of Abbo of Fleury may themselves help to clarify the gender question, as soon as one ceases to view each allegedly 'erroneous' formulation in isolation and places it in a wider context. 'Likewise, there are three grades or orders of men: Of which the first is that of the lay'. Abbo is one of those canonists who favour the tripartite ecclesiological model which has particular regard to the ascetic wing of the church. Though his language is highly ambiguous, there is no question that lay status is for both sexes. 'The first order exists in both sexes of married people', we read at the beginning of his explanation of the three ecclesiastical orders. Most canonists would not have paid further attention to women. Abbo is more aware of the 'second sex' – maybe because of his monastic background. It is significant that he mixes the canonical order system with another traditional concept: that of three grades of perfection. The special reference to widows and virgins is an obvious echo of this perspective. Some Fathers – Jerome for example – had transferred the picture of three different crops in the parable of the sower to the different statuses of Christians: marriage, widowhood, virginity.[8] Though widow (*vidua*) and virgin (*virgo*) are gender-inclusive terms in principle, the classification has special significance for women. Thus a confusion of order and grade (of perfection) might explain why Abbo, demonstrating that there are three orders from both sexes, speaks about women first. Singling out women was no problem as far as the monks (*monachi*) were concerned. The crucial role women played in formative monasticism was already reflected in its own particular terminology: *sanctimoniales* is one contemporary term for the female counterparts of monks. It carries notions of equivalence, and can be translated as consecrated women or women dedicated to God or simply as nuns. We find masculine and feminine equivalents elsewhere within Abbo's collection of canons. Title XIX refers to *monachi* (masc.) and *monachae* (fem.) respectively. Title XXII quotes a decree attributed to Pope Siricius referring to *monachi* (masc.) and *moniales* (fem.). These and other references (cf. title IV, V, XIV, XVIII, XXVI) testify to the predominant equality of male and female monastics as well as to a fluid terminology, especially as far as women are concerned. One must, of course, point out the absence of a separate female form of *laicus*. And it is difficult to link Abbo's female 'continents and widows' and male clerics – at least at first glance. Are they equivalents? I shall return to this point. For the moment it is enough to stress that Abbo's model is ambiguous. However, there is no reason to deduce that Abbo intended to exclude married women from the laity, since he obviously considers monks and virgins[9] and nuns as sharing one status.

A more crucial issue than the terminological question is the respective levels of male and female rights and duties. The tendency to restrict women's rights in opposition to men's legal status is almost a commonplace as far as ancient laws – and not only religious laws – are concerned. In the medieval world, nearly all conceivable contexts were concerned: liturgical as well as juridical competencies, rights and duties in respect of marriage and family life, even the judicial context (not only were women deemed incapable of being judges but also of prosecuting or giving witness).[10] Nevertheless it has to be maintained that such inequality alone cannot be used as an indicator for status conscription. We have to bear in mind the influence of the Roman model. To give an example: in legal terms the difference between citizens and non-citizens was very important in the ancient empire, for instance Roman private law in principle applied only to those inhabitants of the empire who had the status of citizen. Though women were undoubtedly granted Roman citizenship, female citizens did not enjoy the same rights as male citizens, especially in respect of family law and the right to hold offices. Thus, sharing lay status (the status of a normal 'ecclesiastical citizen' so to speak) does not necessarily imply the same rights for both sexes. It is certainly not just accidental that the areas where women and men were most obviously treated in different ways are more or less the same in canon law and Roman law.

However, one should be cautious about accepting the surviving evidence of attempts to restrict women's legal possibilities as the universal norm. Epigraphic sources have made us aware that women had access to several offices at least in some eastern provinces in Hellenistic times despite 'official' legal incapacity. There is also evidence for *de facto* marriages between people whose relationship was considered extra-marital according to Roman law and for *de facto* tutelage and adoption by women. The Church Fathers sometimes seem nearer to the current praxis than the imperial legal sources, for example in their way of treating the relationships of slaves or women's care for children. The discrepancy becomes even more clear in the treatment of rape. Despite very strict legal sanctions, at least in the east, 'rape' seems to have remained a practice to initiate marriages, particularly between partners with different socio-economic background. But a woman might also organise her 'rape' in order to enforce a love marriage against her parents' will.[11] In contrast to imperial legislation, early church law was ready to accept such 'faits accomplis'.[12]

The same ambivalence is no less true for the medieval world. Hagiographical material and other narrative sources demonstrate that women often transgressed the theoretically fostered gender-limits. But also legal sources in the strict sense – council legislation, episcopal and papal decrees, canonistic comments – illustrate the discrepancies between the theory of those who wanted to impose restrictions and a much greater flexibility in practice. Canon law sources repeat the same limitations and prohibitions: this makes clear that forbidden behaviour of women was still occurring. In some cases even the norms changed. There is a lot of evidence for the capitulation of legal theory vis-à-vis practical needs. At a later date, for example, the Inquisitorial process made it necessary to grant women the capacity to testify (and implicitly to prosecute).[13] Specific women enjoyed outstanding privileges. Abbesses,[14] secular rulers and female land-holders were granted more or less the same jurisdictional rights as their male counterparts, at least at times. It is, of course, problematical to treat either abbesses or, for that matter, queens and empresses, as simple lay women. We will return to this point, but only after considering Abbo's 'second order', the clerics.

Though female clerics are not the central issue of this chapter, we cannot simply ignore clerical status completely. Dealing with lay people requires at least some reflection on how the clergy were demarcated. In other words: what is the principal criterion of clerical status? A glance at recent developments in Roman Catholic canon law helps us understand the full problem. Both modern Roman Catholic Codes – the 1917 Code as well as the 1983 Code which is presently in effect – confidently hold to the bipartite model, that is, to the fundamental division of the people of God into clergy and laity. Nevertheless, the perception of cleric (and, as a consequence, also that of lay) has

changed considerably. The 1983 Code has made ordination to the
ministry of deacon the demarcation line between clergy and laity.
According to its perception only ordained persons, strictly speaking
only ordained *men,* as far as they have received diaconal ordination at
least, are to be counted with the clergy. For the 1917 Code ordination
was not a condition *sine qua non* for being a member of the clergy.
The demarcation line between the two ecclesiastical castes was the
purely juridical rite of the first tonsure (*prima tonsura*). Both concepts find support in medieval legal history. And, as we shall see, in
opposition to modern Roman Catholic canon law, neither concept
did at that date necessarily exclude women from clerical status.

Late antique Christianity ritualised the official acknowledgement
of ecclesiastical ministry and leadership respectively. The ceremony
of ordination became 'a sort of publicly celebrated ritual of discernment',[15] thus fostering the development of a more and more onto-
logically interpreted class system. In principle, late antique and early
medieval canons rely on the concept that ordination demarcates the
order of *klerikoi/clerici* from the unordained people, the *laikoi/laici.*
In the earliest times the tonsure was not yet a juridical act detached
from ordination. I need not elaborate in detail on the status of early
Christian widows and deaconesses respectively. For our purpose it
might be sufficient to remember the fact that when investigating early
medieval canon law one has to be aware of legally ordained women
who shared clerical status. As long as deaconesses were ordained in
the Byzantine church, they were seen as part of the (major) clergy according to canon law, a point also underlined by imperial legislation.[16]

The question of female clerics in the west is a more complicated
one. A crucial point is the interpretation of the aforementioned
nineteenth canon of Nicaea (325). The original context of this canon
was the reception of the followers of Paul of Samosata into the
'catholic' church. Paul was a former bishop of Antioch who had been
condemned for his christological teaching as well as for other reasons;
for example, he was reproached for having women singing in church.
For us it is very important that there were also women called 'deaconesses' in his community. The council ordered the reception of presbyters
and male deacons who were ready to join the catholic church as clerics.
But it did not do so for the deaconesses. There are two possible ways to
understand the last sentence of canon 19 of Nicaea. The conjunction
epei used here can be read either as suggesting that deaconesses are
in general to be counted with the laity or that only *unordained*

women, called 'deaconesses', lack clerical status. Byzantine canonists traditionally interpreted the canon in the second way, in the light of the clerical status of the ordained Byzantine deaconess.[17] The Latin translators instead preferred the first reading.[18] It is well known that several Gallic councils – for example, the councils of Orange (441), Epaôn (517) and Orléans (533) – which explicitly refer to deaconesses, demonstrate a hostile attitude towards women's ordination (though these same canons prove that the condemned ordinations happened in practice). There is evidence in other sources of the positive reception of the institution of the ordained or consecrated deaconess,[19] mainly in the Frankish and the Italian context. Most famous is the Frankish queen Radegundis (d. 587) who – after having left court – was made a deaconess and then lived in various monastic communities. This monastic career of Radegundis points, of course, to a crucial question. There is some doubt whether it was thought that the liturgical ceremony would make a woman a cleric or rather give her a special status only within the ascetic and monastic context.[20] The Latin ordination formula provided by the Codex Engelbergensis 54, fol. 90v ff (twelfth-century, but going back to Carolingian times), as well as the widespread tendency to confound the ministry of the ancient deaconess with the office of the abbess (found in the eastern context as well) favour the ascetic interpretation. But though sources remain somewhat ambiguous, there is no reason to exclude the clerical interpretation, particularly as far as the abbesses of communities of canonesses are concerned.[21] Many scholars see their consecration in terms of diaconal ordination.

In any case it is unquestionable that abbesses (sometimes called deaconesses[22]) of houses of canonesses, just like the abbesses of cloistered monasteries, were granted jurisdictional and liturgical competencies which were seen as principally clerical in contemporary canon law.[23] Some sources call specific abbesses 'ordinaria' or even 'metropolitana' (the abbess of Quedlinburg[24] in the tenth century at least) thus using technical expressions for jurisdictional power. Other sources testify that abbesses were entitled to use insignia[25] such as a diaconal stole, maniple, pectoral cross and crosier or even the mitre (sometimes in the form of a crown), throne and baldachin.[26] There are examples in the first as well as in the better-documented second millennium, though there was always a tendency to restrict women's cultic activities and jurisdiction at the same time. A significant example is a decretal decision of Innocent III (1198–1216) concerning abbesses who did not only act as *ordinarii*. They consecrated their own nuns, heard their confession, read the gospel and preached in public.[27] According to the legal opinion of the pope these functions should be reserved to the male clergy. So he argued that the practice described would be an unacceptable novelty. But it is more credible that we are seeing here older practices which, for the male hierarchy, had become more and more suspect. At the least it can be stated without question that hearing confession had not been strictly reserved to priests in the first millennium.

Abbo of Fleury himself betrays a certain ambiguity. In his ep. XIV he cites various ancient canons and sayings of the Fathers in order to underline his commitment to clerical continence. One of the texts cited as witness is entitled 'Concerning clerics who cannot contract marriage' (*De clericis qui nuptias contrahere non possunt*).[28] Within this lengthy section, a passage concerning the deaconess is provided. It begins with the ambiguous phrase: 'Those things which we say concerning clerics may also be held to apply to deaconesses' (*Item ea quae de clericis diximus teneant etiam et in diaconissis*).[29] There is no further comment on the institution of the deaconess. One assumes that the reader was supposed to be in the picture. A further reference is provided by Abbo's Collection of Canons (*Collectio Canonum*). In title XLVIII – 'Concerning the witness of clerics'(*De testimoniis clericorum*) – one reads: 'if anyone has a legal action against a cleric or monk or deaconess or monastery or an archisterium'[30] (*si quis contra clericum, vel monachum, vel diaconissam vel monasterium, vel archisterium habeat aliquam actionem*) ('ex constitutione, cap. 33'[31]).[32] Given such statements, one wonders why the deaconess was not explicitly mentioned in the quotation from Abbo's *Apologeticus* with which I began, where the 'second order' for women is confined to 'the continent or widows'.

Continence as a criterion for those who were entitled to sacral competencies was a controversial issue not only between east and west but also within the west. In the reference system of western reformers from the tenth century onwards, the married deacon of current Roman Catholic canon law, who is legally entitled to have sexual intercourse and procreate children, would not have been a real (major) cleric despite his ordination. On the other hand, within Byzantine canon law, total continence and celibacy respectively are only obligatory for the bishop (and this only since the Trullanum confirmed the respective legislation of Justinian) on one hand and for the deaconess on the other.[33] The double standard for male and female deacons[34] is just as noteworthy as the double standard for bishops and presbyters. While the bishop (*episkopos*) remained the central 'priestly figure' in the east, in the west the presbyter became the main 'priestly figure'. Yet even though the west connected the priest's sacral duties and celibacy, in the east the presbyter's sacramental competencies seem somewhat higher than in the west, where confirmation became reserved to the bishop. Eastern canon law remains true to the antique treatment of cultic chastity.[35] Continence is not a permanent requirement for the ministers of the Sacred but only a temporary one in cases of immediate contact with the Holy. It is a commonplace, of course, that in the west major clerics did not always keep to the stricter norms in practice. Disregard of obligatory continence is a recurring issue at synods as well as in papal decrees.[36]

As people like Abbo, the forerunners of the western second millennium canonists, began to systematise traditional canon law, they had to deal with a variety of demarcation lines between the ordained ministers. Abbo denies clerical status to those ministers who are legally entitled to marry. For him, the normal contemporary nomenclature referring to them as clerics is 'an abuse' (*abusus*).[37] Byzantine sources which speak of the 'lay priest' (*hiereus laikos*) in order to distinguish the married priest from a monastic reflect similar though less radical tendencies.[38]

The gender issues which Abbo's formulation in his *Apologeticus* raises become clearer once we appreciate how important continence was to his perception of what makes a male cleric. The aforementioned Latin 'Order for the making of a deaconess' (*ordo ad diaconam faciendum*) encourages the hypothesis that one might equate the 'continent or widows' with the deaconesses. First, it explicitly refers to a vow of continence; second, it puts the candidate alongside the New Testament saintly widow (H)anna (Cf. Luke 2:36–8).[39]

Continence could not be a substitute for ordination in general, but it was an additional requirement for deaconesses and western male clerics. But things became even more complicated. In a Byzantine text we have the paradoxical expression of clerics 'even if they happen to be laypersons'.[40] The confusion is due to the fact that, in the Byzantine church, the term 'cleric' could refer to every employee on a church payroll even if this person received neither ordination nor an episcopal blessing. Similarly, western developments meant that the tonsure could entitle people without any ecclesiastical ministry to

benefit from clerical privileges. Innocent III had confirmed the growing praxis of disjunction between tonsure and ordination. There are
various ways in which this developed. For example, throughout the
entire middle ages even small children were designated for an
ecclesiastical career.[41] By cutting their hair the ecclesiastical authorities
could confirm this potential claim to clerical status without being
obliged to confer holy orders on them at once. But this status of
being a candidate for the clergy was often not clearly distinguished
from being a cleric. Thus the ritualised first cutting of the hair became
more and more a *rite de passage* from lay to clerical (and monastic)
status. The papal decision, which declared tonsure as the juridical act
of entry to the clergy, became part of Roman Catholic decretal law
and long remained firmly fixed.[42] Since the thirteenth century, canonists have increasingly interpreted the legal term 'clerical status' in the
most extensive way: thus unordained male and female members of
religious orders, and hermits as well as those persons who lived in
religious communities which were similar to orders but did not count
as such in legal terms, were entitled to clerical privileges (even if they
had not taken any vows!).[43]

Another basic issue in relation to clerical definition is the role
of bishops (and partriarchs and popes respectively). They are not
perceived as simple clerics but rather attributed a position *sui generis*
vis-à-vis the whole Christian people of their district (including the
clergy) and vis-à-vis 'their clergy' or other groups singled out of
the 'people of God' (e.g., the poor, widows and orphans, strangers).
In principle Abbo of Fleury counts the bishops with the clergy. Nevertheless, the traditional phrase 'clerics and/or bishops' is to be found
several times in his epistles[44] (and of course, in the source material
arranged in the *Collectio Canonum*).

From the perspective of gender studies it is noteworthy that
medieval canon law reserved the office of bishop to men, though it
did not necessarily exclude women from clerical privileges or, in the
strict sense, from clerical status. One should always be cautious of
monocausal explanations. But the male hierarchic concept of episcopacy seems above all to have been a consequence of the ecclesiastical
reception of the antique house order; that is, the hierarchy and structure of the antique household. In respect to the 'house of God', the
bishop obviously took over the role of the *pater familias*.[45] His jurisdictional power strongly reflects the *patria potestas* of Roman law
which was legally confined to men. Even in late antiquity when men

had to learn more and more to share their privileges with women, this remained unchanged.

But, as mentioned above in relation to houses of canonesses, and also in regular monasteries, there were interesting compromises. Within such female houses women did not only *de facto* act as 'fathers'; in so far as monastic life was ordered according to a specific statute or rule, the abbess (sometimes also called 'mother' (*mater*) or 'superior' (*praeposita*)) could also refer to specific 'legal' provisions, as for example in the rule of Caesarius of Arles which states that 'all should obey the mother after God'.[46] As house-fathers were not just normal members of the family, medieval abbots and abbesses likewise were not just nuns and monks respectively. In any case, they had specific rights and duties vis-à-vis the monastic family which they also represented in public. There could, of course, be differences between actual power on several levels: for example, not every monastery enjoyed jurisdictional autonomy vis-à-vis the local bishop, and some were subordinated to the abbot or abbess of a mother-house or, within the reform-movements, the general-abbot of a monastic congregation. Where female houses were founded by members of ruling families and/or otherwise connected with the secular rulers, this could give them a status comparable to male foundations in worldly terms: for instance, the abbesses of Quedlinburg and Gandersheim became 'Reichsfürstinnen'.[47] Such women, who were in general members of the ruling families themselves, also enjoyed a strong position vis-à-vis the local bishops. When papal authority was growing, monasteries tried to gain confirmation of privileged status from the pope. Some abbesses were then formally granted a share of various episcopal prerogatives as abbots were, though admittedly only a relatively small number of female houses enjoyed full exemption from male jurisdiction (bishop or male monastic superior).

This brings me to the 'third order' in Abbo's formulation. As Abbo nicely illustrates, during the first millennium 'the role of the monks and women religious was seen as a third area of Christian life'.[48] The late antique writer Egeria may serve as an early witness. Her itinerary of a pilgrimage to the Holy Land provides one of the first explicitly inclusive interpretations of the status of 'lay' – 'lay-persons [...] men or women' ('*laici* [...] *viri aut mulieres*')[49], a fact which fostered Faivre's hypothesis that women were not considered to belong to the laity before the fourth century. Egeria, herself a nun, also confronts '*laici*' and '*monazontes et parthenae*',[50] that is, lay people and those living a monastic life,[51] thus applying a criterion of demarcation to the Christian community which in the first millennium was to prove almost as successful as clerical ordination. As pointed out by Osborne, one might even speak 'of a sort of "alternative church" structure'[52] in connection with early monasticism. The Council of Chalcedon (451), for example, points to a certain antagonism between the clerical hierarchy and monasticism.

Both the monastic and the clerical forms of Christian life enjoyed a leadership role. Clearly, the clerical church exerted leadership and authority, and the local *episkopos* (bishop) enjoyed great prestige and obedience from the Christians in his community. Within the monastic enclave, the superior or abbot was willingly given a position of leadership and authority by the monks, and even beyond the confines of the monastery the superior or abbot was often held in the highest esteem. Even the rank and file of monks themselves were held in some repute.[53]

The seventh-century Life of St Brigid of Kildare might illustrate Osborne's observation that some women played an outstanding role in this monastic context.[54] There is even a hagiographic tradition that interpreted Brigid's extremely powerful position in terms of episcopacy.[55] Quasi-episcopal powers for abbesses were not so unusual, as has already been pointed out. In England, for example, Hild of Whitby, the learned founder and head of a double monastery, where several future bishops were educated, seems to have enjoyed a strong position similar to that of Brigid. Like other religious women (e.g. Leoba, according to Rudolph of Fulda) she was also accepted as an authority outside the monastic context: her biographer, Bede, recounts 'that not only ordinary people, but kings and princes sometimes sought and received her counsel when in difficulties'.[56] But it is obvious that he tends to play down her role, not explicitly referring to spiritual guidance and the teaching of men. It seems, however, that he was ready to accept the jurisdiction of a royal abbess, over monks as over nuns, 'perhaps because the power of Northumbrian queens was a part of the unshakeable order of his world'.[57] On the continent, it was likewise mainly in female houses with connections to ruling families that the abbesses acquired the most powerful position, for example the promotion of the abbess of Quedlinburg was associated with the rise of the Ottonian dynasty. Another prominent case is the Cistercian house of Las Huelgas which was founded by Alfons VIII in 1180. The abbess of Las Huelgas was granted full jurisdiction, in temporal as well as in spiritual affairs. Like any bishop in his diocese, she nominated pastors, gave faculties for celebrating the Eucharist, and preached and heard confession in the abbey as well as in several dependent monasteries and the parishes under her jurisdiction. It was she who had to decide upon marriages and ordinations, censures and dispensations.[58]

From the eighth century onwards, western male monasteries became more and more clericalised; that is, the monks became also ordained clerics.[59] The result was two alternative clerical structures on the one hand, and a growing discrepancy between male and female monasticism on the other. The requirement of title XVI of Abbo's *Collectio Canonum* – abbots should be ordained priests – is significant for this change.[60] Though in general it seemed reasonable to treat monks and nuns (or male and female monastic communities respectively) together, in this specific context Abbo could no longer say: 'Whatever we say concerning monasteries of monks, may also be considered to apply to monasteries and archisteria of women' (*Quae autem de monasteriis monachorum diximus, eadem teneant et monasteriis et archisteriis mulierum*).[61]

Nevertheless, women were still much less marginalised in the monastic structure than in the clerical. I elaborated briefly on the outstanding position of the abbess of Las Huelgas – very often a woman of royal origin. Other female houses enjoyed comparable independence from male jurisdiction. So Pope Hadrian IV, confirming the ancient privileges of the abbess of Herford in 1155, could write: 'We forbid that in the said monastery any bishop apart from the Roman pontiff exercise jurisdiction, and indeed that he ever – unless he is invited by the abbess – may presume to celebrate solemn Mass there'.[62] Being aware of these and other examples of female houses with specific privileges, one cannot take the much-quoted restrictive tendencies of second-millennium canon law as standard.[63]

Especially in the West, abbesses did not cease to hold leadership positions comparable to bishops and male abbots within female monastic communities and also over lay persons and male clerics as an effect of the feudal system. In the context of double monasteries, they might occasionally rule over male monastic communities.[64] The most famous example is Brigitta of Sweden's fourteenth-century rule for a double monastery under female leadership. Chapter 14, which clarifies the structure of authority, says clearly that the abbess of the new foundation should be the 'head and lady' (*caput et domina*) of the monastery, 'just as Mary was head and queen of both the apostles and the other disciples after the Ascension. A confessor general is to be chosen by the abbess with the consent of both nuns and friars. He is to rule the male community and uphold the Order, but is not to do anything else without consulting the abbess'.[65] The elaborate symbolism in Brigitta's monastic concept might be new – the attribution of leadership to the abbess had a long tradition. Now and then abbesses had even appeared side by side with bishops and male abbots in regional councils and imperial Diets. The occasional representation of women at such events was a matter of fact in the first millennium. In the Conciliar Movement of the fourteenth century the representation in councils of all the different structural elements of the church (including women) even became a theoretical claim. Konrad of Gelnhausen (d. 1390) explicitly argued that all statuses, orders and sexes (*status, ordines, sexus*) must be represented at a 'holy synod representing the universal Church' (*sacrosancta synodus universalem repraesentans ecclesiam*). 'In the context, one of consideration of the legal rights of corporations or groups, the representation of women claimed here seems to refer to the representation of female monasteries'.[66]

There were of course always differences in the extent to which nuns and especially abbesses could acquire status in the monastic context. Monasteries connected with ruling families were more likely to acquire a strong position, but sometimes there were also other circumstances that served to equalise the status of abbesses and abbots (who enjoyed the same rights as bishops in many respects). The abbey of Conversano was originally a male house. When it was taken over by Cistercian nuns in the thirteenth century, they had the old possessions and privileges of the monastery confirmed by several popes. On special occasions the abbess of Conversano sat on the cathedra (a kind of throne, often specifically episcopal) adorned with mitre and crosier as late as the early eighteenth century. When a new abbess had been elected, the dependent clerics had to bend their knee before her and kiss her hand. Only in 1709 did Rome order some modifications of this remarkable ceremony which fell into disuse thereafter.[67] There were stories interpreting Brigid's power in terms of episcopacy, whilst the data for Conversano derive from a much later time. Nevertheless one should keep them in mind when reflecting on the first millennium, as they give a vivid impression of continuity for 'quasi-episcopal' women.

Such women were an important phenomenon of ecclesiastical life in the second as well as the first millennium. One must, of course, make some distinctions in terms of canonical doctrine. Abbesses who enjoyed full jurisdiction were exceptions according to the categories of canon law which were established during the second millennium. Their rights were defined as privileges. As for the first millennium, it would be dangerous to project back views from later times. As I argued above, monasticism was more likely to be seen as a particular sector within the early medieval order-system than it was after Gratian. And it was only gradually clericalised. Male abbots could be, but were not necessarily, priests. This situation allowed for more fundamental gender equality though there could be great differences between different houses. What one now would call 'universal canon law' is a rare phenomenon in the first millennium. It only emerged gradually from the reception of the canons of particular synods and Church Fathers. In early monasticism, as in the case of female clerics, we have to deal not only with a multifold praxis but also with many different and also competing conceptions of what should be considered legally correct. Nor should second-millennium western canon law be seen only in terms of papal decisions (though they became more and more important for the legal development) and their scholarly interpretation. Consecration formulas, monastic rules and statutes for individual houses, which, for example, define the power of an abbess, as well as traditional local rites (for example, in connection with the enthronement of a new abbess) and symbols (for example, the *insignia* used by the abbess) continued to represent the normative tradition of the church. Moreover, some attention should be paid to hagiographic source materials, particularly in so far as they provided role-models for monastic women which did not always harmonise with ruling canonistic doctrine. As transmitted, these stories contained alternative models – for instance, teaching women and saints who transgressed the canonical ideal of strict enclosure which was enforced with considerable success from the time of Boniface XIII (1294–1303).[68]

Let us turn now to women's participation in worldly rulership. Elaborating on Abbo of Fleury's perception of the second order, I noted the ambivalent position of the bishop. Though he was counted with the clergy in principle, he was also ascribed a position vis-à-vis the clergy. A comparable ambiguity was perceived in the monastic context for abbot and abbess. We have a similar problem with respect to lay persons. According to the well-known Byzantine twelfth-century canonist Theodoros Balsamon, 'the service [*aroge*] of the emperors [*autocratores*] includes the enlightening and strengthening both of

soul and body: the dignity of the patriarchs is limited to the benefit
of souls, and to that only [...]; likewise the care and the thought
given to subjects by the empress is simply directed to the welfare of
the body and only to that (for women are totally lacking in the power
of giving spiritual succour)'.[69] Balsamon's was not, however, the
generally accepted theory. Rather than an accepted given, the relative
status of the Byzantine emperor and the empress was a controversial
issue. Did the emperor enjoy priestly qualities? What about the
empress? As for the western world, it is well known that canonistic
theory wanted to see secular rulers as nothing but simple lay persons.
Abbo and other canonists avoided speaking of a specific status of
kings/emperors and queens/empresses. But that does not mean that
their concept fits early medieval reality. There is good reason to
subscribe to Osborne's view, that rulers were only *reduced* to lay
status at times. 'From the time of Constantine to the so-called lay investiture struggle, the church [...] was not divided into two groups'[70]
(lay and cleric) or three classes (lay, cleric, monastic), it was obviously
a more complex reality. Besides theological tractates, which stress
a sacred status *sui generis* of the king/emperor, the evidence for
liturgical anointing and coronation ceremonies for both kings/
emperors and queens/empresses is remarkable.[71] The rituals are in
some respects reminiscent of episcopal ordination. I do not intend to
enter into the controversy over whether kings/queens and emperors/
empresses were ever attributed any 'priestly' character *sensu stricto* in
terms of ecclesiastical law.[72] Even Balsamon would have denied this.
For our purpose it must be enough to stress that they obviously
enjoyed a status *sui generis* at least in the sense that they were not lay
persons as other lay persons.[73] What I want to investigate is the no less
controversial issue of genderedness of this same status. Though the
existence of a parallel terminology – queen and empress (*regina* and
augusta in Latin, *augousta*, *basilis/basilissa* and *despoina* in Greek) –
bears witness to the inclusion of women in kingship and imperial
status, the significance of these titles is debatable. As for normal lay
women, things become complicated on the level of rights and duties.
The problem is clear in Balsamon: 'the empress is simply directed to
the welfare of the body and only to that (for women are totally
lacking in the power of giving spiritual succour)'.

In Byzantium, the question of full equality – which Balsamon
obviously denied, as far as the ecclesiastical context in a more narrow
sense is concerned – arose first with Pulcheria[74] and became central

again in the eighth century with Eirene.[75] After a time of regency for her minor son, Eirene was not willing to withdraw from the political scene. In order to ensure her position, she had blinded her son – rendering him disqualified from ruling. She was then quite successful as a sole emperor for five years. Her claim to the full authority of *Augustus* is most significantly expressed in the occasional use of male titles (*autocrator, basileus*). However, Kantorowicz's conclusion on the basis of the masculine form 'Basileus Eirene',[76] that at least 'in the body politic there is no sex' (*in corpore politico nullus est sexus*),[77] seems over-optimistic. First, the central question of the empress's equality returned again and again in Byzantine legal history. Second, even Eirene's legitimacy was not beyond question. The problem is well known from the perspective of constitutional history in so far as contemporaries pointed out a link to Charles the Great's investiture with the title of 'Emperor' in the west. The appropriation of imperial dignity by the Franks was justified with regard to the unconventional situation in Constantinople. It was argued that, since a woman cannot rule in her own right, there was no legitimate emperor and so it became possible to transfer the *imperium* to Charles.

Nevertheless, the fact that the 'sole' rule of a woman alone and in her own right could happen and be successful must be interpreted as evidence for a strong position of empresses in general. It appears to have been widely accepted that the married empress and queen had an institutionalised share in her husband's office. As stressed by Janet Nelson, for example, who has investigated western *ordines* for queen-making, the queen's 'partnership of [the king's] realm' was also underlined in the development of the female consecration liturgy, 'even if, at the same time, the prayers differentiated clearly between the king's office of ruling and the queen's supporting role'.[78] As for early Byzantium, there is less theoretical expression for such partnership, as there is not much legal and even less canonistic theory about the status of emperor and empress. But in practice, we find a similar situation.[79] Nor should discussion be confined to married queens and empresses. It is important to point out that many women who were actually ruling were widows or even unmarried women as in the case of the virgin empress Pulcheria. The church historian Sozomen stated that 'she took control of the government, reaching excellent decisions and swiftly carrying them out with written instructions'.[80] It is not completely clear if Pulcheria was considered *only* as the regent of her minor brother, Theodosios. Like him, Pulcheria had dynastic legitimacy. Referring to her virginity, she also claimed ascetic legitimacy. When she was forced to withdraw from the political scene for some years, this was not due to the fact that her brother had reached majority but to tensions between Pulcheria and her brother's wife; that is, the rivalry between the two empresses. Pulcheria made a comeback at her brother's death. In order to cover her rulership, she then married a tribune named Marcion, on condition that he respect her vow of virginity, and conferred upon him the imperial diadem. As far as the west is concerned there is ample evidence for cases more or less comparable to that of Pulcheria in so far as regency and transmission of rule is concerned. An early example, which might remind us that 'the West' is more than the Frankish empire, is reported in the Lombard History of Paul the Deacon.[81] In 590 – about a hundred years after Pulcheria's death – the Lombard people granted their widowed queen, Theodelinde, permission to keep her royal dignity on condition of remarriage with an able Lombard man of her choice.[82] After her second husband's death Theodelinde's position was secure enough to take over the regency for her minor son Adaloald. To some extent, the demand for remarriage after her first husband's death seems to underline the fact that the autocratic rule of a woman was, in general, not tolerated. But, on the other hand, the transmission of rule by a woman was similar in the cases of both Pulcheria and Theodelinde, and in circumstances where the formal rulers, Theodosius and Adaloald, were young, both women were able to take over actual rulership for several years.

From a modern point of view these problems belong mainly to the political sphere. But in early Christian societies the political and the ecclesiastical spheres were deeply linked. Medieval constitutional history cannot be uncoupled from the history of ecclesiastical law, particularly not where the great missionary empires, especially the (eastern) Roman and the (western) Carolingian empires, are concerned. The aforementioned development of liturgical legitimation of kings and – with time[83] – also of queens is significant in this context. From the ninth century onwards, the consecration of queens (anointing and coronation) spread widely from the West Frankish kingdom. It had occasionally been practised before. In the eleventh century it became standard. In so far as the consecration of a queen or empress was a liturgical ceremony, it also throws some light on the status of women in the ritual context. It seems that from the very beginning of Christianity, there was no gender differentiation *in principle* concerning admission to baptism, confirmation and Eucharist, though a more detailed study of sacramental discipline makes clear that gender problems nevertheless did occur (for example, the question of ritual purity often found in medieval legal sources applied much more to women than to men[84]). As for the ritual of monastic profession and/or monastic consecration, as with the consecration of a new abbot or abbess, we have again in principle equality for male and female candidates. But as is well known, there was considerable hesitation about admitting women to clerical ordination. If they were accepted at all, women were limited to the diaconal order. They were clearly excluded from priestly and episcopal ordination. Thus it is remarkable that the sources suggest little hesitation concerning liturgical queen-making.[85] The growing inclusion of royal women in the quasi-sacramental ritual of the consecration of the king was not contested by the ecclesiastical hierarchy.

Special attention should be drawn to imperial and royal women's participation in church policy. All the above-mentioned queens and empresses – Pulcheria, Theodelinde and Eirene – could serve as examples of female involvement in decisions concerning faith and/or church order. It was more than a *de facto* involvement. In canonistic terms it is important that the early medieval ecclesiastical hierarchies often willingly approved women's share in church policy, though there were, of course, also conflicts. The case of Pulcheria is most significant for this ambivalence. As is well known, Pulcheria's share in church policy was marked by the decisions of two imperial synods – Ephesos and Chalcedon. The alliance between the empress and the hierarchy of both Old and New Rome was almost total – with one significant exception: Nestorius, who had become bishop of Constantinople in 428. The theological controversy was over the title for Mary of 'Theotokos' ('the one who gave birth to God'). Nestorius preached against this terminology, which was already established in the capital and favoured by the empress as by large sections of the populace. As we know, Nestorius lost this battle at Ephesos, even though he was a protégé of Theodosius. The synod declared Mary 'Theotokos' and banned Nestorius. Pulcheria's personal enthusiasm for mariological spirituality undoubtedly combined with her theological ambitions in favour of this decision. But it is hard to believe that the personal hostility of the empress, which Nestorius's attitudes towards her had fostered, had no bearing. In contrast to his predecessor on the episcopal throne of Constantinople, Nestorius had treated Pulcheria in a way that made clear that he was not willing to grant her any privileges in relation to other women. The growing conflict became obvious only a few days after Nestorius's episcopal ordination. Under bishop Sisinnius a significant liturgical practice had been introduced. During the Easter liturgy, Pulcheria 'entered the sanctuary of the Great Church to take communion within the company of priests and of Theodosius her brother, an expression of her claim to the priestly character possessed by an Augustus'.[86] As noted above, I do not wish to enter the discussion over whether it is correct to ascribe a 'priestly character' to the Byzantine emperor. As stressed by Pistakis, the permission to take communion in the sanctuary, like other liturgical privileges, can be interpreted in other terms.[87] What is important in our context is that Nestorius denied the empress access to the sanctuary.[88] For her, the practice had been a symbolic expression of equality with the male emperor. For the bishop, it was nothing but the transgression of the canonical ban on women's entering the sanctuary. Pulcheria had her full victory when the Fathers of Chalcedon reversed protocol, acclaiming her before her male counterpart: 'Many years to the Augusta! Many years to the emperor!'[89] This was certainly more than the personal victory of an ambitious woman. It points to the fact that the equal status of empress and emperor was, at least at times, accepted in the ecclesiastical context.

To sum up: most medieval women and men shared lay status in principle, but there were many differences on the level of rights and duties, depending on gender but also on kinship-ties and wealth. More gender equality was reached in the monastic context than in the lay or clerical. In any event, early medieval women were not completely excluded from clerical status. Moreover, there was a tendency to confound clerical and monastic status not only in male monasteries but also in female houses, as witness the confounding of the offices of abbess and deaconess and the tendency to allow for abbesses to share episcopal prerogatives together with their male counterparts. Alongside the abbess, royal and imperial women undoubtedly had an outstanding status within early medieval society, where the political and the ecclesiastical sphere were more intimately linked than in later times. Thus an early medieval abbess usually played a role in the political context, and being a queen or empress elevated a woman over normal 'lay status' in the ecclesiastical context (though in a more restricted sense).

Apparently, there was remarkable interdependence in this acquisition of such an equal status with men, between royal/imperial women and women entrusted with monastic leadership. Quoting Hollis, I referred to the thesis that Bede was ready to accept the jurisdictional power of an abbess over men because he was used to powerful queens. Powerful abbesses belonged to ruling families or were at least heads of monasteries which were somehow connected with reigning dynasties in general, whilst, as Nelson recently pointed out, consecration-rituals for queens echo not only the respective rituals for kings but also the ritual for the consecration of a new abbess.[90] Abbesses and queens and empresses, all enjoyed a *status sui generis* together with their male counterparts. At least to some extent, they were able to transgress normal restrictions for women; most significantly in the jurisdictional capacity granted them, and also in the fact that teaching and spiritual guidance – usually denied to women – could be seen as female prerogatives in connection with these very offices. Abbesses and queens and empresses were quite willingly granted a share in church policy and at times even liturgical privileges relative to 'normal' women.

This positive picture does not, of course, mean that all gender ideology, which led to a different treatment of lay men and lay women in many respects and hindered women's career in the clerical context, was overcome for abbesses, empresses and queens. As far as rights and duties were concerned, neither abbot and abbess nor emperor/king and empress/queen had achieved an unquestionably equal status. But it is one thing to question rights in general and another to refer to a preconceived opinion on female nature as Balsamon did. Such discourses must be clearly distinguished from general disputes on status conscription and respective areas of competencies, in which male office-holders were as much implicated as female (for example, the controversy on the lay status of the king and emperor respectively).

This chapter can claim to be no more than a summary of the most basic gender questions raised by medieval ecclesiastical categorisations. It is far from a comprehensive study. The aim was more modest: to draw attention to differing perceptions and thus to contested meanings, mainly focusing on source material from the early middle ages, that is to say in the time before the specifically western canonistic development (of the eleventh century onwards). I hope to have shown that the study of ecclesiastical legal status must be subtle and nuanced. It must not only deal with variety and difference among canonical conceptions of affiliation to the clergy and the laity respectively in different places and times, but also recognise competing perceptions in contemporary sources from one ecclesiastical region.

A quotation from an early legal source from the Rus may serve as the 'summary of the summary'. This late-Christianised part of the world not only inherited about a thousand years of canonic development when becoming a Christian society itself. Coping with this heritage it also contributed to further complexity. Thus we read in the so-called statute of Vladimir (d. 1015): 'But those are the church-people: abbots, priests (popes), deacons, their children, the pastors' wives and those who belong to the clergy, abbesses, monks, nuns, proskurnici [= the women preparing the bread which is used for Holy Liturgy], pilgrims, doctors [...], those are the people of the church [and] the poorhouses. The metropolitan or the bishop sits in judgement on them'.[91] From a gender perspective the motley crew of male (abbots, priests, deacons, monks) and female (abbesses, pastors' wives, nuns, proskurnici), as well as mixed groups (pilgrims, miraculously cured people, freed persons, blind and crippled ones), is highly significant. When the church of the Rus was founded at the end of the first millennium of Christianity, Byzantine canon law was adopted in principle. At the same time local 'church orders' (*cercovnyj ustavъ*) were produced. Though the transmitted text of the so-called statute of Vladimir cannot go back to the time of this first Christianised ruler of the Rus himself, the central parts must originate in an early stage of official adoption of Christianity. In our context it is noteworthy that the principle of the three orders, cleric/monastic/lay, was introduced to Russian society thanks to Byzantine influence. But, as pointed out by Goetz, one should not overlook particular local developments. The creation of the legal category of 'church people', a highly ambiguous, gender-mixed category that combines traditional forms of categorising with a new judicial reality, is one of them.[92]

As I have tried to show, the study of medieval categorisation must cope with a complexity which transgresses the simple bipartite division of Christian society favoured by western canonistic doctrine (at least after Gratian). The tripartite system – which won the battle in Byzantium but is testified to in western sources as well, by Abbo of Fleury, for example – whose classification I took as a starting point for this chapter, does more justice to the importance of the ascetic and monastic tradition. But things are even more complex. We can see this when dealing with the specific status of the bishop, the abbot and abbess respectively, or with men and women of imperial or royal status. Our short excursion into the particular development of the Rus, where the category of 'church people' bears witness to a system which transgresses all usual models, is further evidence for a complexity which becomes the more remarkable the more one pays regard to the specific problems concerned with the categorising of women. A gendered approach to the middle ages forces us to see more than unfixed and competing order models, and produces awareness of ambiguities within the principal categories themselves, particularly when differentiating between principal status conscription and the much more crucial level of rights and duties.[93]

Notes

1. Abbo of Fleury, *Apologeticus*, in *Patrologia Latina*, ed. J. P. Migne, vol. 139, p. 463 (henceforth *PL* + vol. number); trans. K. B. Osborne, *Lay Ministry in the Roman Catholic Church: Its History and Theology* (Paulist Press, New York, 1993) p. 236.
2. Cf. Gratian, *Decretum*, C.12 q.1 c.7.
3. Osborne, *Lay Ministry*, p. 280.
4. Even in the second millennium the bipartite model has never completely won the battle in any eastern canon law system including the recent Code for the various eastern Catholic churches. The Codex Canonum Ecclesiarum Orientalium of 1990 has kept the *religiosi* as a third group *sui generis*.
5. See M. Zimmermann, 'Weder Kleriker Noch Laie – Die Frau in der Kirche', *Concilium*, 21 (1985), pp. 406–11
6. Cf. E. M. Synek, 'Laici – viri aut mulieres: Bemerkungen zum patristischen Laienbegriff', *Österreichisches Archiv für Kirchenrecht*, 43 (1994), pp. 102–34.
7. '*quod semper masculinus etiam femininum sexum continet*', D. 32.62. See also D. 1.7.10; 1.9.1 pr.; 3.5.3.1; 31.45 pr.; 32.81 pr.; 50.16.1; 50.16.101.3.
8. Cf. Jerome, *Adversus Jovinianum* I, 3 (*PL* 23, pp. 223–4). For further references see, for example, M. Bernards, *Speculum Virginum: Geistigkeit und Seelenleben der Frau im Hochmittelalter* (Böhlau, Cologne, 1982), pp. 40–72.
9. As long as Abbo is speaking in a canonical context, one has to suppose that he is not referring to young, unmarried women in general but to vowed (consecrated) virgins. For further orientation see the standard work on this topic, R. Metz, *La Consécration des vierges dans l'Église Romaine: Étude d'histoire de la liturgie* (Bibliothèque de l'Institut de Droit Canonique de l'Université de Strasbourg t. 4, Presse Universitaire de France, Paris, 1954).
10. For a summary of the most important issues concerning whether women were more or less legally discriminated against in the western context, see D. Müller, 'Vir caput mulieris: Zur Stellung der Frau im Kirchenrecht unter besonderer Berücksichtigung des 12. und 13. Jahrhunderts', in *Vom mittelalterlichen Recht zur neuzeitlichen Rechtswissenschaft: Bedingungen, Wege und Probleme der europäischen Rechtsgeschichte*, Rechts- und Staatswissenschaftliche Veröffentlichungen der Görres-Gesellschaft N.F. t. 72, ed. N. Brieskorn et al. (Schöningh, Paderborn, 1994), pp. 228–41.
11. Cf. J. Evans-Grubbs, 'Abduction Marriage in Antiquity: A Law of Constantine (CTh IX.24.1) and its Social Context', *Journal of Roman Studies*, 79 (1989), pp. 59–83.
12. Cf. c. 11 of Ancyra; 67th Apostolic Canon; so-called cc. 22; 38 and c. 42 of St Basil.
13. Cf. Müller, 'Vir', pp. 230–31; see also Müller, *Frauen vor der Inquisition: Lebensformen, Glaubenszeugnis und Aburteilung der deutschen und französischen Katharerinnen*

(Veröffentlichungen des Instituts für Europäische Geschichte t. 166, P. v. Zabern, Mainz, 1996).

14. See, for example, the decisions of Hadrian IV (1155) or Paul III (1549) on the abbess of Herford. Cf. A. Cohausz, *Herford als Reichsstadt und papstunmittelbares Stift* (Bielefeld, 1928); H. van der Meer, *Women Priests in the Catholic Church? A Theological-Historical Investigation* (Temple University Press, Philadelphia, 1973), pp. 117–18.

15. Osborne, *Lay Ministry*, p. 30.

16. In the Codex Theodosianus XVI,2,27 as well as in the Codex Iustinianus I,3,20 the norms for deaconesses are to be found under the title *'De Episcopis et Clericis'*; see also the Novellae 3,1.2; 6,6; 123,13.21.30.43; 131,13. The Libri Basilicorum remain faithful to the late antique perception. Most significant is Novella 3 and its reception into the second title of the third book of the Libri Basilicorum. The terminology used here ('deacons, male and female ones') definitely points to an equalised status.

17. Cf. H. Kotsonis, 'A Contribution to the Interpretation of the 19th Canon of the First Ecumenical Council', *Revue des etudes byzantines*, 19 (1961), pp. 189–97.

18. See F. Gillmann, 'Weibliche Kleriker nach dem Urteil der Frühscholastik', *Archiv für Katholisches Kirchenrecht*, 93 (1919), pp. 239–53, p. 239–40, n. 4.

19. See, for example, the recent studies of J. Ysebaert, 'The Deaconess in the Western Church of Late Antiquity and their Origin', *Instrumenta Patristica*, 14 (1991), pp. 421–36; A.-A. Thiermeyer, 'Der Diakonat der Frau: Liturgiegeschichtliche Kontexte und Folgerungen', in: *Frauenordination. Stand der Diskussion in der katholischen Kirche*, ed. W. Gross (Wewel, Munich, 1996), pp. 53–63, pp. 61–2; A. C. Lochmann, 'Studien zum Diakonat der Frau' (doctoral thesis, Siegen, 1996), pp. 146–58; for epigraphic evidence: U. Eisen, *Amtsträgerinnen im frühen Christentum: Epigraphische und literarische Studien* (Forschungen zur Kirchen- und Dogmengeschichte t. 61, Vandenhoeck und Ruprecht, Göttingen, 1996), pp. 188–92.

20. Already most of the twelfth- and thirteenth-century canonists preferred the second interpretation. See the summary in F. Gillmann and A. Ludwig, 'Weibliche Kleriker in der altchristlichen und frühmittelalterlichen Kirche', *Theologisch-praktische Monatsschrift* (1910), pp. 1–24, pp. 16–19; in modern times it is again favoured by A.-G. Martimort, *Les Diaconesses: Essai historique* (Edizione Liturgiche, Rome, 1982).

21. Cf., for example, J. Funk, 'Klerikale Frauen?', *Österreichisches Archiv für Kirchenrecht*, 14 (1963), pp. 271–90, pp. 280–82; B. U. Hergemöller, 'Klerus, Kleriker', in *Lexikon des Mittelalters* t. 5 (Artemis, München, 1991), col. 1207–11, col. 1208. There seems to be further evidence for some continuity of a female clergy in the institution of the canoness in general and even in the privileges of the Cistercian and Carthusian nuns of the second millennium. See K. H. Schäfer, 'Kanonissen und Diakonissen', *Römische Quartalschrift*, 24 (1910), pp. 49–80; Gillmann, 'Kleriker', p. 239, n. 2; recently: A. Ulrich, 'Die Kanonissen: Ein vergangener und vergessener Stand der Kirche', in *Liturgie und Frauenfrage: Ein Beitrag zur Frauenforschung aus liturgiewissenschaftlicher Sicht*, ed. T. Berger and A. Gerhards (EOS, St Ottilien, 1990), pp. 181–94 (with literature).

22. Cf., for example, *Petrus Abaelardus*, ep. 8 (*PL* 178, p. 267): 'septem vero personas ex vobis ad omnem monasterii administrationem necessarias esse credimus [...], portariam scilicet, cellerariam, vestiariam, infirmariam, cantricem, sacristam, et ad extremum diaconissam, quam nunc abbatissam nominant'.

23. Not to mention the fact that abbesses frequently transgressed the limits of competences the regional bishops were willing to grant. See, Müller, 'Vir', pp. 223–45; pp. 239–40.

24. Cf. 'Annales Quedlingburgenses' (*MGH.SS* 3, 75).

25. A short survey on the historical development of the use of such insignia and their legal significance is provided by L. Carlen, *Orte, Gegenstände, Symbole kirchlichen Rechtslebens: Eine Einführung in die kirchliche Rechtsarchäologie* (Universitätsverlag Freiburg Schweiz, Freiburg/CH, 1999), including bibliographical references.

26. Cf. the survey of A. Pantoni, 'Abbadessa', in *Dizionario degli Istituti di perfezione* t. 1 (Città Nuova, Rome, 1974), col. 14–22, col. 21.

27. Cf. Liber extra 5.38.10.
28. Cf. Justinian, Nov. 6,6 (summarium habet in Coll. LXXXVII,5 (inde Nomoc. L tit. 24) et Nomoc. XIV tit. 1,28; 8,14; 9,29.30).
29. Abbo of Fleury, ep. XIV (*PL* 139, p. 451).
30. Terminus technicus for the main seat of a monastery.
31. Cf. Nov. 123,21 = Basil. B III, t. 1, cap. 37.
32. Abbo of Fleury, *Collectio Canonum* XLVIII (*PL* 139, p. 505).
33. The ancient interdict on marriage after ordination is binding for all male clerics from the subdeacon onwards.
34. For the development of obligatory episcopal celibacy in Byzantium, see S. Troianos, 'Zölibat und Kirchenvermögen in der früh- und mittelbyzantinischen Gesetzgebung', in *Eherecht und Familiengut in Antike und Mittelalter*, ed. D. Simon (Schriften des Historischen Kollegs/Kolloquien t. 22, Oldenbourg, Munich, 1992), pp. 133–46, and C. Pitsakis, 'Clergé marié et célibat dans la législation du concile in Trullo: Le point de vue oriental', in *The Council in Trullo Revisited*, ed. G. Nedungatt and M. Featherstone (Kanonika t. 6, Pontifico Istituto Orientale, Rome, 1995), pp. 263–306; for a survey of possible reasons for the origins of the celibacy claim for deaconesses, see E. M. Synek, *Oikos. Zum Ehe- und Familienrecht der Apostolischen Konstitutionen* (Kirche und Recht t. 22, Plöchl, Vienna, 1999), pp. 211–18.
35. E. Fehrle, *Die kultische Keuschheit im Altertum* (Religionsgeschichtliche Versuche und Vorarbeiten t. 6, Töpelmann, Gießen, 1910).
36. See, for example, G. Denzler, *Das Papsttum und der Amtszölibat* (Päpste und Papsttum t. 5, I–II, Hiersemann, Stuttgart, 1973; 1976).
37. 'Sequitur clericorum ordo, quo in tribus gradibus specialiter distinguitur, hoc est, diaconorum, presbyterorum et episcoporum: nam omnes qui sunt inferioris gradus per abusionem clerici vocantur, dum eis sicut et laicis ex indulgentia permittitur sociari conjugibus': Abbo of Fleury, *Apologeticus* (*PL* 139, p. 464).
38. For example, G. Dagron, 'Remarques sur le statut des clercs', *Jahrbuch der Österreichischen Byzantinistik*, 44 (1994), pp. 33–48, p. 35.
39. 'Deus qui Annam filiam Phanuelis [...] in sancta et intemerata viduitate servatis': quotation from Thiermeyer, 'Diakonat', p. 61.
40. L. Burgmann, 'Palatium canonibus solutum: Vier Texte zum byzantinischen Kirchen- und Verfassungsrecht aus dem Codex Zavordensis 121', in *Cupido legum*, ed. Burgmann et al. (Löwenklaugesellschaft, Frankfurt, 1985), p. 22 (trans. J. H. Erickson, 'Bishops, Presbyters, Deacons: An Orthodox Perspective', *Kanon*, 13 (1996), pp. 148–64, p. 159): the text refers to *kubukleisioi* (imperial title conferred on patriarchal chamber- lains) and *chartularioi* (officials in various bureaus). Cf. A. Kazhdan, in *The Oxford Dictionary of Byzantium*, vol. 1, ed. Kazhdan et al. (Oxford University Press, New York and Oxford, 1991), p. 416, and vol. 2, p. 1155.
41. Cf. L. Trichet, *La tonsure: Vie et mort d'une pratique ecclésiastique* (Édition du Cerf, Paris, 1990).
42. Liber extra 1.14.11.
43. W. M. Plöchl, *Geschichte des Kirchenrechts*, t. 2 (Herold, Vienna, 1962), p. 179.
44. For example, ep. XII *Clerici vel episcopi* (*PL* 139, p. 439:); ep. XIV *Episcopi et clerici* (*PL* 139, p. 443); see also the treatment of the bishop as 'sui generis' column 450; ep. I *Archiepiscopus cum suis clericis* (*PL* 139, p. 420).
45. Cf. E. Dassmann, *Ämter und Dienste in den frühchristlichen Gemeinden: Hereditas* t. 8, (Borengässer, Bonn, 1994) pp. 49–95.
46. See, for example, the rule of Caesarius of Arles, ch. XVI (*PL* 67, 1109: '*matri post Deum omnes obediant*'); ch. XIX (*PL* 67, 1110: '*quae aliquid habebant in saeculo, quando ingrediuntur monasterium, humiliter illud offerent matri, communibus usibus profuturum*').
47. Cf. for example, H. Goetting, *Das Bistum Hildesheim. t. 1 Das reichsunmittelbare Kano- nissenstift Gandersheim* (Germania Sacra) (De Gruyter, Berlin, 1973).
48. Osborne, *Lay Ministry*, p. 41.

49. Egeria, Itinerarium 24,1 (ed. Fontes Christiani t. 20, p. 224).

50. 'Monazontes et parthenae' is usually translated as 'monks and virgins' but it is not at all clear that Egeria uses the first term for men only and the second for women . It is well possible that both terms were applied in an inclusive way for men and women.

51. As for synonyma in Egeria's work, see Fontes Christiani, t. 20, p. 224, note 3.

52. Osborne, Lay Ministry, p. 262.

53. Osborne, Lay Ministry, p. 263.

54. The prologue of the Second Life (according to the Bollandist ranking, chronologically the first Vita) informs us that it was the holy woman who called an anachorete as bishop to ordain priests and to join her in church-leadership. After Colaeus' episcopal ordination he and the 'beatissima puellarum principalis [...] suam rexerunt principalem ecclesiam. [...] Quam semper Archiepiscopus Hibernensium Episcoporum, et Abbatissa, quam omnes Abbatissae Scottorum venerantur, felici successione, et ritu percepto dominantur': Vita S. Brigidae Prol. (ed. AASS. Boll. Febr. t. I, 135).

55. For references see J. Ryan, Irish Monasticism: Origins and Early Development (1931; Four Courts Press, Dublin, 1992), p. 183.

56. Bede, Church-History 3,23 (PL 45, 209: 'tantum autem erat ipsa prudentiae, ut non solum mediocres quique in necessitatibus suis, sed etiam reges ac principes nonnumquam ab ea quaererent consilium, et invenient').

57. S. Hollis, Anglo-Saxon Women and the Church (Boydell Press, Woodbridge, 1992), p. 269.

58. J. M. Escrivá, La abadesa de Las Huelgas (Madrid, 1944).

59. Of course, that does not mean that in the second millennium all male religious were priests. The monasteries had non-ordained inmates also in later times, the so-called 'fratres conversi' or 'lay brothers'. But though they were seen as members of the monastic family, they were not considered to be monks in the strict sense and were thus also excluded from various rights such as the election of the abbot for example. Mutatis mutandis, the division between so-called choir-nuns and working 'lay sisters' reflects a related development within the female houses.

60. Abbo of Fleury, Collectio Canonum XVI (PL 139, 486).

61. Quotation from the 'Liber Legum' = 'Liber Novellarum' (cf. Nov. V,9) provided by Abbo of Fleury, Collectio Canonum XIV (PL 139, 484) under the title 'De electione abbatis'.

62. Pope Hadrian IV, confirming the old privileges of the the abbess of Herford (1155), cf. Cohausz, Herford, p. 25.

63. So recently J. Wogan-Browne, 'Queens, Virgins and Mothers: Hagiographic Representations of the Abbess and her Powers in Twelfth- and Thirteenth-Century Britain', in Cosmos, vol. 7, Women and Sovereignty, ed. L. O. Fradenburg (Edinburgh University Press, Edinburgh, 1992), pp. 14–35, at p. 14.

64. Cf. S. Hilpisch, Die Doppelklöster: Entstehung und Organisation, Beiträge zur Geschichte des alten Mönchtums und des Benediktinerordens t. 15 (Aschendorff, Münster, 1928); K. Elm and M. Parisse (eds), Doppelklöster und andere Formen männlicher und weiblicher Religiosen im Mittelalter, Berliner Historische Studien, t. 18 (Dunckher & Humblot, Berlin, 1992).

65. S. Borgehammar, 'St. Brigitta, an Architect of Spiritual Reform', in Brigittiana, 5 (1998), pp. 23–47, p. 28.

66. W. Brandmüller, Papst und Konzil im Großen Schisma (1378–1431): Studien und Quellen, (Schöningh, Paderborn, 1990), p. 165: 'Mit der geforderten Repräsentation der Frauen dürfte, vor dem Hintergrund des korporationsrechtlichen Denkens gesehen, wohl die Vertretung von Frauenklöstern gemeint sein'.

67. Cf. G. Mongelli, Le abbadesse mitrate di s. Benedetto di Conversano (Monvergine, 1960).

68. Cf. the recent study of E. Makowski, Canon Law and Cloistered Women: Periculoso and Its Commentators 1298–1545 (Catholic University of America Press, Washington, 1997).

69. Balsamon, Meditata sive responsa, PL 138, 1017, trans. E. Barker, Social and Political Thought in Byzantium. From Justinian I to the Last Paleologous: Passages from Byzantine Writers and Documents (Clarendon Press, Oxford, 1957; repr. 1961), p. 106.

70. Osborne, *Lay Ministry*, p. 312.
71. A bibliographical survey is provided by Carlen, Rechtsarchäologie, pp. 120–21, see also J. N. Nelson, 'Early Medieval Rites of Queen-Making and the Shaping of Medieval Queenship', in *Queens and Queenship in Medieval Europe*, ed. A. J. Duggan (Boydell Press, Woodbridge, 1997), pp. 301–15.
72. For the Byzantine context, the ascription of 'priestly character' to the emperor was recently disputed by K. G. Pitsakis, 'L'Empereur romain d'orient: un laïc', *Kanon*, 15 (1999) pp. 196–221 (with literature). Pitsakis argues that liturgical privileges cannot prove the priestly character of the emperor; according to ecclesiastical conceptions he would have been nothing but a lay person.
73. Cf. Osborne, *Lay Ministry*, p. 212.
74. Cf. the detailed treatment by K. G. Holum, *Theodosian Empresses: Women and Imperial Dominion in Late Antiquity* (Berkeley University Press, Berkeley, 1982).
75. Cf. R.-J. Lilie, *Byzanz unter Eirene und Konstantin VI (780–802)*, Berliner Byzantinische Studien, t. 2, (P. Lang, Frankfurt, 1996).
76. And two western counterparts from much later times – 'Maria Rex Hungariae' (late fourteenth century) and Maria Theresia.
77. E. Kantorowicz, *The King's Two Bodies: A Study in Mediaeval Political Theology* (Princeton University Press, Princeton, 1957; repr. 1997, note 93).
78. Nelson, 'Queen-Making', p. 312.
79. Cf., for example, L. James, 'Goddess, Whore, Wife or Slave: Will the Real Byzantine Empress Please Stand Up?', in *Queens*, ed. Duggan, pp. 123–39.
80. Holum, *Theodosian Empresses*, p. 97; cf. Sozomenos, Historia Ecclesiastica, 9, 1, 5–6, *Die griechischen christlichen Schriftsteller der ersten Jahrhunderte*, ed. J. Bidez and G. C. Hansen (N.F. 4, Berlin, 1995, p. 391).
81. Ed. L. K. Bethmann and G. Waitz (= MGH.SRL t. 1).
82. Cf. J. Hofmann, 'Die selige Langobardenkönigin Theodelinde – "Brückenbauerin" zwischen getrennten Völkern und Kirchen', *Zeitschrift für Kirchengeschichte*, 108 (1997), pp. 12–31; p. 19; see also Hofmann, *Frauen, die die Kirche prägten: Lebensbilder aus den ersten sechs Jahrhunderten* (Extemporalia t. 16) (EOS-Verlag, St Ottilien, 1998), pp. 127–53.
83. For the most recent research, see Nelson, 'Queen-Making', *passim*.
84. A study by E. Synek will be published in the next volume of *Kanon* (Kovar, Eichenau, 2000).
85. But see the apparent resistance to the consecration of Queen Aelfthryth in 973, which required a royal decree. It is not clear whether resistance here came from lay or clerical quarters.
86. Holum, *Theodosian Empresses*, p. 145.
87. Cf. Pitsakis, 'L'Empereur', pp. 203–9.
88. Cf. c. 44 Laodicea.
89. ACO II,1,2,123.12; 1,70.39; Holum, *Theodosian Empresses*, p. 215.
90. Nelson, 'Queen-Making', pp. 309–10.
91. The text of the so-called statute of Vladimir is provided by L. K. Goetz, *Geschichte des russischen Kirchenrechts*, Kirchenrechtliche Abhandlungen, t. 18/19 (Enke, Stuttgart, 1905), pp. 14–18; p. 18, and Goetz, *Staat und Kirche in Altrussland: Kiever Periode 988–1240* (Duncker, Berlin 1908), pp. 151–4, p. 154 respectively. As for the question of authenticity and transmission, see L. Müller, 'Die Russische Orthodoxe Kirche von den Anfängen bis zum Jahre 1240', in *Die Orthodoxe Kirche in Rußland: Dokumente ihrer Geschichte (860–1980)*, ed. P. Hauptmann and G. Stricker (Vandenhoeck und Ruprecht, Göttingen, 1988), pp. 35–133; p. 111, note 27 (with literature).
92. For a more detailed study of living conditions etc., see A. M. Ammann, *Untersuchungen zur Geschichte der kirchlichen Kultur und des religiösen Lebens bei den Ostslawen*, Das östliche Christentum N.F. t. 13 (Augustinus, Würzburg, 1955).
93. Gary Macy's article 'The Ordination of Women in the Early Middle Ages', *Theological Studies*, 61 (2000), pp. 481–507, appeared after mine was completed.

5

'Halt! Be Men!': Sikelgaita of Salerno, Gender and the Norman Conquest of Southern Italy

Patricia Skinner

It is relatively uncommon to have a surviving narrative work written by a named woman prior to 1200; still rarer is it to find in such a work a woman's view of another woman of similar rank and status to her own. Such a situation occurs, however, in the *Alexiad*, in which the twelfth-century Byzantine princess Anna Komnena writes a eulogising biography of her father, the emperor Alexius I. In passing, she also describes an earlier princess, Sikelgaita of the southern Italian city of Salerno, in four separate passages of the work.[1]

Sikelgaita first appears in a typically feminine guise, where she is seen persuading her husband, the Norman leader Robert Guiscard, not to make war on the Byzantines.[2] Shortly afterwards, however, Sikelgaita appears in a very different role. Robert, having decided to go to war after all,

> arrived at Otranto [from Salerno]. There he stayed for a few days waiting for his wife Gaita (she went on campaign with her husband and when she donned armour she was indeed a formidable sight). She came and he embraced her, then both started with all the army again for Brindisi.[3]

Sikelgaita's warlike credentials are emphasised at greatest length by Anna in the remarkable passage from which this chapter takes its title, when she persuades the Normans to continue fighting having been put to flight by the Byzantines:

> There is a story that Robert's wife Gaita, who used to accompany him on campaign like another Pallas, if not a second Athena, seeing the runaways and glaring fiercely at them, shouted in a very loud voice, 'How far will ye run? Halt! Be men!' – not quite in those Homeric words, but something very like them in her own dialect. As they continued to run, she grasped a long spear and charged at full gallop against them. It brought them to their senses and they went back to fight.[4]

Sikelgaita's final appearance in the *Alexiad* is at Robert's deathbed off the island of Kefalonia: 'His wife reached him as he was breathing his last, with his son weeping beside him. The news was given to his other son whom he had named heir to his domains previously'.[5]

Anna's accessible yet conflicting portraits of Sikelgaita create the image of a valkyrie-like woman who defied gendered roles some twenty years before the crusades made warlike women a more visible (and fashionable?) phenomenon. Anna alternates between fascination and horror at Sikelgaita's activities – the Lombard woman is at once barbaric (the reference to her 'dialect') and an object of admiration, inspiring as she gallops round on horseback urging on the army with a long spear.

The value of Anna's portrayal has been largely overlooked as an entry point into an exploration of the issues of gender, warfare and Norman expansion in the Mediterranean. By the time that the exploits of Robert Guiscard's army impacted on the Byzantine empire, in two separate campaigns of 1081–2 and 1084–5, he had been married to Sikelgaita some twenty-five years and had become the lord of much of southern Italy. A study of Sikelgaita's own public career can aid in understanding the process of conquest and political takeover in the latter region, and can also explain why she made such an impact on subsequent historiography both locally and in the works of outsiders such as Anna.

Anna writes of the Lombard Sikelgaita as both wife and warrior, and at the same time plays with gender to create an army of effeminate Normans who need a woman to make them fight. Anna, who was an educated and literate woman, is here reversing an insult more commonly used of the Byzantines by western authors,[6] and using Sikelgaita – a non-Norman from whom the goading would therefore have added impact – as the means with which to make her point.

The Norman expansion in Europe appears to have provoked discussions about masculinity (or its lack) in a number of sources. For example, the pro-Norman monk Amatus of Montecassino, whose *History of the Normans* will feature strongly in this chapter, includes a statement from the German emperor's chancellor Frederick of Lorena, sent to gather forces to fight the Normans in southern Italy, that, 'If I had a hundred effeminate knights, I should fight against all the knights of Normandy'.[7] Amatus, like Anna, was reversing the common perception of the Normans as invincible warriors, but here he points up the absurdity of Frederick's rash boast prior to a humiliating dispersal of the army even before it met its foe.

No single narrative exists of the Normans' entry into and takeover of the southern half of the Italian peninsula from the 1030s onwards. Its history is recounted by three authors: Amatus, Geoffrey of Malaterra, monk of one of Robert's own monasteries, and the poet William of Apulia, and the spread of Norman power was a complex process involving more than one leader with numerous territories to overcome. The largest political entity in the south at this time was the Lombard principality of Salerno, which, under its prince Guaimarius IV, extended over much of the southern half of the peninsula. Only the far south and a few coastal strips remained, as they had been since the sixth century, in Byzantine hands. This partly explains Anna Komnena's interest in the Normans, for their expansion threatened Byzantine territories here before they became ambitious and crossed the Adriatic sea onto the Byzantine mainland late in the eleventh century.

Amatus's approach to the invaders is uncompromisingly favourable, but surprisingly little has been written about him or his work. Scholars of the Norman conquest of the south have been content to use his evidence, acknowledging the difficulties inherent in relying on a text known only through a fourteenth-century Old French translation, but have been reluctant to address the circumstances of its composition.[8] Cowdrey considers it a eulogy of the two Norman leaders, Robert Guiscard and Richard of Capua,[9] and certainly Amatus is at pains to justify the Normans' expansion. A vision of archbishop John of Salerno is used as a device to emphasise the righteousness of the Norman mission: 'This land of God was given to the Normans due to the perversity of those who held it and through the ties of kinship which they made with them; the just will of God gave them the land'.[10]

The 'ties of kinship' mentioned were between the Normans and the rulers of Salerno: Guaimarius IV realised the danger that the newcomers posed to his territory and sought to contain it by marrying off two nieces and a daughter to the Norman leaders, William Iron-Arm (d. 1046), William of the Principate and Drogo. Guaimarius had by 1042 associated his son, Gisulf, in power with him, but the latter was no military match for his father or the Normans, and the death of Guaimarius in 1052 precipitated the need for more allies. By this time Robert Guiscard had emerged as the Norman leader in the region, and a further marriage took place between him and Sikelgaita, Gisulf's sister. This union was pivotal to the eventual Norman takeover of Salerno (see Figure 1).

A key issue to note about Amatus's picture of these events is that its date of composition, on which the consensus appears to be 1072 to 1080, sets it apart from other narratives in that it describes the main actors while they were still alive. This significantly alters its value and meaning: how Amatus dealt with Sikelgaita's position as wife of the man who displaced her brother as ruler when all three were still alive, was just one problem which will be discussed below.

Besides the chroniclers, there is a considerable body of charter evidence – that is, written records of transactions in lands and privileges – which, through analysis of their place of writing and preservation, content and personnel, can reveal much about the gradual expansion of Norman power. They have been exploited in studies of southern Italy many times before, but few historians have taken as their starting point a gendered analysis of the material, considering not only the transactions themselves, but the family relationships revealed, the titles and language used by the participants, the need to fulfil multiple family roles in a single charter, and the sometimes conflicting claims that these exercised upon an individual. The main exception to this tradition, Huguette Taviani-Carozzi, characterises

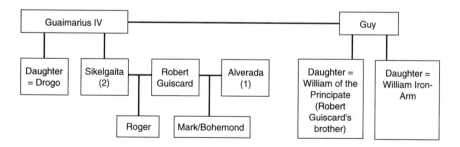

Figure 1: The Salernitan princely family and the Normans.

the Norman immigration into southern Italy as 'essentially a male immigration',[11] necessitating marital alliances to establish them in power. Her discussion of Robert's marriage to Sikelgaita in 1058, however, did not consider how that marriage created a route into power not only for Robert, but for Sikelgaita too.

Unlike Amatus's story of Frederick of Lorena, Anna's tale about Sikelgaita may have been an entirely credible image of the Lombard princess. Anna's sources included not only Byzantine generals (including her own husband), but also Normans who, after their leader's death in 1085, chose to serve the Byzantine emperor rather than return to Italy.[12] Sikelgaita's long association with Robert provided ample opportunity, as Amatus and other sources demonstrate, to build her own reputation.

Sikelgaita was born in 1040. When her brother Gisulf offered her in marriage to Robert in 1058, he was following in a long tradition of marital strategies which stretched back over two centuries (they are clearly visible, for example, in the tenth-century *Chronicon Salernitanum*).[13] Potential enemies were regularly turned into kinsmen by marriage – but then the kinsmen themselves often became enemies. This marital game had, as we have seen, been played more recently in marriages of Gisulf's cousins and other sister to members of Robert's family.

To marry Sikelgaita, however, Robert had to put aside his first wife, the Norman Alverada, by whom he already had a son named Mark/Bohemond. Amatus explains that Robert found his marriage to Alverada was consanguineous,[14] but given that Robert's half-brother Drogo had previously married Sikelgaita's sister, this explanation is, to say the least, disingenuous. Robert's supposed religious qualms about his marriage to Alverada have largely been dismissed by historians; instead, his marriage to Sikelgaita is normally discussed in terms of its greater political advantages. Matthew says the marriage was 'certainly for political reasons', but also that Sikelgaita, once married, 'clearly aimed to secure Guiscard's succession for her oldest son [by Robert], Roger, whose Lombard connections gave him certain advantages, particularly after Guiscard's capture of Salerno itself in 1076'.[15] Matthew here acknowledges that the marriage may have had mutual advantages, but does not explore Sikelgaita's role in the arrangement. At eighteen years old, and hedged round by the constraints that Lombard family law placed on women[16] whatever their social class, she may not have had much choice when her brother married her off (in other, contemporary, Lombard documents this is the brother's responsibility, after the death of the father, in which the sisters have little say). But with Robert's power in the ascendancy – he was invested with the duchy of Apulia, Calabria and Sicily by Pope Nicholas II in 1059 – Sikelgaita both as wife and widow appears to have forged a role for herself that was more than simply political pawn.

Amatus deals with Sikelgaita's delicate position as the transmitter of power between the Salernitan princely house and the new Norman regime with some skill. Having already castigated the Lombard dynasty, and subsequently characterised Sikelgaita's brother Gisulf as 'born of a viper-like race'[17] and 'like a snake',[18] the monk nevertheless has to present Sikelgaita herself as worthy of her husband and new status. He mirrors Robert's wealth, humility and bravery with her nobility, beauty and wisdom, and states that as a pair they were well matched.[19] This was not, then, simply a eulogy of Robert.

Sikelgaita is absent from the historical record in the first seven years of her marriage. During this time she gave birth to two sons by Robert: Roger Borsa, born in 1060, and Guy, a more shadowy figure in the historiography.[20] Thereafter, Sikelgaita appears alongside Robert in his charters. In 1065, she and Robert were present at the dedication of the new church of St Maria at Matina in Calabria; he is recorded in the charter as 'duke of Calabria and Sicily and count of Apulia' – he had not yet taken over Salerno. In a second charter of the same year, Robert and Sikelgaita confirmed the same church in all its possessions and rights. She is recorded here as 'daughter of Guaimarius of Salerno', and her signature (or sign) is included at the end of the document.[21] There is a clear issue of identity here: Sikelgaita is presented by the notary as the daughter of a great prince in prefer-ence to the wife of a warrior and *parvenu* who as yet only controlled southern Italy in name. But her identity in this public document may have served as a signal legitimising Robert's claim to the last major territory remaining out of Norman hands.

A gap of eleven years then ensues where she does not appear in Robert's documents, although these are so poorly preserved that her absence may not be significant. In fact, if Amatus is reliable, she was frequently at Robert's side in these years, when he was engaged in the conquest of Sicily. After the submission of Val Demone in 1066/7, Geoffrey Ridell (the future duke of Gaeta) was sent to fetch Sikelgaita so that Robert could display his victories to her.[22] She reappears during his second campaign of conquest in the early 1070s, when a pestilence struck during the siege of Palermo. At the same time 'the wine at the court of the duke failed; and whilst they still had delicious meats to eat, he and his wife had to drink water'.[23] While this passage is anecdotal in treatment, it does suggest that Sikelgaita was an important and relatively constant presence at Robert's mobile court. Her importance is further reinforced in an episode which happened in 1073, while Robert was away in Puglia. Amatus relates that he fell ill, and that rumours of his death reached Rome. This prompted Pope Gregory VII to write a letter of condolence to Sikelgaita, which Amatus reproduces in full, encouraging her to have her son Roger receive his father's inheritance from the papal hand. This letter, which does not survive in Gregory's registers, has been discussed at face value in several studies: the circumstances of its transmission, however, beg questions to which I shall return below. By 1076, reflecting Robert's newfound status as conqueror of much of the South, Sikelgaita had a new identity, content to sign Robert's charter in favour of the bishopric of Melfi as 'Sicaildis his wife' under Robert's signature.[24]

Why was Sikelgaita such a constant presence beside Robert? The power of her late father throughout much of the southern Italian mainland made her an essential political ally and rendered her presence in documents necessary to Robert's position as heir apparent (or, at least, father of the heir). Although there is a seven-year gap between her marriage and her first documented appearance beside him, it is likely that this early absence was due to the need to provide Robert with a son to consolidate his claim to Salerno, but also to reinforce her position as his wife. Later documents from the abbey of the Holy Trinity at Cava in which Sikelgaita appears are an extension of this claim, for her family had founded the house and their continued patronage is signified by her status as co-donor in a number of charters made by Robert. But we must also remember that it was also in Cava's interest to secure the goodwill of the Norman leader: Sikelgaita's role might also be read as intercessor for her family's house with the new ruler.

In 1076, Robert finally took Salerno itself, a process which Amatus describes in dramatic detail as the climax to his chronicle and casts as an epic battle of wills between Gisulf and Robert, with Sikelgaita centre stage. Indeed, Amatus weaves her loyalties together in a tense drama involving a confrontation with her brother when she is intervening to try to make peace between Gisulf and Robert: Gisulf 'threatened that, once her husband was dead, he would make her wear black clothes'.[25] Robert, having decided to end Gisulf's reign once and for all, goes on the attack, and Gisulf seeks refuge in the *rocca* above Salerno along with his other sister.[26] Even now, Sikelgaita could not entirely ignore her natal family, and is recorded providing them with food supplies at the request of her sister, although 'she could not now give her goodwill'.[27] This episode is interesting for the gendered messages it sends out. As a dutiful sister, Sikelgaita was fulfilling her expected role in showing mercy to her siblings and bringing them supplies, but Amatus's additional comment makes it clear that she was no longer part of their world.

With Gisulf's defeat, Sikelgaita entered a new phase of her life after 1076. The modern editor of the *Codex Cavensis* comments explicitly on her 'great influence' on Robert and his actions.[28] A close reading of the language of the charters to Cava suggests that Sikelgaita's influence was strong by the late 1070s. In July 1079 Robert's gift of the church of St Matthew at Roccapiemonte to Cava was made *per interventum domne S[ichelgaite] coniugis nostre* (at the intervention of lady S our wife).[29] In September of the same year a gift to Robert's *fidelis* Gratianus was made *per interventum domne S[ichelgaite] ducis, dilecte coniugis nostre* (at the intervention of lady S the duke, our dear wife).[30] In August 1080, Robert confirmed Cava's rights over a number of monasteries *per interventum d(o)m(n)e S[ichelgaite] ducisse, dilecte coniugis nostre* (at the intervention of lady S the duchess, our dear wife).[31]

Robert's dependence on his wife in these years is clear as he inserted himself into the patronage network around Salerno. The donation to Gratianus, however, is particularly arresting, as Sikelgaita is clearly identified there as 'duke' and not, as in the 1080 charter, as 'duchess'. The latter charter clearly shows that *ducissa* was known and used as a title, so why the earlier use of *dux*? Was this an acknowledgement by Robert (or his scribe) that Sikelgaita's power around Salerno was at least as formidable as his own? The word is being used deliberately, and may have contributed to or acknowledged Sikelgaita's growing authority.

The question centres on how the title would have been perceived: as we shall see later, there is evidence to suggest that *dux* was not so much a masculine as a gender-neutral title. There are precedents for the use of apparently masculine titles by female rulers, and they seem, rather than to present a woman undertaking a male role, simply to convey that the woman is, at that moment, in a position of relatively unchallenged authority. For example, Theophanu (d. 993), widow of the German emperor Otto II, used the title *augustus* in a charter of 990, and it was apparently not uncommon for masculine forms to be used for women by the German chancery. Later on, marquise Matilda of Tuscany (d. 1115) would also be described as *dux* in some narrative sources.[32] The difference between both women and Sikelgaita is that the latter was a married woman constantly beside her husband: the authority accorded her through titles, therefore, seems to be another facet of her legitimising role in Robert's military rule.

Besides intervening in her husband's charters, Sikelgaita also appears to have retained her own property which she is seen managing alone. In a precious document of 1079 (which is dated 'the sixth year of Robert and Roger's rule' – that is, suggesting that Robert and his son by Sikelgaita had ruled the region around Salerno *before* the city itself fell in 1076), she gave lands which she had inherited and bought near Maiori to the church of St Trophimena there. She identifies herself in the document as 'Sikelgaita the duchess, wife of Robert', and a local judge and two witnesses sign the document.[33] This suggests that she remained active in local patronage in her own right. The dating clause is significant: as the second wife of Robert, Sikelgaita would have been very concerned to ensure that her son inherited the Salernitan patrimony, and to date her charter to extend Roger's rule backwards seems to be a calculated part of her campaign (which is echoed in more dramatic terms in Amatus[34]) for him to do so. As such, it is a revealing glimpse of her understanding of the power of the written document.

Robert and Sikelgaita also patronised the monastery of Montecassino, and along with their son Roger gave it the church of St Peter in Taranto in 1080, followed by a gift of property in Amalfi made by Robert and Sikelgaita in 1082.[35] They were commemorated by the abbey's chronicle as major benefactors, and appear in its necrologies, such as Leo of Ostia's produced in 1098/9.[36] Their generosity had been one of the motives for Amatus to write his *History:* in his prologue he justifies writing about 'secular men' (*'li seculer'*) by recalling their gifts to the abbey. The latter consisted both of valuable land and vast amounts of moveable treasure and money.[37] Their benefactions extended also to the archbishopric of Salerno, given a castle in 1080, and to the church of St Laurence in Aversa, given the church of St Oronzo in Taranto in 1082.[38]

The next five years appear to have been largely taken up with the Byzantine campaigns recorded by Anna Komnena, according to whom Sikelgaita was at Robert's deathbed, somewhere off the islands of Corfu or Kefalonia,[39] in 1085. Bohemond, Robert's eldest son, was sick in Italy as Robert died, and in his absence Sikelgaita was able to have Roger named the heir.[40]

The political sensitivity of the moment, and the more general problem of stepmother/stepson relations in high politics, have their parallels elsewhere, but Sikelgaita's position at the time of her widowhood may have given rise to another story mythologising her even more than Anna. Orderic Vitalis, writing at the monastery of St Evroul in Normandy, tells of Sikelgaita's attempt in 1085 to poison Bohemond using poisons taught to her by the doctors of Salerno. Found out by Robert, who was on his deathbed, she was forced to send an antidote to Bohemond but then, 'Terrible to relate, she administered poison to her husband'.[41] These stories may be apocryphal, and Chibnall speculates that Bohemond himself, who had survived to go on the First Crusade but remained weak for the remainder of his life, was responsible for spreading the rumours surrounding his father's death. But it does reflect a very real problem for Sikelgaita – how to remain in power (or ensure that Roger did) against an older, and militarily competent, adversary.

Once widowed, Sikelgaita next appears issuing a document at Bari in Puglia in 1086, giving control over the Jewish community in the city to its archbishop. Her son Roger was present, but the charter was also witnessed by her stepson Bohemond.[42] And Sikelgaita herself once more, as in 1079, appears as *dux*. This title, alongside her very ruler-like activity of patronage over a Jewish community (her father had made a donation of the Jews at Capua in a similar way in 1041[43]), suggests that as a widow she was not inclined to give up power to either her son or her stepson. Cowdrey refers to a further two charters in which she uses the title, and interprets its use as Sikelgaita 'exercising a *de facto* regency on her son's behalf'. This only ended, he believes, when Sikelgaita reached agreement with Bohemond, and thereafter 'allowed Roger Borsa to be duke in his own right'.[44]

Sikelgaita was clearly perceived to be powerful as a widow and a mother, and the notary of the Bari document knew enough to realise that the use of *dux* was a credible title for the widowed duchess. It also had a more recent precedent than the Cava charter of 1079. In 1083, Sikelgaita had represented her husband in a court case over

Cava's rights in a number of monasteries in the Cilento, and the decision was recorded as having been made *iussu supradicti domine nostre ducis* (at the order of the abovementioned mistress our duke), an eclectic mix of gendered endings which again recognise that Sikelgaita was not simply the representative of ducal power, but actually shared in it, for all that she is never identified as a 'consort'.[45] But the usage in this document confirms the gender-neutral status, at best, of the term *dux*.

Chronicle and charter evidence combine to create an image of Sikelgaita which builds her up as a formidable partner in Robert Guiscard's reign and a considerable influence during the early years of that of her son, Roger. She died on 16 April 1090, and was buried at her own request in the atrium of the abbey of Montecassino.[46]

Sikelgaita has largely remained in the shadow of her husband's exploits in traditional historiography, but the varied, and trans-gendered, identities which she was credited with and created for herself are to some extent the product of the political uncertainty of the Norman conquest, which briefly opened opportunities to her as a ruler. But is her case exceptional? As a warrior she might not be unique: Amatus describes a stand-off between Gisulf and his brother Guy, in which the latter sought refuge with his family in the *rocca* above Salerno. Guy subsequently came to court to negotiate over the cession of the fortress, only to be taken hostage and threatened with blinding if his family did not give up the stronghold. Guy's wife, though, had other ideas: 'The wise woman, strong in soul, remained firm and fought, and encouraged her people to fight'.[47] Only when Guy asked her to did she give up the fortress.

Images of warrior women are by no means unusual in the twelfth-century Mediterranean, nor do they seem to attract censure, as in sources further north.[48] But these southern Italian examples are early and suggest, as does Sikelgaita's use of masculine titles, that a period of political upheaval could create temporary spaces for aristocratic women to exert their power in new ways.[49] But did Sikelgaita's relative freedom of action (for example, making property transactions without the intervention of a Lombard-style male guardian or *mundoald*), owe more to her existing status as a royal princess than to her Norman marriage?

It is hard to answer this question. Logic dictates that a princess and heiress in the Lombard princely dynasty would find her freedom more constrained rather than less, and that therefore it was as consort to Robert, and freed from paternal or fraternal control, that Sikelgaita's change of status occurred. But Robert was still a ruler – did marriages to less illustrious Normans transform the opportunities available to other Salernitan women?

A survey of the documents from the Cava archive after 1100 suggests that, despite a number of documented Norman men, little changed initially for Salerno's women in terms of their property-holding. There is limited evidence of local women's interaction with the Normans and one or two more mixed marriages, but there is not any clear-cut evidence of any large-scale transformation in the way Lombard women identified themselves, the legal customs they followed, or the way in which they managed land.[50] In very well-documented Campania, the Norman conquest has been characterised – correctly in my view – as one of Norman assimilation to local practices.[51]

Not all local ruling women were prepared to accept the inevitable, however. Left a widow in 1061 with a young son for whom she was acting as regent, duchess Maria of Gaeta forged an anti-Norman pact with neighbouring small towns in 1062. Her action was to little avail – prince Richard of Capua took over the city that year. Dating clauses of Gaetan documents show that Maria's young son, Atenolf II, was permitted a token role as late as 1064, but Maria herself temporarily disappears after the takeover. Richard handed over control of Gaeta to his son-in-law William of Montreuil, but William rapidly revolted, repudiated Richard's daughter and sought to marry duchess Maria. She was therefore still perceived as having power, and the key was that she was mother of the rightful duke. The revolt failed, but its message is significant – women were recognised by the Normans as trans-mitters of authority over the political fragments of southern Italy.[52]

Further south more disturbance is argued to have taken place, but on the basis of much less documentary evidence. It is difficult to tell what role(s) a certain Guimarga, 'lady and possessor of Tygane' in 1080, or 'Emma, *domina* of the territory of Eboli' in 1090, played; the latter's name suggests a Norman immigrant, but one who wielded power. Guimarga is more ambiguous – was she a resident noble-woman who took advantage of the Norman advance to carve out her own small territory, or did she, too, arrive with the incomers? Only more work will clarify this issue.

These two cases do, however, highlight the difference in the quality of evidence available – Sikelgaita's career and duchess Maria's revolt can be analysed because chroniclers thought them worthy of discussion. Sikelgaita's legend and memory, in particular, seem to have survived in a number of different traditions.[53] For example, her name rose sharply in popularity in local documents during and after her lifetime. This might have been a way for the indigenous population to express their ethnic identity in the face of the newcomers, a resistance which seems to have crumbled and given way to a whole flood of novel women's names, many French or Norman, a couple of generations later.[54] Her fame spread throughout the Mediterranean and Frankish worlds, and acquired a different gloss with the twelfth-century authors who recorded her.

Before concluding, I should like to suggest a different reading of the one contemporary chronicle we have. Throughout this study, the work of Amatus of Montecassino has been used as a means of filling in the gaps in the charter evidence, providing evidence of Sikelgaita's power as a result of her marriage in 1058. The work could be read as much as a eulogy of her as of Robert, but could the *History of the Normans* in fact be the history as Sikelgaita herself saw *and shaped* it? The evidence is circumstantial, but builds into a picture of the chronicle as a highly politicised piece with far more than simple eulogy or glorification of Montecassino under Desiderius in mind.

Amatus's agenda, I suggest, was not only to promote Lombard acceptance of the Norman conquest,[55] but also, and possibly primarily, to establish Sikelgaita and her son, Roger, as the successors to Robert over and above his first wife Alverada and firstborn son Bohemond. And, unlike parallel examples from other parts of Europe, Sikelgaita did not wait until her husband's death to begin this process. Instead, she drew upon her existing links with Montecassino's abbot, Desiderius, who had briefly been a monk in her family's foundation at Cava between 1048 and 1049,[56] and possibly with Amatus as well (he had been bishop of Paestum/Capaccio before entering the monastery,[57] and so might well have frequented the court of her father), to produce a text which underlined her claim and that of Roger. The date of writing supports this. Amatus began his work around the year 1072, precisely the critical time in the complicated family life of Robert, as Roger reached the aged of twelve or thirteen, the threshold of majority, and became a genuine contender for power with Alverada's son Bohemond, who may have been in his early twenties. Sikelgaita's charter to St Trophimena, discussed above, reveals that she was consciously backdating the start of Roger's rule to this same period,

1072/3. Could she have encouraged Amatus, or his abbot, Desiderius, to collude in her propaganda campaign?

Objections might be raised that Amatus's work contains almost nothing about this rivalry. Its internal evidence, however, suggests that deliberate choices were made about the way in which the women were portrayed. The Appendix lists the key passages in the work. Amatus's scheme builds towards the takeover of Salerno by Robert as the climax to the story, but he also needs to emphasise Sikelgaita as Robert's chosen partner to aid him in this enterprise. Sikelgaita, therefore, has to be detached from her Lombard loyalties in the text, and Book VIII appears to achieve this. Gisulf, her brother, has been described in negative terms from Book III onwards, and his lack of reason and his cruelty in the first twelve chapters of Book VIII enable Sikelgaita to be portrayed first as intercessor (a role she later repeats in Anna Komnena's portrait) and, when that fails, as a merciful sister having pity and providing the refugees in the *rocca* with food. Her goodwill, however, is now withdrawn: Amatus has enabled her to remain charitable without compromising her political position, which is now firmly with her husband.

This has already been made clear with the insertion of the letter from Gregory VII: it reinforces Sikelgaita's responsibility to ensure her son inherits Robert's position as servant of the papacy, and thereby authorises his accession ahead of his older half-brother. The authenticity of the letter has, to my knowledge, never been seriously called into question; even if it is real, its inclusion in its entirety in the chronicle further supports the view that Sikelgaita actively contributed to, and provided material for, Amatus's composition.

There is also symmetry in the arrangement of the text: it was apparently dedicated to Desiderius, although the dedicatory letter is now lost, and the abbot becomes Sikelgaita's surrogate father in the final chapter. Detached from her own Lombard family, she becomes part of the wider spiritual family of Montecassino. Her decision to be buried in the abbey precincts is the logical conclusion, therefore, to life of mutual beneficence.

The story of Roger's participation in 'Balalardus's' revolt (*c.* 1073/4) remains to be analysed in detail. Amatus emphasises Sikelgaita's anger at Robert's nephew, and her subsequent reminders to Robert about his nephew's disloyalty and arrogance towards her and her son. But why include a passage which also implicated Roger? This fulfilled another need: to demonstrate that Roger was now capable of participating in military and political enterprises as a young man, just as his elder half-brother Bohemond had been for some years. His actions parallel those of Robert Curthose, son of William the Conqueror, whose rebellion has been analysed as an example of a young man attempting to escape his role as subordinate youth and achieve full adult, and masculine, status.[58] But the story was essential to developing Roger's public image as future duke: the text minimised the aspect of filial disloyalty by emphasising 'Balalardus' as the instigator of the rebellion.

Throughout the period covered by Books III to VIII, the *History of the Normans* can be read as the story of Robert Guiscard's rise, even as that of a 'Christian hero',[59] but those passages featuring Sikelgaita emphasise her constant presence with him, her own prestige and power and her final choice of identities as daughter of Montecassino and wife of Robert. By 1080, which is thought to be when Amatus completed his work, the urgency with which the project had begun had diminished: Roger was an adult, Sikelgaita a regular participant in the local and wider pattern of donations which maintained her status, and Robert planning his first Byzantine campaign.

In hindsight the *History* might appear to be about soliciting further gifts for Montecassino from this couple and their eldest son – these certainly continued and increased in size. But this function, a satisfactory *raison d'être* for modern historians of institutional relationships, who have shown little interest in subjecting the abundant sources of the period to a gendered scrutiny, ignores the delicate political situation in 1070s southern Italy. The writing of texts was a political act in itself. Even if we accept that Desiderius was the prime mover behind Amatus's work (as its dedicatee), the prologue suggests that other debts had to be repaid, and Desiderius's close relationship with Sikelgaita after she was widowed in 1085 may simply have continued a longstanding friendship.

Periods of conquest and warfare are often discussed by historians as a time when women will end up as victims: southern Italian sources include episodes of distress caused to women by the Normans' habit of taking male prisoners and ransoming them. Marriages in these periods, too, are seen in terms of conquest, with women given to the invaders as the spoils of war or peace-offerings (a theme developed in particular by feminist historians such as Gerda Lerner).[60] Indeed, the masculinity of the conquerors often depends on their ability to take the women of those conquered. But it has been demonstrated effectively in the case of England that such 'victims' are also powerful transmitters of power and legitimacy, and that elite women could use written texts to shape their image and authority.[61]

This is why Anna Komnena's image of Sikelgaita telling the *Normans* to be *men* is such an evocative one. Sikelgaita is essentially on the losing side in the process of Norman infiltration to the south. Her marriage to Robert, however, removes her from her family, and in particular from association with her weak brother who had been unable to repeat the military achievements of his father. Instead, she became a powerful and respected figure alongside her husband and son. Almost unnoticed, however, is the clear loosening of control over Sikelgaita's own property, and her new freedom to manage it herself. This went hand in hand with the development of her public image through a contemporary text, the writing of which, I believe, she strongly influenced.

The dynamic of the Norman conquest, when viewed with the lens of gender, was the supplanting of one aggressively masculine group – the Lombards, with their tight familial control over women and their property – by another, the warlike Normans. Its effect, ironically, may have been to allow certain women more space politically and economically. Did it offer women an alternative system of laws and customs to live by? In the early period perhaps not visibly, but a Lombard woman could demand up to a quarter of her husband's property as a morning-gift or *morgengabe* – this has intriguing possibilities if Lombard women attempted this successfully with Norman husbands, thereby perhaps creating powerful female landowners like the shadowy figures further south.

Sikelgaita is of course exceptional, but she also demonstrates the limits that such apparent moments of political emancipation had. Unlike her later contemporary Matilda of Tuscany, she had brothers to contend with, and only her husband's superior military force furnished her with the role of duchess. Once established, she may have experimented with masculine titulature, but rarely acted alone. She relied on a monastic writer to create a textual identity which asserted her new roles, but ended up with a new paternal figure in the shape of Desiderius. As such, her career was hedged round by patriarchal constraints. But to Anna Komnena, herself restricted in movement and activity after a failed *coup*, the tales which reached her of the princess must have struck a chord. Ironically, her version of the ambivalent and ambiguous identities that Sikelgaita left to posterity were more accurate than she could have imagined.

Appendix: Structure of the *History of the Normans*

Prologue:	justifying writing about secular matters because of rewards received from those written about. Lost dedication to Desiderius.
Bks I–II:	events prior to Robert's arrival in the south.
Bk III, 2:	Robert's marriage to Alverada (*c.* 1048?) 'Against his brother's wishes', thus bad.
Bk IV, 18:	Robert's repudiation of Alverada and marriage to Sikelgaita, his perfect partner.
Bk IV, 32:	Sikelgaita accompanies Robert to Puglia from Calabria.
Bk V, 24:	Sikelgaita brought to Sicily to see Robert's victories.
Bk VI, 18:	story of wine shortage, a device to remind reader of Sikelgaita's continued presence with Robert?
Bk VII, 3:	Guy of Salerno with Robert on campaign because of Robert's love of Sikelgaita, Guy's sister.
Bk VII, 8:	letter of Gregory VII to Sikelgaita, emphasises Roger's position as heir.
Bk VII, 16:	Sikelgaita and her sons present at a major event, the peace between Robert and Richard of Capua.
Bk VII, 19–21:	Roger aids 'Balalardus', Robert's nephew, in a rebellion. Sikelgaita persuades Robert of his nephew's ill-will on account of the injury she has suffered from him (Balalardus had been the only one not to recognise Roger's position as heir when the rumour of Robert's death had spread in 1073).
Bk VIII, 1–12:	Gisulf as tyrant.
Bk VIII, 13, 15:	Sikelgaita as mediator between Robert and Gisulf.
Bk VIII, 24:	Robert enters Salerno, Gisulf flees to *rocca*.
Bk VIII, 26–7:	climactic dialogue between Robert and Gisulf; Sikelgaita passing food to *rocca*.
Bk VIII, 30:	Gisulf surrenders, Sikelgaita ordered by Robert to give him leaving gifts.
Bk VIII, 36:	Robert and Sikelgaita's goodness to Montecassino; Sikelgaita 'daughter of Desiderius'.

Notes

1. Anna Komnena, *Alexiad*, trans. E. R. A. Sewter (Penguin, London, 1969).
2. *Alexiad*, I.12.
3. *Alexiad*, I.15.
4. *Alexiad*, IV.6.
5. *Alexiad*, VI.6.

6. For example, the tenth-century bishop and diplomat Liutprand of Cremona thought the Greeks 'soft, effeminate creatures ... idle liars of neither gender': Liutprand of Cremona, *The Embassy to Constantinople*, ch. 54, in *Liudprand of Cremona: The Embassy to Constantinople and Other Writings*, trans. F. A. Wright, ed. J. J. Norwich (Everyman, London, 1993), pp. 202–3. The crusader Geoffrey de Villehardouin, writing in the early thirteenth century, also characterises the Byzantine inhabitants of Abydos as 'men who have not sufficient courage to defend themselves': Geoffrey de Villehardouin, *The Conquest of Constantinople*, ch. 7, in Joinville and Villehardouin, *Chronicles of the Crusades*, trans. M. R. B. Shaw (Penguin, London, 1963), p. 58.

7. V. De Bartholomeis (ed.), *Storia de'Normanni di Amato di Montecassino* (Tipografica del Senato, Rome, 1935) (hereafter *Amato*), Bk III, ch. 24.

8. Since W. Smidt, 'Die *Historia Normannorum* von Amatus', *Studi Gregoriani*, 3 (1948), only V. d'Alessandro, 'Lettura di Amato di Montecassino', *Bullettino dell'Istituto Storico Italiano e Archivio Muratoriano*, 83 (1971), pp. 119–30, has problematised the source. Few secondary histories utilising Amatus have discussed the source *per se*. H. Taviani-Carozzi, 'Le Mythe des Origines de la Conquête Normande en Italie', in *Cavalieri alla Conquista del Sud*, ed. E. Cuozzo and J.-M. Martin (Rome/Bari, Laterza, 1998), pp. 57–89, includes an extended discussion of Amatus's models, but does not address the issue of the purposes of his text; the contributions to the Bari congress in 1973, *Robert il Guiscardo e il suo Tempo* (Dedalo, Rome, 1975; repr. Bari, 1991), did not include any specific work on the narrative sources; similarly sparse are D. Matthew, *The Norman Kingdom of Sicily* (Cambridge University Press, Cambridge, 1992); J.-M. Martin, *La Vita Quotidiana nell'Italia Meridionale al Tempo dei Normanni* (Rizzoli, Milan, 1997); G. A. Loud, *Church and Society in the Norman Principality of Capua, 1058–1197* (Oxford University Press, Oxford, 1985); and R. H. C. Davis, *The Normans and their Myth* (Thames and Hudson, London,1976). See also E. Joranson, 'The Inception of the Career of the Normans in Italy: Legend and History', *Speculum*, 23 (1948), pp. 353–96.

9. H. E. J. Cowdrey, *The Age of Abbot Desiderius* (Oxford University Press, Oxford, 1983), p. xx.

10. *Amato*, Bk III, ch. 38.

11. H. Taviani-Carozzi, *La Principauté Lombarde de Salerne, IXe–XIe Siècle* (École Française de Rome, Rome, 1991), vol. II, p. 932.

12. G. A. Loud, 'Anna Komnena and her Sources for the Normans of Southern Italy', in *Church and Chronicle in the Middle Ages: Essays Presented to John Taylor*, ed. G. A. Loud and I. N. Wood (Hambledon, London, 1991), pp. 41–5.

13. U. Westerbergh (ed.), *Chronicon Salernitanum* (Studia Latina Stockholmensia, Stockholm, 1956).

14. *Amato*, Bk IV, ch. 18.

15. Matthew, *Norman Kingdom*, p. 18.

16. The seventh-century law of the Lombard king Rothari, which classified women as minors, requiring a male guardian or *mundoald* in any legal transaction, was still respected in Lombard-dominated areas of the south: Rothari, law 204, in *The Lombard Laws*, trans. K. F. Drew (University of Pennsylvania Press, Philadelphia, 1973), p. 92.

17. *Amato*, Bk III, ch. 44.

18. *Amato*, Bk IV, ch. 42.

19. *Amato*, Bk IV, ch. 18.

20. Genealogical table in H. Takayama, *The Administration of the Norman Kingdom of Sicily* (Brill, Leiden, 1993), p. 222.

21. A. Pratesi, *Carte Latine di Abbazie Calabresi Provenienti dall'Archivio Aldobrandini* (Studi e Testi 197, Vatican City, 1958), documents 1 and 2.

22. *Amato*, Bk V, chs 24–5.

23. *Amato*, Bk VI, ch. 18.

24. L.-R. Menager (ed.), *Recueil des Actes des Ducs Normandes d'Italie*, I (Società di Storia Patria per la Puglia, Bari,1981), document 23.

25. *Amato*, Bk VIII, ch. 13.
26. De Bartholomeis, in *Amato*, p. 368, identifies Gisulf's sisters as Sica and another whose name is unknown. In fact Gisulf's sister Gaitelgrima is identified in a later charter from Cava dated 1104: Cava, Holy Trinity, Archive, *Arca* XVII, document 100. She is also documented with her husband Hugh in 1093 giving gifts to the church of St John at Nocera for the soul of her deceased husband, Jordan I of Capua (d. 1090): Cava, Holy Trinity. Archive, *Arca* XV, document 100. It is unclear from Amatus, however, which sister Gisulf fled with.
27. *Amato*, Bk VIII, ch. 26.
28. S. Leone and G. Vitolo (eds), *Codex Diplomaticus Cavensis*, X (Badia di Cava, Cava de Tirreni, 1990), (hereafter *CC*, X), p. xxiii.
29. *CC*, X, document 119 (= Menager, *Recueil*, document 27).
30. *CC*, X, document 124 (= Menager, *Recueil*, document 28).
31. *CC*, X, document 138.
32. Theophanu: O. Engels, 'Theophanu, the Western Empress from the East', in *The Empress Theophano: Byzantium and the West at the Turn of the First Millennium*, ed. A. Davids (Cambridge University Press, Cambridge, 1995), pp. 28–48. Matilda: P. Skinner, *Women in Medieval Italian Society, c. 500–1300* (Longman, forthcoming), ch. 5.
33. R. Filangieri di Candida (ed.), *Codice Diplomatico Amalfitano*, II (Vecchi, Trani, 1951), document 592.
34. *Amato*, Bk VIII, ch. 13.
35. Menager, *Recueil*, documents 31 and 42.
36. Loud, *Church and Society*, p. 127.
37. Details in H. Bloch, *Montecassino in the Middle Ages*, 3 vols (Harvard University Press, Cambridge, MA, 1986), vol. I, pp. 85, 276, vol. II, p. 748 and Cowdrey, *Age*, pp. 8 and 19.
38. Menager, *Recueil*, documents 34 and 40 respectively.
39. Kefalonia's northern port of Fiscardo is a local claimant to Robert's memory.
40. Matthew, *Norman Kingdom*, p. 18.
41. M. Chibnall (ed. and trans.), *The Ecclesiastical History of Orderic Vitalis*, IV (Oxford University Press, Oxford, 1973), Bk VII, ch. 7, p. 29. M. Chibnall, 'Women in Orderic Vitalis', *Haskins Society Journal*, 2 (1990), pp. 105–21, at p. 108, illustrates that poisoning is a common theme in Orderic's work.
42. F. Nitti di Vito (ed.), *Codice Diplomatico Barese*, I–II (Vecchi, Bari, 1897–9), document 30.
43. Taviani-Carozzi, *Principauté*, p. 448.
44. Cowdrey, *Age*, p. 180.
45. Menager, *Recueil*, document 43. The term *consors regni* had been commonly used in the northern kingdom of Italy to denote the power of the queen from the late ninth to early eleventh century, but it does not appear to have been used of women rulers in the south. On the significance of the term: C. G. Mor, '*Consors regni*: la regina nel diritto pubblico italiano dei secoli IX–X', *Archivio Giuridico*, 35 (1948), pp. 7–32; criticised by P. Delogu, '*Consors regni*: un problema carolingio', *Bullettino dell'Istituto Storico Italiano*, 76 (1964), pp. 47–98.
46. Bloch, *Montecassino*, vol. I, p. 84.
47. *Amato*, Bk IV, ch. 42.
48. M. McLaughlin, 'The Woman Warrior: Gender, Warfare and Society in Medieval Europe', *Women's Studies*, 17 (1990), pp. 193–209.
49. This is not a startling revelation: Pauline Stafford's work on female rulership, classically in her *Queens, Concubines and Dowagers: The King's Wife in the Early Middle Ages* (University of Georgia Press, Athens, Georgia, 1983; repr. Leicester University Press, London, 1998), and most recently in *Queen Emma and Queen Edith* (Blackwell, Oxford, 1997), has long served as a guide to rereading medieval political history with a gendered lens.
50. I surveyed the evidence in P. Skinner, 'Figlie di Sichelgaita: Donne a Salerno nel Dodicesimo Secolo', paper read at the conference *Salerno nel XII Secolo*, Raito di Vietri, 16–20 June 1999 (forthcoming).

51. G. A. Loud, 'Continuity and Change in Norman Italy: The Campania during the Eleventh and Twelfth Centuries', *Journal of Medieval History*, 22 (1996), pp. 313–43; J. Drell, 'Cultural Syncretism and Ethnic Identity: the Norman "Conquest" of Southern Italy and Sicily', *Journal of Medieval History*, 25 (1999), pp. 187–202.

52. On Maria, P. Skinner, *Family Power in Southern Italy: The Duchy of Gaeta and its Neighbours, 839–1150* (Cambridge University Press, Cambridge, 1995), pp. 153–7.

53. Her legend continues to be cultivated by local writers in Salerno: D. Memoli Apicella, *Sichelgaita: tra Longobardi e Normanni* (Elea Press, Salerno, 1997), is a creative blend of historical evidence and invention.

54. P. Skinner, '"And her Name was …": Gender and Naming in Medieval Southern Italy', *Medieval Prosopography*, 20 (1999), pp. 23–49.

55. As argued by Cowdrey, *Age*, p. 25.

56. Cowdrey, *Age*, p. 115.

57. Cowdrey, *Age*, p. xx.

58. W. M. Aird, 'Frustrated Masculinity: The Relationship between William the Conqueror and his Eldest Son', in *Masculinity in Medieval Europe*, ed. D. M. Hadley (Longman, London, 1999), pp. 39–55.

59. Cowdrey, *Age*, p. 26.

60. G. Lerner, *The Creation of Patriarchy* (Oxford University Press, Oxford, 1986), esp. pp. 76–100, though her model is based on ancient examples.

61. Stafford, *Queen Emma*, pp. 28–52.

6

The Metamorphosis of Woman: Transmission of Knowledge and the Problems of Gender

Anneke B. Mulder-Bakker

Guibert of Nogent (*c*. 1064–*c*. 1125), in his autobiography *De Vita Sua* (On his own Life), has pertinent observations concerning the transmission of knowledge, in particular sacred knowledge, by himself, his mother and his uncle – a cleric, a lay woman, and a lay man respectively. Speaking of the formative influences on his mother's religious life, he notes that, widowed and alone after her children had left the nest, she opted for the solitary life. He then depicts her conversion in a way that is pivotal for his ideas concerning female schooling and the transmission of knowledge.[1] Evaluating this picture against his characterisation of both his own training as a cleric and an abbot, and his uncle's conversion to an eremitic life, we gain valuable insights into male and female (religious) education and thus into the transmission of knowledge and the problems of gender.[2] In the following I will investigate the perceived inequality of male and female education, focusing geographically on the lands of Loire and Rhine[3] and distinguishing between: (a) the way knowledge was acquired; (b) the media in which it was set down; (c) the content of the knowledge; and (d) the way it was transmitted to others. Subsequently I will test my findings on an example from the late middle ages, Christine de Pizan.

After Guibert's mother had left family and friends and had a little cell built next to the abbey church of St Germer de Fly – a family monastery, it seems, in which many members of her family and household also found their spiritual home – she organised for herself a personal director. Guibert writes:

> When she arrived at the monastery, she saw an old woman dressed in monastic habit whose appearance gave every evidence of piety. She coerced this woman into living with her, showing her the submission of disciple to master ... Step by step, then, she began to imitate the austerity of that older woman; she took up the same frugality, settled for the simplest foods, did away with the luxurious mattresses to which she was accustomed and was content to sleep on a straw mat, covered with a simple sheet. Although she was still quite beautiful and showed no sign of aging, she made every attempt to look as if she had reached old age with an old woman's wrinkles. Her flowing hair, which usually is an essential component of feminine charm, succumbed under the scissors' repeated assault. A dark cloak with unusually broad folds, dappled with innumerable patches and repairs, served as proof, along with a small, undyed coat, and shoes with hopelessly irreparable soles, that the One whom she was endeavouring to please with such unassuming apparel was within her.[4]

The old nun functioned as her personal teacher. Guibert's mother learned the seven penitential psalms from her – significantly, 'not by reading them but by listening', not *videndo sed audiendo* – and grew into a wise and holy mother who attracted many visitors. 'All who had known her before, especially men and women of the nobility, enjoyed her conversation immensely and found her playful and restrained at the same time.' She was especially commended for being *faceta et temperans*, concise and moderate.[5] Guibert speaks of her having visions and prophetic gifts, foretelling the future and reading other people's minds. She appears to have been a prophetess and a holy recluse. She must have been in her thirties at the time.

One of the visions his mother had was a dream in which she saw herself imitating Mary just as she had imitated the old nun. In her dream she saw Mary going to the altar of the abbey church, kneeling down in prayer, and herself following exactly the Holy Mother's example.

> Suddenly she saw a woman of unparalleled beauty and majesty walking up the middle of the church toward the altar. She was followed by what looked like a young maiden whose deferential appearance seemed entirely appropriate for whom she followed [this is Guibert's mother] ... Drawing close to the altar, the Lady knelt in prayer; and she who had been seen walking behind her, a noble lady of the court, did the same.[6]

Guibert's mother heard Mary speaking to her son and herself repeating the words in the same way as she had learned to repeat the words of the old nun before. The mother's religious education, therefore, in the typology of Guibert, consisted in imitating exemplary people. An education on the job, so to speak, it was acquired not by studying books but by listening to people, not *videndo sed audiendo*, and by mulling things over in her heart, ruminating on what she had heard. That is why she was said to have learned the psalms by listening to the old nun. She may have read the texts for years in her own prayer book or heard them read aloud by her own chaplains, but only now were they stored in her heart: *quos saporose, ut sic dixerim, diebus et noctibus ruminabat* – day and night she turned them over in her mind, chewing them with savour.[7]

The mother's education was an imitation of the good deeds and morals of older persons, an *imitatio morum*, to quote Theodulfus of Orleans when he describes the training of young priests in Carolingian times. These young students lived in the house of the bishop and took him as their example; they received their priestly training *per morum imitationem in sacerdotio subrogantur* – by imitating the habits of priests they became candidates for the priesthood.[8]

Guibert's description suggests that his mother's religious training coincided with her schooling in general. We get the impression that she was unable to read and write and for this reason had to resort to oral instruction. Her training was therefore a learning by doing, a gaining of wisdom by experience, *experientia*. In this way she acquired knowledge which can be qualified as wisdom, *sapientia*, not *scientia*, the scholarly knowledge of books.

Because Guibert clearly presents his mother as an ideal type, we can infer the following. (a) Women were supposed to acquire knowledge by imitation; they were not supposed to occupy themselves with reading and bookish learning. Even the Psalter they learned by listening to an older voice. (b) The knowledge they gained was therefore a type of wisdom, practical wisdom, which (c) was preserved in the heart. (d) The women then transmitted the knowledge they had acquired by responding modestly but adequately to the questions of visitors seeking guidance for their lives – in any case, the women who became recluses saw this as their task.

About his own education Guibert speaks in quite different terms. As a little boy at home he learned the basics of reading, he says[9] – presumably from his mother. This means that she, despite what has been said before, must have had the ability to read and possibly also to write. As he reached school age, his mother hired a personal teacher for him. Both Guibert and his mother kept in close contact with this dedicated man; the teacher even withdrew with the mother to the convent when she opted for the solitary lifestyle. Guibert had a low opinion of his teaching abilities, however. An autodidact, the teacher retained incorrectly what he had once learned badly late in life.[10] Guibert received his intellectual training only later, in adolescence, in the same convent which his mother and his teacher had entered. Here he read day and night, even stealthily under the blankets when the other boys were asleep. According to his own memoirs, he fully immersed his soul in the study of verse-making and love lyrics. He even competed 'with Ovid and the pastoral poets, striving to achieve an amorous charm in my way of arranging images and in well-crafted letters'.[11] More important is that here he also experienced the special encouragement of a teacher, this time Anselm, later bishop of Canterbury, who was a familiar visitor in St Germer. 'He was so determined to make me benefit from his learning, and he pursued this end so persistently, that I might have seemed to be the only reason for his frequent visits.'[12]

Like his mother, it is clear, Guibert received his education in the personal interaction of teacher and pupil, but his curriculum, in contrast to his mother's, consisted mainly of bookish knowledge, *scientia*, the learning of the schools.

The scraps of factual evidence that slip through the net of Guibert's value scheme lead us to suspect that his mother was not nearly as unschooled as Guibert tried to portray her. She was very probably able to read and possibly to write as well; she kept a concerned eye on her son's education and maintained close contact with his teacher. In addition she had chaplains in her employ from whom she would certainly have learned the Psalter and other religious literature, even if she had not been able to read.[13] She was therefore not actually dependent on the nun for acquiring knowledge of the Bible later in life.

We can further conclude: (a) Guibert also came by his knowledge mainly through personal contact with an older tutor, in other words, through *imitatio morum*. The lessons provided by his first teacher he even describes as mainly moral wisdom: 'he seemed more a parent than a tutor, more my soul's caretaker than my body's'.[14] But (b) the content of his formal education consisted of book learning – Latin grammar and the stylistic skills of the classical authors which could be found in books and learned by imitating classical verse or writing fictional letters. He was subsequently taught principles of scholastic theology in his talks with Anselm. Unlike his mother, Guibert (c) preserved this knowledge in his memory *and* in self-composed texts. Upon reaching adulthood, he (d) would transmit what he knew in public sermons and authoritative Latin treatises.

In Guibert's time the wave of new hermits and new monasteries reached northern France. Guibert is obviously highly impressed. He sings the praises of knights converting to the eremitic life, of princes burning charcoal in the woods, mortifying their flesh, or withdrawing to new and holy monasteries. He mentions Thibaut of Champagne, Simon of Valois, Bruno of Cologne and in particular his uncle Evrard of Breteuil, who 'imitated' Thibaut, 'the model from whom Evrard had drawn his inspiration'. This Evrard, 'in the prime of his life' adopted a religious lifestyle, fled to foreign parts where his name was utterly unknown and had the courtly habit of collecting dicta and sayings of the masters – this last point is of particular interest to us. 'If he happened to meet people whom he knew to be famous scholars, he would coerce them into writing something, in prose or in verse, for his benefit in a little book he often carried with him for this purpose ... Even if he did not discern the meaning himself he would soon obtain from those to whom he had given these maxims an unequivocal opinion as to which of these sayings were the most pertinent, either in their meaning or in the way they were turned.'[15]

This lay man, then, like Guibert's mother, (a) learned the religious lifestyle by imitating an older example. Secondly, (b) he was not supposed to acquire book learning himself but was praised for having assembled the dicta and maxims of others in a *liber amicorum* of sorts, the oldest one I know of. He (c) did not read the booklet himself but listened to learned men explaining the meaning and moral lessons to him. He subsequently (d) entered a strict reformed monastery, a move which no doubt made contact with the outside world all but impossible.

These are my three examples – the mother, the son and the uncle. Each of them provides us with insight into the general process of the acquisition of knowledge by the group to which they belonged: the categories of females, clerics, and males. Through them we are also shown the nature of the knowledge they acquired, and the ways in which it was preserved and transmitted. Each of these issues calls for some further discussion.

In a period when schools and universities had not yet pervaded society, both boys and girls acquired most of their knowledge in the personal 'exchange between an older voice of experience and a younger audience'.[16] Most youngsters learned on the job. The young priest was trained by assisting the old one, the squire by bearing the shield of his knight, the maid by serving her lady. *Imitatio morum* was central to all education, in the monastery as well as in the household and in urban trades. According to Anne Clark Bartlett, 'imitation – the fashioning and reconstruction of the self in accordance with the multiple models provided by the holy family, male and female saints, aristocratic ideals, and an assortment of textualised personages – was the chief aim of virtually all forms of medieval (and particularly devotional) discourse'.[17] Indeed, a courtly writer like Thomasin von Zerclaere, in his *Der Waelsche Gast* of the early thirteenth century, advised young knights to choose a virtuous knight, a man with *wistuom, tugende unde sin*, and imitate him in all things.[18] The boy was told to identify with his role model and follow his example in minute detail.[19] Whenever he had to act himself while his hero was not physically present, he was supposed to search his memory to discover how the knight had acted in similar circumstances or how he might have acted. For a knight in training it was important to store up in his memory as many good examples as possible. These were in the first place drawn from people he knew, but they could also be found in stories told about great heroes from the past or in texts he had read about predecessors, such as *Der Waelsche Gast*.[20]

Acquiring knowledge in these circles can therefore be characterised as appropriating the collective memory of the virtuous deeds of all good people in the present and stories about good people in the past. Transmission of knowledge amounts to passing on the stories piled up in the house of memory. Schooling is a matter of making the young observe the good examples in their surroundings and having them read (or listen to) virtuous stories from the past. Schooling is training youngsters to ponder and store up these memorabilia in their hearts.

Knowledge is here the fruit of personal communication. Even if it is recorded in a book, this is considered secondary, as no more than a mnemonic device, not as knowledge, which is by nature written knowledge.[21] Thomasin, for example, stylises his book as a person, calling it a welcome 'guest'.[22] In the monastic milieu – an environment in which everyone learned to read and write and which we would for this reason consider more text-oriented – Hugh of St Victor described the three-stage process of reading-meditation as follows: 'first, one focuses on the example, next one acts in imitation of it, and then one internalises the imitation so that one's own vital power (*virtus*) is permanently changed'.[23] Striking here is that he hardly seems to distinguish between the non-literate imitation of knights and the classroom training of monks. Women, too, appear to have shared in this *imitatio morum*. Guibert's mother imitated Mary, and Elisabeth of Spalbeek took Christ as her role model by reviving his passion on Fridays, standing with her arms held wide for hours.[24]

This *imitatio morum* therefore appears in every educational setting, and nearly all written texts place themselves in the service of the exemplum effect. German nobles took as role models the heroes of the past by replaying their battles, which were described in detail in epics and romance, the 'matière de Rome' and the 'matière de Bretagne'. In religious circles, dicta and sayings of the Church Fathers as well as Lives and legends of the saints were used to preserve and transmit exemplary religious knowledge. Thus, we might add, many saints' Lives should not in the first place be viewed as instruments in the canonisation procedure but as a means of storing good examples – a function they shared with epics and historical writing. So far, men and women, students and apprentices were more or less equals.

As for the nature of the knowledge acquired, we can conclude that in all of the cases mentioned above it was experiential knowledge, practical wisdom; this kind of knowledge, shared by Guibert, his mother, and his uncle, was held in high esteem by all. When Guibert, as an adult man, writes prestigious scholarly treatises (*scientia*) but fails to attain the position of abbot, he himself declares that on closer consideration this was as it should be, because he was still lacking the proper frame of mind. Only after acquiring *sapientia* was he entrusted with the leadership of Nogent.[25] His mother, despite her lack of schooling, did possess that wisdom: 'To hear her talk about these matters you would have thought her a mellifluous bishop rather than the illiterate woman she was'.[26]

Generally speaking, people preserved this knowledge in their memory, *memoria*, and in the case of women this was evidently located in their heart. Books, if people had access to them, served as mnemonic devices. And their appearance confirms this. We have only to think of Thomasin's booklet with its little pictures and poems, or the beautifully illustrated Books of Hours. Those who were literate read the text, those who heard it read aloud or who were unable to read looked at the pictures and remembered the accompanying text. To quote Carruthers: 'Medieval culture remained profoundly memorial in nature, despite the increased use and availability of books ... Writing ... was always thought to be a memory aid'.[27] This holds true for the high middle ages as well as for the later period, for illiterate people and scholars alike. Michael Clanchy, too, maintains that reading means hearing the text aloud, while looking at the lettering and images on the pages; repeating the text aloud with one or more companions, until it was learnt by heart. The ultimate stage of this reading was contemplation, when the reader 'saw with his heart'.[28] Images and sculptures, symbolic objects or 'lieux de mémoire' served in like fashion as memory aids.

Writing a book in this memorial society was, according to Carruthers, a matter of *inventio* and *meditatio*. Searching one's mind for memory images and bringing together the variously stored bits of knowledge, pondering these scattered images and arranging them into a single, composite whole – these were essential to the process. In an illustrative passage by the monk Eadmer, we observe Anselm struggling with this while thinking out his *Proslogion*. He grew almost desperate 'partly because thinking about it took away his desire for food and drink' and partly because it even distracted him from giving full attention to the matins. He feared, therefore, that the devil was leading him astray.

> Then suddenly one night during matins the grace of God illuminated his heart, the whole matter became clear to his mind, and a great joy and exultation filled his inmost being. Thinking therefore that others also would be glad to know what he had found, immediately and ungrudgingly he wrote it on writing-tablets and gave it to one of the brethren of the monastery for safe-keeping.[29]

Anselm, as a cleric and scholar, was entitled to set down his discoveries in a learned treatise. (Later we shall see that he composed a book in essentially the same way as women mystics wrote their works.) For the lay man Evrard, it was acceptable to have a book of wise sayings, although he was not supposed to write it himself nor to understand the message of it. Guibert's mother was not even supposed to have such a book.

The proper form of knowledge for lay persons was non-literate, a knowledge embedded in a culture we could define as memorial. Coleman speaks of an 'aural' culture, stressing the communal listening act of 'public reading and the reading public'.[30] In this way she upholds the status of lay culture, placing it on a par with the monastic culture studied in older scholarship. In his fine work *The Love of Learning and the Desire for God,* Jean Leclercq, himself a Benedictine monk, claimed this memorial culture as a 'monastic culture', the exquisite achievement of Benedictine order. This is an understandable but, in my opinion, much too limited characterisation.[31] Memorial culture is the culture of all educated people in times when teaching is a matter of telling exempla – whether of knightly heroes, fairies, or the apostles of the faith – and when to learn means to meditate on these stories and store them in one's memory.

Not all knowledge, however, was amassed wisdom, *experientia* preserved in the mind or in written mnemonics. There was also a corpus of specifically written knowledge. Works of classical authors and theology, scripture and Scripture, were by definition book learning. Written down in Latin and transmitted in the schools, at least from the twelfth century onwards, this knowledge was thought out in rational discourses, constructed by means of logical argumentation, underpinned with authorities, *auctoritates,* and developed in scholastic scholarship. From the thirteenth century onwards, if we may trust Clanchy, it was preserved in real books, that is, in codices designed for page-turning and passage-comparison, complete with indices, headings and a convenient layout. These books were the products of a literate mentality and an intellectual culture. They are qualitatively different from the mnemonic devices of memorial culture.[32]

In today's scholarship we tend to take these books and the corpus of knowledge written down in them as characteristic for all knowledge. We assume that cathedral schools and universities were the centres of education par excellence, and that classroom teaching and scholastic treatises were the norm. We study university teaching when we want to study education in general, and we turn to scholastic knowledge to collect common forms of wisdom.[33] Non-academic learning and education which took place outside the schools we tend to view as peripheral phenomena, deviating from the norm. Parisian scholars of the time were, in fact, unanimous in claiming this. Instead of taking their word at face value, however, we should investigate whether and to what extent their claims were accepted in society. Moreover, was classical and sacred knowledge the exclusive domain of the clergy? And was it always taught in a classroom setting and written down in Latin, in scholastic treatises? And was it only to be preached from the pulpit?

A pastoral writer such as Caesarius of Heisterbach (d. *c.* 1240), not bound to scholastic theology and the claims of the Parisian scholars, shows us that such is not the case. God uses two different routes to pass divine knowledge to mankind. Caesarius distinguishes between learning, the *scientia* of the schools written down in books, and God-given knowledge which is not dependent on books but directly transmitted, infused so to speak, by God or his Mother; it is passed down in visions and divine conversations. He explains that God, Lord of all knowledge, determines himself how and to whom he benignly grants his sacred knowledge. He gives it to one person or takes it away from another, just as he chooses. Caesarius gives examples of priests bereft of wisdom and lay brothers endowed with the gift of speech. He speaks of lay people's spirit of prophecy and mystic raptures. As if to test and subsequently to legitimise such visions, he tells the story of a priest in his own abbey in his own time – a trust-worthy example therefore – who had a dream about Christ's birth. It is strikingly similar to Bridget of Sweden's Christmas vision. Notwith-standing his initial doubts – events cannot happen twice, can they? – the priest, and thus the common faithful, learn to understand that such dreams are highly meritorious, especially when they are preceded by holy meditation: *meditatio.* As real as the Bible itself and church writings, and of equal historical value, they constitute solid know-ledge. The content of these visions is not essentially different from theological or scriptural knowledge, only the format and the route along which it is gained differ – although here, too, some question marks should be placed, as we will see presently.[34] In Caesarius's opin-ion, priests were to be concerned with learning. Devout lay believers might obtain knowledge of equal value but along a different route; they acquired this independently of the church and the schools.

Anne Clark's brilliant study of the *Book of Visions* of Elisabeth of Schönau (d. *c.* 1165), written down by her brother Ekbert, gives facts and figures.[35] Elisabeth, after she had begun to distribute her visions, urged her brother to come to her convent and mediate between her and the outside world. Ekbert was a learned priest who had studied under the Parisian doctors. He started to collect all the evidence of his sister's visions and 'worked over these records, translating, polish-ing, revising, until he had a text that satisfied his judgement about what was appropriate to be published'. But he did more. Aware of the limits of his own bookish learning and deeply convinced of his sister's 'access to knowledge beyond that which he had gained in studies in

Paris', he questioned Elisabeth about what she saw and presented her with unsolved academic problems.[36] Elisabeth interviewed her angel about them and received answers. Here the two ways of acquiring knowledge are portrayed as working together harmoniously and complementing each other.

Elisabeth had been commanded by the angel to commit to writing what she had heard:

> On a certain day while I was in a trance, [the angel] had led me as if to a meadow in which a tent was pitched and we went into it. And he showed me a great pile of books kept there and said, 'Do you see those books? All of these are still to be dictated before the judgement day.' Then, raising one from the pile, he said, 'This is the *Book of the Ways of God* [*Liber Viarum Dei*] which is to be revealed through you after you have visited sister Hildegard [Hildegard of Bingen] and listened to her.' And indeed it began to be fulfilled in this way immediately after I returned from her.[37]

That is why she decided to record her visions in a book, imitating an older example, Hildegard, and asking her brother, a cleric, to assist her. Other mystic women such as Hildegard of Bingen herself and Mechtild of Magdeburg and many others were urged to do the same. Dreams and visions, or to use the medieval term, prophecies, were not private conversations between the Lord and his beloved – as modern scholars often tend to believe – but divine knowledge to be spread to the faithful.[38] To quote from Alcuin Blamires's outstanding studies on scholastic thought in these matters: prophecy, according to Aquinas, was a truth revealed to some person for the edification of others. These divine truths had to be couched, therefore, in utterances of speech for transmission to others and/or laid down in books. However, in the event that a woman was the receiver, she was not to be trusted with the teaching herself because of her inferior social status. A male cleric had to stand in for her, and the church had to test beforehand whether she had received real prophecies.[39]

To come back to God's instructions to women mystics to write down his revelations in books: it strikes me that in Eadmer's description of Anselm thinking out his *Proslogion*, the sudden illumination in the church closely resembles the females' illuminations during visions and dreams. Even of Aquinas we know that he worked out his theology while lying prostrate and praying at night. If we recall Caesarius's description of how the priest in his abbey received a Christmas vision in a dream which was preceded by holy meditation, the parallels become ever more striking. I conclude from this that the two routes along which divine knowledge was passed down to men and women on earth had more in common than we usually assume. It is modern scholarship that 'rationalised' the scholastic thought of the men and 'mysticised' feminine thinking.

Two factors do differ, however: the media in which the revelations were recorded and the ways in which they were taught to others. Guibert's mother did not write things down herself and only spoke to visitors in private conversations. Clerics such as Anselm or Aquinas were entitled to compose theological treatises, to preach or to teach students. Some of the lay mystics did write, at least after they had reached a certain age and sometimes with the help of male scribes; but their texts differ radically from the writings of clerical authors. Their texts appear 'simple and emotional', written 'artlessly' and in the vernacular, without the references to *auctoritates* required in serious work. We can not be sure, however, whether this is because the women had no knowledge of these things or because they were not allowed to show such knowledge and therefore kept it hidden. Anne Clark Bartlett singles out 'just this sort of "strategic ignorance" as a means of resistance to male authority'.[40]

A further thought. *Clerici* were not only men of divine knowledge; medieval clerkliness, or 'style clergial' as it was qualified in French, also comprised classical learning, the results of the *translatio studii* from Greece and Rome to France and the medieval world. And here, too, clerkly women intervened in the discussion. Christine de Pizan (*c.* 1364 – after 1429) is certainly the most illustrative for the questions raised in this context.[41] Characterising her own literary education, she uses modes and metaphors similar to those we encountered in the religious women, but as an eloquent author conversant with male scholarship, she includes interpretation and comment for the sake of clarifying their significance. She, moreover, adds one important new element which puts all the others into a meaningful framework, namely the effect of the female life cycle.

After being widowed at age twenty-five and struggling for her own independence for another fourteen years, she looks back to her formative years in the 'serious' books she now publishes, namely her *Livre du Chemin de long Estude* (1402–3), *Mutacion de Fortune* (1403) and *L'Avision Christine* (1405). She tells us that as a child of a loving father who discovered in her an eager pupil, and a devoted mother who attached greater importance to her moral upbringing, she acquired a great deal of knowledge but never enjoyed a higher education. That was simply not considered suitable for a girl. As she puts it: 'I was born female, because of which I could not have it [the treasure of great learning], still – I was not able to prevent myself from stealing scraps and flakes, small coins and bits of change, that have fallen from the great wealth that my father had'. Therefore, 'I gained nothing except furtively, and I have acquired a poor hoard, as is well evident in my work'.[42] Evidently she believed – also in her later years – that her lack of schooling accounted for the fact that her books did not meet the literary standards of her time. Once married and the mother of three children, she found little time to further her development: 'For although I was naturally and from my earliest youth inclined to learning, the preoccupation with the duties common to married women and also frequent child bearing kept me from it. Also, great youth, that sweet enemy of good sense, will often not allow children of even great intelligence to devote themselves to study because of the desire to play.'[43] Only after she had become a widow and had to bear the full responsibility for her family did she return to her books. 'Then, in this solitude some memories of Latin and of the noble sciences came back to me, along with various learned sayings and refined rhetoric which I had heard in the past from my dear departed friends, my father and my husband, even though I was too frivolous then to retain much.' This sounds very much like Guibert's talk about his mother. She, too, was said to have first acquired her knowledge of the Psalter and other religious writings after being widowed. Christine continues: 'just like a child whom one first teaches the alphabet, I began with the ancient histories from the beginnings of the world, the histories of the Hebrews, the Assyrians ... all the way to the Romans, the French ... and many other writers of history ... Then I started to read the books of the poets and as my knowledge kept on increasing, I was glad to have found a style that was natural to me; I delighted in their subtle coverings and noble subject matter hidden under delightful moral fictions and in the beautiful style of their verses and prose, ornamented by polished rhetoric adorned with subtle language and surprising proverbs.'[44] She worked, in other words, on her classical education and an appropriate style of writing, and subsequently began to give birth to books as she had borne children before.

These passages call to mind the oldest poetics in the vernacular, written by the Antwerp clerk Jan van Boendale (*c.* 1350). Dismissing the light verse and fictions of the oral writers and appropriating the learned tradition of the Latin authors, Boendale insists that a serious vernacular writer 'must know his [Latin] grammar ... because those who do not realize what kind of an art grammar is – laymen, for example – can never be successful writers, as they lack the grounding which is the sign of the true writer'. Grammar for him seems short-hand for a learned style (*style clergial?*) and classical learning, exactly the skills Christine got conversant with. It implies 'references to author-ities as well as instructive examples [*auctoriteite ende exemple*]'.[45] Who-ever composes in this way is, according to Boendale, a 'Poet, that is, someone who desires his teachings and his writings to be known by all, and to stand forever' – but in the vernacular. A poet of this kind can measure up to the learned clerics of the university, whose mono-poly on learning Boendale vigorously opposed.[46] Fiona Somerset speaks in this connection of 'an extra-clergial position'.[47] This is pre-cisely the position occupied by Christine.[48] In the fourteenth century non-ecclesiastical authors begin laying claim to the moral and didactic authority of classical learning. Boendale claims this authority for town clerks like himself; Christine appropriates it as a wise old widow.[49]

She is about forty at the time and joins the public debate by writing historical and political-philosophical works.[50] This again recalls Guibert's mother, who also started to acquire knowledge after she had been widowed, and then grew into a public figure, a sought-after counsellor, when she was in her forties or fifties. Both remind us of women such as Hildegard of Bingen, Julian of Norwich and Margery Kempe, who also began public careers in old age. In *Le Livre du Chemin de long Estude*, an allegorical work describing Christine's own education, she tells how in a dream – here she resembles the women mystics with their visions – Sybille of Cumae, 'who was neither young nor pretty but aged and very calm' and wearing 'a wide tunic' took her by the hand.[51] This woman led her up the ladder of 'imagination' and 'speculation'.[52] The parallel with Guibert's mother's instruction by the old nun is again striking.

I deduce from this that, according to general consensus, women may have received a reasonably good education in their youth and gained further knowledge later, but that such was not valued as formal education and learning. It was seen as informal knowledge, wisdom of sorts, scraps and flakes that fell from the table of the learned but never enabled women to think and write properly. Just as Hildegard of Bingen confessed her illiteracy in the twelfth century, Christine did so in 1400. Widowhood, however, changed female status dramatic-ally. Christine describes how after her husband's death and a long period of utter distress, Fortune came to her in a dream (again a

dream!). Fortune 'touched me all over my body ... I felt myself
completely transformed ... I found my heart strong and bold, which
surprised me, but I felt I had become a true man.'[53] Later Christine
returns to this metamorphosis. It is apparently no mere idiomatic
expression – convincing herself to 'take it like a man' – but the beginning of a new phase in her life.[54] In her autobiographical first book,
Le Livre de la Mutacion de Fortune, Christine explains that by publishing this book, a work of scholarship and not light verse, she moved
from being female to becoming male: 'de femelle devins masle'.
Fortune made her 'en homme naturel parfaict'.[55] Christine alludes
here to the general notion of the *aetas perfecta* in a man's life.[56] In her
widowhood, as she has taken up the responsibility for her family and
an income, she feels that she holds a position which allows her to
behave as a man, to enter the world of learning, to acquire the knowledge needed for participation in public debate, and to advise others.
When she subsequently reaches the age of perfection, the *aetas perfecta*,
she feels entitled to publish serious books – not the love lyrics of
youth – to enter public discussions and, indeed, public life. What is
more, she is accepted in these new roles. This is why I wonder whether
women more generally, once they had fulfilled their matrimonial
duties and raised their children, once they had become widows and
had reached their own *aetas perfecta*, were allowed, like men, to enter
the public world and perform more communal tasks. Could they, indeed, behave as a man: 'homme je suis, assez le demonstent mes pas'?

In medieval texts which deal with the division of ages in human
life, the life cycle treatises, we learn that men, when they were in their
thirties or forties, were assumed to enter this *aetas perfecta*. They
were old enough now to have learned self-control, and having taken
on domestic responsibilities, they could enter the sphere of worldly
affairs and undertake more civic tasks. Visual images often depict them
with a purse and the signs of public dignity.[57] This is what Christine
is referring to, I argue, when she speaks of her turning 'en homme
naturel parfaict'. She, too, has reached the *aetas perfecta*. Women of
that age were more or less past the years of fertility and thus, for the
males in their surroundings, free of the threatening qualities associated with sexual incitement. They were equals of the restrained men
of their age. This will have facilitated their entrance into the world
outside the family.

As an encore, we may wonder whether women like Christine and
Guibert's mother may even have been perceived in the eyes of their

fellow countrymen as beyond the female status as such. Ethnologists tell us that in non-western societies people often distinguish more than two genders. Besides male and female they recognise a third category of more or less ungendered children and/or elderly people.[58] Does *aetas perfecta* perhaps refer to such a non-female status? Or does it mean that men *and* women are now conceived as belonging to the same 'asexual' gender, termed perfect? Considering the possible implications of the life cycle, we can also begin to understand why Hildegard of Bingen, having received visions from early youth, only informed Bernard of Clairvaux and the pope when she was in her forties.[59] Women had a greater chance of being accepted as religious leaders when they had reached the *aetas perfecta*. This does not mean, however, that elderly women could simply assume the same positions as men. Christine, for example, is bold enough to maintain that she, like her learned father, can counsel princes and administrators because she is able to foresee the consequences of their deeds; but at the same time she confesses that she owes this gift to the Sibyl – she is, in other words, a prophetess – while her father, scholar that he was, derived his knowledge from astrological books. Christine remains a 'simple person'.[60] She feels legitimated by the spoken word of the Sibyl, whereas her father was authorised by the written *auctoritates*. Women in the later middle ages – even a learned woman such as Christine – stopped dead in inspirational and vernacular wisdom, men grew away from them with their bookish learning.

To search for the connections between the stray observations so far: in an oral or aural society,[61] in which knowledge is transmitted in the exchange between an older voice of experience and a younger one, and which consequently places the highest value on personal example, women occupied a potentially pivotal position. Since time immemorial women had been seen as mediators between man and the gods; they prognosticated and foresaw the consequences of men's actions and for this reason were expected to intervene and to direct.[62] They were also the keepers of social memory.[63] In the circle of the peasant and the bourgeois family they were the storytellers,[64] and in the courtly milieu they were the patrons of poets and artists – they owned books and loved to read, they conversed with the clergy. 'Bookish pursuits were a matter for women and priests'.[65] In the actual life of this society, where the men were often out on campaign or already dead, women played a primordial role.[66] Guibert and his mother provide valuable testimony on this point. When it came to gaining wisdom in this world, by an *imitatio morum*, men and women stood side by side.

Because books were seen mainly as mnemonic devices, they were not prohibited for women, although having them and reading them was not specifically endorsed either – just as this was not considered meritorious for lay men. Only in the field of written knowledge – both classical and divine – were lay women and lay men barred from the sources. But even in this field a learned author such as Thomasin of Zerclaere appropriated the classical part, the seven liberal arts, for his courtly audience. He translated Latin knowledge into the vernacular, recreated it in the form of dicta and sayings of a Roman Guest, *Der Waelsche Gast*, and offered it to his German hostess, 'die Hausfrau'. I have not, by the way, come across women who wrote such books in this period themselves.

In the field of sacred learning, God benignly opened two different routes along which men and women, clergy and laity, could acquire his divine knowledge. Elisabeth of Schönau and her brother Ekbert are graphic illustrations of the value and prestige of both routes. Never-theless, Elisabeth's case also demonstrates that women were not trusted to further transmit this knowledge themselves. Church authorities tried to prevent them from committing their revelations to paper in (Latin) treatises following the academic and scholastic style. Misogyny worked its way through to the gates of the Highest. In view of this, the peculiar, non-scholarly style of books of visions produced by female mystics is hardly surprising.

The conclusions drawn so far are by now more or less common knowledge in medieval Gender Studies. Two observations must be added, however. Modern investigations almost always focus on female religious, virgin nuns who devoted themselves to Christ from early youth: Hildegard of Bingen and Elisabeth of Schönau, Beatrice of Nazareth and Ludgart of Aywières, Catherine of Siena and Julian of Norwich. As Rosalynn Voaden shows in her contribution to this same volume, these women's lives followed a straightforward course, at least in contemporary representation. Secluded from society, they lived in lifelong devotion to the Lord. They underwent no sudden conversions in early adulthood comparable to religious men, or trans-formations later in life comparable to married women. Actually, they are not representative figures for medieval society at large. Guibert's mother and Christine de Pizan illustrate quite different life cycles, and theirs is much more typical for the medieval condition, also in contemporary reflection. 'For women and girls there is, according to the moralistic didactic texts, only one form of existence; it is also their "profession", and its individual phases were supposed to flow naturally, one from the other. The young girl was to grow up making every effort to become a desired object for marriage and thus, in the future, a good ... wife, lady of the house, and mother'.[67]

These women show that they did undergo radical conversions, metamorphoses in fact, as Christine coined it, in the course of their lifetime. Left behind as widows (when they did not remarry and resume their spousal state), they became heads of families and felt entitled to participate in public life. In the field of learning this meant that whatever knowledge they might have acquired in their youth at home, undervalued though it was in terms of education, was now publicly recognised as something to build on and to use in the public sphere. Just as men who had reached their forties were expected to restrain their emotions and perform civic duties, these widows claimed public roles. Christine was exactly in her fortieth year when she proclaimed her maleness – and was accepted in her new role. Bridget of Sweden was about the same age, as was Hildegard of Bingen. These women broke out of the secluded and domestic lifestyle imposed on them in their youth – a lifestyle that modern scholarship considers the norm for all medieval women of all ages – and entered the male world of religious leadership and public debate. Guibert's observation is astounding enough to merit repetition here: 'To hear her talk about these matters you would have thought her a mellifluous bishop rather than the illiterate woman she was'.[68]

Women's age and the female life cycle prove to be of vital import- ance when evaluating transmission of knowledge and the problems of gender.[69] If mothers survived childbirth, they could expect to outlive their spouses, sometimes for several decades.[70] Both Guibert's mother and Christine lived on for at least thirty or forty years, a longer time than they had spent in their traditional family roles.

However, dramatic changes hung over them in the later middle ages. As cathedral schools and universities developed into ever more important power blocks, *studium* became, next to *regnum* and *sacerdotium*, state and church, the third 'formative force of society'. For women it became increasingly difficult to gain access to the world of higher education, and certainly to the possibility of propagating their knowledge by writing books. The university 'arose as an alliance of teaching and learning males and was, for the first eight centuries of its history, off-limits for women. The consequences of this exclusion continue to make themselves felt in our educational system today.'[71] Fortunately women did not stand alone in resisting the monopolistic aspirations of academics and clerics. In the commercial towns of the Low Countries and in administrative capitals, learned clerks claimed their part of classical knowledge as clerkliness. Deschamps in France, Maerlant and Boendale in the Low Countries, and Chaucer in England appropriated the classical authors and wrote moralistic and didactic works in the vernacular and in the *style clergial*. Women were their born allies.

They proved to be rather self-confident allies, as well. The Wife of Bath in fiction and Christine de Pizan in actual history learned their lessons and knew how to play their social roles. They followed in the footsteps of many generations of foremothers and, after the death of their consorts, grew into wise and learned widows. The female life cycle and the public role of these wise old widows – it promises to be a challenging new field of study.[72]

To end with a political note in this politically engaged journal: even in our own academia the effects of the 'deviant' female life cycle make themselves felt. In the Netherlands, where less than 10 per cent of the chairs are held by women, I observe men in their fifties sitting back, waiting till early retirement will release them, while many women of that age keep growing and investing ever more energy in teaching and research. But, given the ranking system based on the male life cycle, they are never rewarded for this – they are simply too old. In my own society they are even pushed firmly to the sidelines. Here, too, seems to be a challenging new field – this time not of historical research but of political action.

....

Notes

I wish to thank Dr Myra Scholz for correcting and improving my English. A first version of this chapter was presented as a paper at a workshop of the research group 'Transmission of Knowledge and the Problems of Gender', a joint project of the Dutch School for Medieval Research and the Medieval Institute of Notre Dame University in the US. A volume of studies on the topic will be published in due course. Several parts of this study elaborate on my 'The Prime of Their Lives: Women and Age, Wisdom and Religious Careers in Northern Europe', in *New Trends in Feminine Spirituality: The Holy Women of Liège and Their Impact*, ed. J. Dor et al. (Brepols, Turnhout, 1999), pp. 215–36.

  1.   Guibert de Nogent, *Autobiographie*, ed. and trans. with an introduction by E. R. Labande, *Les Classiques de l'Histoire de France au Moyen Age 34* (Belles Lettres, Paris, 1981); in English, *Self and Society in Medieval France: The Memoirs of Abbot Guibert of Nogent*, trans. J. F. Benton (1970; repr. Medieval Academy Reprints for Teaching 15, Toronto,

1984), and *A Monk's Confession: The Memoirs of Guibert of Nogent*, trans. P. J. Archambault (Penn State University Press, Pennsylvania, 1996). My translations are based on Archambault. See, for Guibert, T. Lemmers, *Guibert van Nogents Monodiae: Een twaalfde-eeuwse Visie op Kerkelijk Leiderschap* (Verloren, Hilversum, 1998).

2. Guibert and his relationship with his mother have recently been the object of psycho-historical research, see J. Kantor, 'A Psychohistorical Source: the Memoirs of Abbot Guibert of Nogent', *Journal of Medieval History*, 2 (1976), pp. 281–304, and C. D. Ferguson, 'Autobiography as Therapy: Guibert de Nogent, Peter Abelard and the Making of Medieval Autobiography', *Journal of Medieval and Renaissance Studies*, 13 (1983), pp. 187–212. I follow Lemmers, *Monodiae*, pp. 64–8, in declining this approach and analysing the mother's portrait in the context of its own time.

3. Since R. W. Southern, *The Making of the Middle Ages* (1953; repr. Yale University Press, several edns), these lands have been seen as the social, economic and cultural core of western Europe, with Paris as its capital.

4. Archambault, *A Monk's Confession*, p. 46.

5. Labande, *Autobiographie*, p. 51; Archambault, *A Monk's Confession*, p. 47.

6. Archambault, *A Monk's Confession*, p. 56.

7. Labande, *Autobiographie*, p. 51; Benton, *Self and Society*, p. 76.

8. P. Brommer, *Capitula Episcorum I* (Monumenta Germaniae Historica: Capitula Episco-porum I, Hannover, 1984), p. 168,4.

9. Labande, *Autobiographie*, p. 12: 'Traditus ergo literis apices utcunque attigeram, sed vix elementa connectere noram, cum pia mia mater erudiendi avida disposuit mancipare grammatico'.

10. Archambault, *A Monk's Confession*, pp. 15–20.

11. Archambault, *A Monk's Confession*, pp. 58–9.

12. Archambault, *A Monk's Confession*, p. 61.

13. Archambault, *A Monk's Confession*, p. 15: 'those clerics named chaplains who celebrate the Divine Office in her household'; and p. 43: 'the chaplains in her home were kept constantly busy, so that there was hardly a moment when the praise of God was not being sung'.

14. Archambault, *A Monk's Confession*, p. 19.

15. Archambault, *A Monk's Confession*, pp. 25–8.

16. M. Warner, *From the Beast to the Blonde: On Fairy Tales and Their Tellers* (Vintage, London, 1995) made this older voice the object of her research.

17. A. Clark Bartlett, *Male Authors, Female Readers: Representation and Subjectivity in Middle English Devotional Literature* (Cornell University Press, Ithaca, 1995), p. 32.

18. Thomasin von Zerclaere, *Der Waelsche Gast*, ed. F. W. van Kries (4 vols, Göppingen, 1984–5), here v. 6838. See for a general introduction to the theme the illuminating study of H. Wenzel, *Hören und Sehen: Schrift und Bild: Kultur und Gedächtnis im Mittelalter* (Beck, Munich, 1995) pp. 15–47.

19. Thomasin, *Der Waelsche Gast*, vv. 647–52: 'man sol gern volgen dem man/der bezzer ist ze sehen an/denne ze hoeren; daz ist der/der also hat der zuehte ler/daz er nach siner rede guot/baz danner spreche tuot'.

20. To quote a book of morals from the Low Countries: memory is a storehouse of good stories. Eye and ear are the doors. Stored up in this house are not only the memories of living heroes and of good deeds done (the eye), but also stories about great men in the distant past (ear), see *Nederrijns Moraalboek*, Part I, *Moralium Dogma*, ed. M. Gysseling, *Corpus van Middelnederlandse Teksten*, vol. II, 6 (Nijhoff, The Hague, 1987), p. 355. This text is based on the *Bestiaire d'Amour* of Richard de Fournival.

21. Wenzel, *Hören und Sehen*, p. 16: 'Die handschriftliche Kommunikation des Mittelalters bleibt hinorientiert auf die Kommunikation im Raum der wechselseitigen Wahrnehmung, auf die Konfigurationen handelnder Personen und auf die körpergebundenen Codes verbaler und nonverbaler Verständigung'.

22. Wenzel, *Hören und Sehen*, pp. 204–25.

23. Hugh of St Victor, *De Tribus Maximis Circumstantiis Gestorum*, cited by M. J. Carruthers, *The Book of Memory: A Study of Memory in Medieval Culture* (Cambridge University Press, Cambridge, 1990), p. 186.

24. W. Simons, 'Reading a Saint's Body: Rapture and Bodily Movement in the *Vitae* of Thirteenth-Century Beguines', in *Framing Medieval Bodies*, ed. S. Kay and M. Rubin (Manchester University Press, Manchester, 1994), pp. 1–23.

25. Archambault, *A Monk's Confession*, p. 72: 'For the very first time, Lord, I tried to experience that blessed solitude of mind, where one finds your presence'.

26. Archambault, *A Monk's Confession*, p. 73.

27. Carruthers, *Book of Memory*, p. 156.

28. M. Clanchy, *From Memory to Written Record: England 1066–1307* (1979; rev. ed. Blackwell, Oxford, 1993), pp. 186 and 283–93.

29. *The Life of St Anselm by Eadmer*, ed. and trans. R. W. Southern (Nelson, Oxford, 1963), pp. 29–30, quoted by Carruthers, *Book of Memory*, pp. 199–200.

30. J. Coleman, *Public Reading and the Reading Public in Late Medieval England and France* (Cambridge University Press, Cambridge, 1996).

31. J. Leclercq, *L'Amour des Lettres et le Desir de Dieu: Initiations aux Auteurs Monastiques du Moyen Age* (Cerf, Paris, 1963); in English, *The Love of Learning and the Desire for God: A Study of Monastic Culture*, trans. C. Mistahi (Fordham University Press, New York, 1974).

32. Clanchy, *From Memory to Written Record*, pp. 160–61.

33. See for instance W. Rüegg (ed.), *Geschichte der Universität in Europa* (Beck, Munich, 1993), vol. I, and S. Jaeger, *The Envy of Angels: Cathedral Schools and Social Ideas in Medieval Europe* (University of Pennsylvania Press, Philadelphia, 1994), and criticism of their view in E. Kleinau and C. Opitz (eds), *Geschichte der Mädchen- und Frauenbildung* (Campus Verlag, Frankfurt, 1996), vol. I.

34. Caesarius von Heisterbach, *Dialogus Miraculorum VIII, 2*, ed. J. Strange (Lempertz, Cologne, 1851; repr. Gregg P., New Jersey, 1966), vol. II, p. 83.

35. A. L. Clark, *Elisabeth of Schönau: A Twelfth-Century Visionary* (University of Pennsylvania Press, Philadelphia, 1992).

36. Clark, *Elisabeth of Schönau*, p. 17.

37. *Die Visionen der hl. Elisabeth und die Schriften der Aebte Ekbert und Emecho von Schönau*, ed. F. W. E. Roth (Verlag der Studien aus dem Benedictiner- und Cistercienser-Orden, Brünn, 1884), p. 91; quoted in English translation in A. L. Clark, 'Holy Woman or Unworthy Vessel? The Representations of Elisabeth of Schönau', in *Gendered Voices: Medieval Saints and Their Interpreters*, ed. C. M. Mooney (University of Pennsylvania Press, Philadelphia, 1999), pp. 35–51, here p. 43.

38. G. M. Jantzen, *Power, Gender and Christian Mysticism* (Cambridge University Press, Cambridge, 1995), in particular ch. 5.

39. A. Blamires, 'Women and Preaching in Medieval Orthodoxy, Heresy and Saints' Lives', *Viator, 26* (1995), pp. 135–52; see also his *The Case for Women in Medieval Culture* (Clarendon Press, Oxford, 1997).

40. Bartlett, *Male Authors*, p. 23; cf. the illuminating study of D. N. Baker, *Julian of Norwich's Showings: From Vision to Book* (Princeton University Press, Princeton, 1994).

41. N. Margolis, 'Clerkliness and Courtliness in the Complaints of Christine de Pizan', in *Christine de Pizan and Medieval French Lyric*, ed. E. J. Richards (University Press of Florida, Gainesville, 1998), pp. 135–54; L. Walters, '*Translatio Studii*: Christine de Pizan's Self-Portrayal in Two Lyric Poems and in the *Livre de la Mutacion de Fortune*', in the same volume, pp. 155–67; L. Walters, 'Fathers and Daughters: Christine de Pizan as Reader of the Male Tradition of Clergie in the Dit de la Rose', in *Reinterpreting Christine de Pizan*, ed. E. J. Richards (University of Georgia Press, Athens, 1990), pp. 63–76, here p. 71: 'As a clergesce [a female clerk] proposing nothing less than a fundamental revision of the presuppositions of literary tradition, she was trying to secure women's place in literary tradition and to free the literary representation of women from misogynist conventions'.

42. Christine de Pizan, *Le Livre de la Mutacion de Fortune par Christine de Pizan*, ed. S. Solente (4 vols, Soc. des anciens textes français, Paris, 1954–64). I quote from the English translation, *Book of Fortune's Transformation*, published in the Norton Critical Edition, *The Selected Writings of Christine de Pizan*, ed. R. Blumenfeld-Kosinski (Norton, New York, 1997), pp. 88–109, here p. 95.

43. Christine de Pizan, *L'Avision Christine*; I quote again from the English translation, *Christine's Vision*, in *The Selected Writings*, pp. 173–201, here p. 192; also for the following.

44. *Christine's Vision*, p. 193.

45. W. P. Gerritsen et al., 'A Fourteenth-Century Vernacular Poetics: Jan van Boendale's "How Writers Should Write" (with a Modern English translation of the text by Erik Kooper)', in *Medieval Dutch Literature in its European Context*, ed. E. Kooper (Cambridge University Press, Cambridge, 1994), pp. 245–60, here pp. 253–4; also for the following.

46. See, on Boendale and his circle, W. van Anrooij, 'Recht en Rechtvaardigheid binnen de Antwerpse School', in *Wat is Wijsheid? Lekenethiek in de Middelnederlandse Letterkunde*, ed. J. Reynaert (Prometheus, Amsterdam, 1994), pp. 149–63, and my forthcoming 'Household Books: Ladies of the House and Their Roles in Late-Medieval Urban Culture', in *Household, Family, and Christian Traditions*, ed. J. Wogan-Browne and A. B. Mulder-Bakker.

47. F. Somerset, *Clerical Discourse and Lay Audience in Late Medieval England* (Cambridge University Press, Cambridge, 1998), pp. 13–19.

48. Cf. J. Blanchard, 'Christine de Pizan: une laïque au pays des clercs', in *Et c'est la fin pour quoy nous sommes ensemble: Hommage … J. Dufournet*, ed. J.-C. Aubailly et al. (Champion, Paris, 1993), pp. 215–26.

49. Cf. R. Krueger, 'Christine's Anxious Lessons: Gender, Morality, and the Social Order from the *Enseignemens* to the *Avision*', in *Christine de Pizan and The Categories of Difference*, ed. M. Desmond (University of Minnesota Press, Minneapolis, 1998), pp. 16–40, here p. 22, where she stresses the role of the Sibyl, an 'ameresse de sapience' in leading a 'colliege de grant science des femmes qui prophetiserent'.

50. Cf. B. M. Semple, 'The Critique of Knowledge as Power: The Limits of Philosophy and Theology in Christine de Pizan', in T*he Categories of Difference*, pp. 108–27.

51. Christine de Pizan, *Le Livre du Chemin de long Estude*; in English, *The Path of Long Study*, in *Selected Writings*, pp. 59–87, here p. 66.

52. Christine de Pizan, *Path of Long Study*, p. 80.

53. Christine de Pizan, *Book of Fortune's Transformation*, p. 106.

54. Cf. J. Blanchard, 'Christine de Pizan: les Raisons de l'Histoire', *Le Moyen Age*, 92 (1986), pp. 417–36.

55. Christine de Pizan, *Livre de la Mutacion*, ed. Solente II, vv. 142, 1456.

56. According to Jerome, Christ had bided his time until he had reached the perfect age, the *aetas perfecta*, so that he could provide man with a pattern. Roger Bacon, in the thirteenth century, commented: 'The soul attains to another regimen until the thirtieth year is completed – because then man flourishes in the full strength of mind and body, according to divine wisdom, the blessed Jerome and others; and philosophy and personal experience bear witness that this is so'; quotations in M. Dove, *The Perfect Age of Man's Life* (Cambridge University Press, Cambridge, 1986), p. 53.

57. See, besides Dove, *The Perfect Age,* also J. A. Burrow, *The Ages of Man: A Study in Medieval Writing and Thought* (Clarendon Press, Oxford, 1986).

58. H. Moore, 'The Cultural Constitution of Gender', in *The Polity Reader in Gender Studies*, ed. H. Moore et al. (Cambridge Polity Press, Cambridge, 1994), pp. 14–27.

59. One more example: Margery Kempe decided to live on her own in her fortieth year and only thought of writing a book when she was in her sixties and her husband had died; cf. C. W. Atkinson, *Mystic and Pilgrim: The Book and the World of Margery Kempe* (Cornell University Press, Ithaca, 1983), pp. 17–18.

60. Semple, *Critique of Knowledge*, pp. 115–19.

61. Coleman, in her *Public Reading*, characterises medieval society as a society in which reading to the family or a group is a specific type of literature and transmission of knowledge.

62. Outstanding studies have been published recently on early medieval queens and princesses; see, for example, P. Stafford, *Queens, Concubines and Dowagers: The King's Wife in the Early Middle Ages* (1983; repr. Leicester University Press, 1998); P. Stafford, *Queen Emma and Queen Edith: Queenship and Women's Power in Eleventh-Century England* (Blackwell, Oxford, 1997) and the volumes edited by John Carmi Parsons such as *Medieval Queenship* (Alan Sutton, Phoenix Mill, 1993).

63. P. Geary, *Phantoms of Remembrance: Memory and Oblivion of the First Millennium* (Princeton University Press, Princeton, 1984), in particular pp. 71–3.

64. Cf. Warner, *From the Beast to the Blonde*.

65. B. Lundt, 'Zur Entstehung der Universität als Männerwelt', in *Geschichte der Mädchen- und Frauenbildung*, vol. I, pp. 103–18, here p. 113. Cf. H. Grundmann, 'Die Frauen und die Literatur im Mittelalter: Ein Beitrag zur Frage nach der Entstehung des Schrifttums in der Volkssprache', *Archiv für Kulturgeschichte*, 26 (1926), pp. 129–61; Joachim Bumke, *Mäzene im Mittelalter: Die Gönner und Auftraggeber der höfischen Literatur in Deutschland: 1150–1300* (Beck, Munich, 1979), ch. 5; and Clanchy, *From Memory to Written Record*.

66. Geary, *Phantoms of Remembrance*, p. 52: 'there is a very clear difference between the image of the role of women in remembering and the image that emerges from documents of practice. Instead, they betray specific ideological traditions as well as pressing political agendas of their authors'.

67. Ingrid Bennewitz, '"Darumb lieben Toechter/seyt nicht zu gar fürwitzig ..." Deutschsprachige moralisch-didaktische Literatur des 13.–15. Jahrhunderts', in *Geschichte der Mädchen- und Frauenbildung*, pp. 23–41, here p. 29.

68. Archambault, *A Monk's Confession*, p. 73.

69. This theme still receives very little attention in the studies on old age which have begun to be published recently; see for example D. Ketzer and P. Laslett (eds), *Aging in the Past: Demography, Society and Old Ages* (University of California Press, Berkeley, 1995), p. 50.

70. Geary, *Phantoms of Remembrance*, p. 66, quotes the demographic study of Hajdu, estimating that more than 60 per cent of married noble women outlived their husbands in twelfth-century France and often for almost twenty years.

71. Lundt, 'Universität als Männerwelt', pp. 102–3.

72. A working group of the Groningen 'Cultural Change' Programme has begun to work on this theme; see their planned volume *The Prime of their Lives*.

7

Visions of My Youth: Representations of the Childhood of Medieval Visionaries

Rosalynn Voaden and Stephanie Volf

The political philosopher Hannah Arendt observed that, 'Stories reveal the meaning of what would otherwise remain an unbearable sequence of sheer happenings'.[1] For medieval visionaries, stories were essential. They told the stories of their revelations, but they, sometimes with their confessors, also constructed stories of themselves, of their lives. They told these stories, in the words, images and concepts which their culture gave them, both to make sense of those things, the divine revelations, which had happened to them, but also to help their audience make sense of the incursion of the divine into the affairs of humanity. We propose to look at one part of their stories, their reminiscences of childhood, an aspect of their stories which is particularly revealing of the influence of gender on perceptions of holiness in the late middle ages.

When Bridget of Sweden (*c.* 1303–73) was six years old, she saw, while wide awake, an altar opposite her bed, with a woman in shining garments sitting above the altar. The woman held a crown, which she offered to Bridget. Bridget left her bed and went to the altar, where the lady placed a crown on the child's head, so that Bridget could feel it surrounding her head. When she returned to her bed, the vision had disappeared, but she states that she could never forget it.[2]

Henry Suso (1300–1366), a contemporary of Bridget's, entered a Dominican monastery at the age of twelve. Despite this environment, he writes that his youth was spent in conflict.[3] He 'began in the first flower of his young life to be entangled in worldly vanities. The treacherous delights of the world were dragging him down, and he longed to stray from the preservation of his soul's health into the land of unlikeness'.[4] He does receive visions during his adolescence, visions which urge him to a more spiritual life, but he forgets these experiences and, as he writes, 'once again, evil thoughts grew up in his mind and undid these benefits'.[5]

These visions are characteristic of the ways in which late medieval perceptions of the nature of men and women influence the representation of childhood. Bridget experienced her first vision of the Virgin Mary at six years old, and claims never to have forgotten it. Suso describes his youth as misspent, and full of lost opportunities to draw closer to God. Bridget is responding to a culture wherein women were believed to be essentially bodily and emotional, easily led into error and prone to deceive others. In an attempt to separate herself from this tradition, she is obliged to represent herself as precociously pious, as chosen from infancy, and as always mindful of God. Suso, on the other hand, is free to describe his early errors and worldly yearnings because of the prevailing conviction of the spiritual and intellectual superiority of males, and because there existed a frequently revisited hagiographic tradition of erring males returning to the fold upon which he could model himself. The inherent and increasing cultural suspicion of women fuelled a need for them to justify and defend their visionary status in a way not required of men. Women did this in a variety of ways, one of which was to offer their childhood as an exemplary period of spiritual formation. Male visionaries did not face the same kind of suspicion of their essential nature and did not have to dispel assumptions that they were inclined to deceit and easy prey for the devil. Accordingly, representations of childhood were less vital in establishing male piety, which tended to be viewed as a given in a way which was not true of women. Males could spring fully formed into the arena of sanctity, shaking off any previous indiscretions, in a manner not possible for women.

It must be pointed out that, in both secular and sacred life, opportunities for medieval women to exercise authority and to function as public figures were, not surprisingly, extremely restricted. Indeed, the general belief prevailed that women were encumbered with bodies which incited lust, oozed bodily fluids and housed minds incapable of ratiocination and subject to uncontrollable emotions. The long Christian tradition of misogyny – a tradition which still persists – is rooted in the writings of St Paul.[6] Various Church Fathers embellished the tradition and medieval theologians subsequently built upon it, emphasising the corporeal nature of women, especially as related to Paul's injunction against women teaching and preaching in public (1 Corinthians 14:34).[7]

However, there was one significant exception to this rule, one area in which medieval women did have access to power of a kind, and where they were permitted an effective, if restricted, public function. Women could be chosen as visionaries and prophets. Christianity holds that God can, if he wills it, transcend natural law and intervene directly in human affairs through such avenues as miracles and revelations. Although the disruptive potential of revelation has led the institutional church to be somewhat suspicious of claims of communication with God which bypass the ecclesiastical hierarchy, nevertheless the church cannot ignore the possibility of divine revelation. Nor can it ignore the belief that, as a sign of his omnipotence, God can and does choose the most unlikely vessels through which to communicate, among whom are included women, fools and madmen. The effective result was that, while women were forbidden to teach in public, or to preach, those women who were deemed authentic visionaries or prophets were granted a voice, a voice which was listened to because of its divine source, rather than silenced because of the body from which it emanated. Moreover, visions are inevitably accompanied by a divine command to communicate the vision; the visionary is always told by God that she sees or hears these things not just for her benefit, but for the education of others. She is therefore impelled by divine injunction into the public sphere. Although her public arena was limited, direct communication of her revelations being largely restricted to other women, with a larger audience being reached only through written versions, visionary experience could, and sometimes did, confer on women a status and authority quite exceptional in the male-dominated world of medieval Christendom.

However, this status and authority were conditional on validation both of her status as a visionary, and of her revelations. This validation was necessary for any visionary, male or female; but it was doubly necessary for women because of traditional Christian beliefs about the essential nature of women. In the formative era of the Christian church, the patristic theologian, Augustine of Hippo (354–430) developed a precise categorisation of varieties of vision, as mystical experience was generally termed.[8] Augustine's taxonomy influenced virtually all subsequent thought on vision, and had profound consequences for women visionaries in the middle ages. He divided vision into three types.

> Hence let us call the first kind of vision corporeal, because it is perceived through the body and presented to the senses of the body. The second will be spiritual,[9] for whatever is not a body, and yet is something, is rightly called spirit: and certainly the image of an absent body, though it resembles a body, is not itself a body any more than is the act of vision by which it is perceived. The third kind will be intellectual, from the word intellect.[10]

After defining the different types of vision, Augustine then ranked them. This hierarchy had a profound effect on the perception of contemplative experience, indeed of all spiritual experience, by locating the zenith of that experience out of the body and out of this world, by privileging the transcendent over the immanent. Augustine states: 'spiritual vision is more excellent than corporeal, and intellectual is more excellent than spiritual'.[11] This hierarchy is based on the reliability of each kind of vision. Corporeal vision can err, either through the distortions of the natural world – think of how a stick seems to bend when put in water – or because of the deficiencies of the viewer. Spiritual vision can also err, because of the deceptions practised by evil spirits, deceptions which go undetected by the visionary; Satan can appear as an angel of light. Such misapprehensions cannot occur with an intellectual vision:

> if man has not only been carried out of the bodily senses to be among the likeness of bodies seen by the spirit, but is also carried out of these latter to be conveyed, as it were, to the region of the intellectual or the intelligible, where transparent truth is seen without any bodily likeness, his vision is darkened by no cloud of false opinion ...[12]

Other patristic authors and subsequent theologians adopted Augustine's classification system, varying the terms somewhat, but maintaining both the vital distinction between sensual and intellectual apprehension, and the superiority of the latter over the former.

These two prevailing beliefs – in the essential corporeality of women, and the superiority of intellectual over spiritual vision – had a powerful influence on the experience and reception of vision. While one might assume that union with the divine would escape cultural determinants and transcend the usual categorisations of gender and class, inevitably one finds that it is culturally constructed. In the middle ages, mystical experience replicated the reigning gender paradigm, whereby women were perceived as sensual, emotional and bodily, and men were seen as intellectual and capable of a higher level of spiritual achievement. For a variety of reasons, including exposure to the models offered by other women visionaries, and a lack of Latin literacy, which restricted their access to works on intellectual vision, the majority of medieval women who had mystical experiences had spiritual visions – that is, they saw, or communicated with divine figures, and sometimes saw visions of heaven or hell. The significant issue for the ecclesiastical authorities was that their visions came through their bodily senses, those senses which, especially in a woman, were so easily deceived. So, despite the fact that their status as visionaries did grant them a voice and a degree of authority, their gender was still a factor and their credibility as visionaries was unstable. An elaborate system of *discretio spirituum* (discerning the spirits) evolved as a means of validating visions.[13] Inevitably, testing visions meant testing visionaries, and the greater part of the system of *discretio spirituum* involved observations of the behaviour of visionaries: were they humble, were they under the authority and leadership of a cleric, did they seek notoriety or profit from their visions? While any spiritual vision, whether received by a man or by a woman, was potentially deceptive, women's visions tended to be more rigorously examined and women visionaries held in greater suspicion than their male counterparts. The fifteenth-century theologian and chancellor of the University of Paris, Jean Gerson, effectively summarised this tendency when he wrote:

> First, every teaching of women, especially that expressed in solemn word or writing, is to be held suspect, unless it has first been diligently examined by another ... and much more than the teaching of men. Why? The reason is clear; because not only ordinary but divine law forbids such things. Why? Because women are too easily seduced, because they are too obstinately seducers, because it is not fitting that they should be knowers of divine wisdom.[14]

To take an obvious instance, the stipulation that the visionary be under the supervision of a cleric was bound to have a different effect when the visionary was a woman. Virtually all male visionaries were themselves clerics; submitting themselves to a spiritual director, to a brother cleric, would have been an entirely different experience than it was for a woman. Women, of course, never were members of the clergy; a woman's submission to a spiritual director carried with it her ordained submission to the male due to her essentially flawed nature. As a result of that crucial gender difference, she was inevitably and always the suspect other.

To return to the principal topic of this chapter, we intend now to examine an area of gender difference which has received little attention, but which sheds considerable light on the different ways in which male and female visionaries are constructed: the stories told of the childhoods of medieval visionaries as they appear both in their *Vitae* (Lives), and in their visionary narratives.[15] A *Vita* is the biography of the visionary, often written by a confessor or spiritual director. Sometimes these were attached to the account of their revelations, and sometimes they were freestanding works. In either case, the purpose was to establish the extraordinary piety, even the sanctity, of the visionary and to validate their status as mouthpiece of God. A visionary narrative is the record of visions or revelations; it is often interspersed with reflections, details about the life of the visionary and the circumstances under which the visions were received and written. Some visionaries wrote their own narratives; this is, not surprisingly, much more frequently the case with male visionaries. Female visionaries, typically lacking Latin literacy, usually dictated their revelations to a spiritual director, a confessor, or some other cleric. In both cases, the visionary made a direct contribution to the composition of the visionary narrative, whether by writing it, dictating, or by recounting the visions to an audience – sister nuns, for example – who kept a record. The construction of the visionary in both narrative and *Vita* is calculated to satisfy reigning cultural expectations about holiness and gender, and the way in which childhood is represented is a significant factor in this construction. While both *Vitae* and visionary narratives are to some degree inevitably influenced by hagiographic motifs and conventions, the use of these conventions can be viewed as a response to specific cultural issues and anxieties.

This chapter is based on an examination of visionary narratives and *Vitae* of twenty-seven female and thirteen male visionaries from Britain and Europe, ranging from the late eleventh to the early fifteenth century.[16] These visionaries experienced a variety of types of vision: prophetic, apocalyptic or revelatory. Our reading of these narratives and *Vitae* indicate that, across this broad chronological and geographical span, the differences between the childhood representations of male and female visionaries are persistent and ubiquitous and are shaped by prevailing beliefs about the nature of men and women, and about the nature of vision. The type of vision – prophetic, apocalyptic or revelatory – seems to have no bearing on how the childhood of the visionary is represented. Our research supports the view that the consistent, primary factor influencing representations of childhood is the gender of the visionary. One obvious difference of great significance is that while male visionaries rarely include reminiscence of their childhood in their narratives, women offer childhood memories relatively consistently. Similarly, in their *Vitae*, little detail is given about the childhood of men, and what is given rarely transcends conventional motifs of precocious piety, while the biographers of female visionaries frequently include copious and specific examples of youthful holiness.[17] For men, it would seem, childhood was relatively irrelevant in terms of validating their adult spirituality. Men were assumed free of any essential taint, beyond that of original sin, which affects all of humanity. Rather, the most significant factor in the construction of male visionaries is a dramatic conversion experience which serves to mark their adult commitment and receptivity to God. Perhaps modelling their own perceptions of youth on Augustine's negative view of the child's sinful, fleshy nature,[18] male visionaries seem to mark their separation from childhood, rather than carrying it with them into adulthood. This may well be because women and children tended to be grouped together in medieval theology, believed to be generally capable only of an inferior level of spirituality. Male children obviously grew into a mature spirituality; therefore there would be little to gain for a male visionary in depicting his childish piety. For women, on the other hand, given the prevailing beliefs about their essential nature, childhood reminiscences offered an opportunity to reaffirm their association with the purity of virgin childhood and to depict themselves, or be depicted, as emerging from the womb with their eyes fixed firmly on God. Charting piety in this fashion appears to have acquired legitimation in Franciscan spirituality of the late thirteenth century, which was based in affective piety, a belief in the undivided will, and in the active life, not in the intellectual search for divine knowledge advocated by the Dominicans. The Franciscans viewed scholasticism and its foundation in Aristotelian philosophy with suspicion, insisting that love for Christ and the way in which this emotion subsumes and directs the will was the more certain way to God. The Dominican theologian Thomas Aquinas (1225–74), on the other hand, contended that humans were better able to understand the nature of God through reason, a faculty not normally attributed to the female, but primarily to the male.[19] Thus, men were distinguished from their tainted, inconstant, and irrational sisters, and were therefore more likely to seek God through logical inquiry than through the emotional, affective modes of devotion favoured by women.

When the childhood of male visionaries is mentioned, they tend to be represented as excessively concerned with material things in their youth and as ignoring opportunities to draw closer to God. Women are constructed as exhibiting exceptional piety from an extremely early age, and as maintaining that piety, sometimes in the face of great opposition, throughout their lives. Men nearly always undergo a radical conversion experience during or after adolescence, a period of youth which is rarely mentioned in association with women, and often after years of academic study. This experience separates them drastically from their previous way of life and sets them on the path to God. It is usually at this point, after or coincident with the conversion experience, that male visionaries begin to experience and recount their visions.

In contrast, women are often depicted as having their first visions as children. While they frequently also undergo a later conversion experience, this serves as a reinforcement of their previous inclinations and way of life, rather than as a separation. These first visions are frequently received at a very early age, around six or seven, and sometimes when they are so young that they do not realise the significance of the event. Hildegard of Bingen (1098–1179) recalls seeing, at the age of three, 'such a great light that my soul quaked'.[20] Two years later she amazed her nurse by looking at a pregnant cow and accurately predicting that her calf would be 'white, and marked with different coloured spots on its forehead, feet and back'.[21] Margaret of Ypres (1216–37), at age five, smelled a wonderful odour during mass and understood that Christ had come upon the altar. After this, she asked the astonished abbess at the convent where she was being educated to be allowed to receive communion. The request was granted, and the child embarked on a life of penitential asceticism.[22] The five-year-old Christina of Stommeln (1242–1312) saw Christ in the guise of a child, who taught her the rudiments of the spiritual life and various prayers.[23] Catharine of Siena (1347–80), at around the age of seven, saw a vision of Christ in the street, when she was on an errand with her brother. A ray of light shone out from Christ's heart and fell upon Catharine.[24] When Bridget of Sweden was ten, the aunt who looked after the motherless girl entered her bedroom to find Bridget kneeling in prayer, naked. The aunt prepared to beat her with a stick for what she saw as frivolity, but the stick immediately broke into tiny fragments. Understandably taken aback, the aunt enquired what Bridget was doing, to which she replied: 'I arose from bed to praise him whose custom is always to help me ... The Crucified One whom I saw'.[25]

As a result of their visions, many young girls conceived a desire to dedicate their virginity to God, either as nuns or as lay women. Others committed themselves to lives of exceptional piety, even if they were eventually obliged to marry. Unlike males, many of whom represent themselves as rejecting, or showing disdain for, Christian virtues in their youth, women's desire conforms to the dominant Christian ideology privileging virginity over marriage. Even as children, women depict themselves as rejecting the secular world, whereas men are more likely to embrace it enthusiastically. Delphine of Puimichel (1284–1360), left an orphan heiress at seven, resisted the attempts of 'the carnal friends and people of the world' who tried to lure her into 'the vanities of the period, the ornaments of the body and worldly ways'.[26] Such rebellion as women do exhibit appears around puberty, and is roused by the prospect of marriage. Their resistance is typically against any contact with the carnal world, as opposed to males who seem to feel some freedom to experiment with its delights in their youth. Delphine, taken to Marseille at twelve to be married, ran away and hid. She did not emerge until she was promised by the Virgin Mary that, while Christ had raised her to be a wife, he would protect her virginity.[27] When Catharine of Siena was fifteen, she cut off her hair in an effort to make herself unmarriageable.[28] She also deliberately scalded herself in hot springs where she had been taken on holiday by her mother in an effort to distract the girl from her desire to join an order of Dominican tertiaries, apparently hoping that her scarred flesh would serve as a further deterrent to suitors.[29]

Even women who do not recount childhood visions are commonly described as exhibiting an exceptional desire for religious commitment while very young. Mechtild of Hackeborn (1241–98/99) was seven when she was taken by her mother to visit Mechtild's sister, abbess at the neighbouring convent. When it was time to leave, Mechtild went to each member of the community of nuns and begged to be allowed to stay. 'And they gladly agreed. And so she stayed there, without her mother's assent, for neither by coaxing nor threatening could her mother nor any other member of her family distract her from her purpose.'[30] Lutgard of Aywières was saved from marriage by the embezzlement of her dowry, and happily entered the convent at twelve years old.[31]

Often there is a domestic specificity to the childhood experiences of these women which lends them verisimilitude. While the scenes described may well employ hagiographic motifs, nevertheless it is important to note that this type of motif is primarily used of women visionaries, seldom, if ever, appearing in relation to male visionaries. This may well result from the traditional association of women with the domestic, but it is significant that male visionaries rarely reflect the household involvement which they must have experienced as little boys. Again, this would suggest that for males it is separation from childhood, marked by a definitive post-adolescent conversion experience, which is paramount, and which signals their entry into mature spirituality. Among the domestic scenes described in relation to women visionaries is the scalding of Dorothy of Montau at age six (1347–94) by a careless maid, an incident which seems to have precipitated her extraordinary piety.[32] She quickly and enthusiastically embraced an ascetic life, begging her mother to be allowed to fast (permission was denied until she was nine), mortifying herself and spending long hours in prayer, and 'spiritual callisthenics', in which she contorted her body into unnatural and painful positions.[33] One of the signs of Catharine of Siena's otherworldly preoccupation was her inability to concentrate on domestic tasks. Her sister-in-law, Lisa, found the meat burning on the spit while the young Catharine had fallen into a trance. She rescued the meat, but when Lisa returned to the kitchen, she discovered that Catharine, still in ecstasy, had fallen into the fire. Lisa pulled her out, miraculously unscathed,[34] Bridget of Sweden, at twelve, was having difficulty with her needlework, which she was engaged upon in the company of other girls her own age. An unknown girl appeared beside her, and helped her, before disappearing, leaving Bridget in possession of a piece of work 'not the work of a girl of such tender age but ... something divine'.[35]

Women visionaries are often described as indulging in childhood games which can be seen as preparation for the holy lives they were to lead. Marie d'Oignies (d. 1213) is described by her admirer and biographer, Jacques de Vitry, as secretly following the monks who passed in front of her father's house, placing her little feet in the footprints of the monks.[36] Catharine of Siena reputedly formed a group of playmates who flagellated themselves with knotted ropes. She began fasting when she was around five years old, and a number of sources recount that as a little girl she ran away from home to live in a cave, in order to emulate the Desert Fathers.[37] Douceline of Marseille (d. 1274) would, as a tiny child, 'kneel with her bare knees upon little stones which she found, join her hands together towards God, turn her eyes towards Heaven, not even knowing what to say'.[38] Sometimes a point is made that women visionaries as children rejected the company of other girls. Marie d'Oignies rejected the fine clothes given her by her parents, and refused to play with other little girls.[39] Juliana of Mont Cornillon (1193–1258) had 'no desire to play the games that children of that age usually enjoy. For already she rose above the habits of her age, being free of all insolence and childish mischief'.[40] When Douceline of Marseille was supposed to be playing with other children, she would hide away in the most secret places she could find, in order to pray.[41] Lutgard of Aywières 'fled dishonourable jokes and unseemly girlish love talk entirely'.[42]

All of these incidents – childhood visions, precocious piety, spiritual games, vows of virginity and resistance to marriage – have the effect of portraying the woman visionary as imbued with an essential purity and predisposition to holiness. This is not generally the case with male visionaries. As stated above, there are far fewer accounts of the childhood of male visionaries. Where biographical or autobiographical information is given for this period, it is usually a record of an ill-spent youth or young manhood dedicated to secular, materialistic pursuits and pleasure, from all of which the visionary recoils when he finally dedicates himself to God. Conversion experiences tend to be post-pubertal events, and accounts of visions experienced as a child are unusual. When they do occur, they are often presented as significant only in the young boy's rejection of them.[43]

A telling example of the absence of childhood reminiscence in a male visionary's narrative is found in the work of John of Rupecissa (*c.* 1310 – *c.* 1364), also known as Jean de Roquetaillade. Although little known today, he was an apocalyptic visionary of some renown who produced copious accounts of his revelations and prophecies. A Franciscan, he was evidently perceived as skirting too close to heresy by some of his superiors. As a result, he spent most of his adult life in Franciscan jails, suffering severe persecution and deprivation – but still permitted to write and disseminate his revelations. Accounts of his visions were interspersed with detailed, often horrific, chronicles of his life and trials which carry the unmistakable ring of truth. As a modern editor of his works, Robert Lerner, points out, 'Rupecissa's entire record as a visionary is too vivid and too grounded in specific contexts to be doubted'.[44] In 1349 he was incarcerated in the Sultan's Prison in Avignon, in order to defend himself before a papal commission against charges of heresy. The chairman of the commission, Cardinal Guillaume Court, ordered John to write an account of his visionary insights.[45] The result was the *Liber Secretorum Eventuum*, a remarkably open account of his prophetic system and beliefs, especially given that this document was intended to aid in his defence against charges of heresy. Despite the crucial nature of this work, when one might suppose he would marshal all possible evidence in his support, he makes no mention of his childhood here, or in any other of his works. Evidently only those incidents which occurred after his conversion experience had relevance for his construction as a visionary and prophet. His conversion vision occurred probably in 1332, when he was in his early twenties, just after his entry into the Franciscan order. He states that, prior to this, he had been studying 'mundane philosophy' at Toulouse for five years as a layman.[46] In a fashion characteristic of male visionaries in their radical separation from the worldly pursuits and unworthy interests of their youth, Rupecissa dismisses his early studies and his entire life prior to his conversion experience.

Childhood memories are also absent from the narrative of Robert d'Uzès (d. 1296), who, unlike John of Rupecissa, was a visionary with a wide contemporary reputation for holiness.[47] When he entered the Dominican order in 1293, after serving as a priest as a young man, each priest was ordered to celebrate a Mass of the Holy Spirit for him, and each convent a Mass of the Blessed Virgin. Robert experienced the characteristic conversion vision. At a time when he was brooding about his future path, the figure of a monk appeared to him in a vision during mass, and counselled him to abjure all of his inheritance – which was considerable, since Robert's family were the *seigneurs d'Uzès* – and to embrace a life of apostolic poverty.[48] Robert's revelations offer precise descriptions of his location and activity when he experienced a vision, and he often mentions his family home, or family members who were present at the time or somehow involved in his visions.[49] With this level of attention to detail, and his openness to referring to his family, the fact that he doesn't mention his childhood suggests, once again, that for males this period of their lives was irrelevant to the construction of a visionary self.

Henry Suso, the Rhineland visionary mentioned early in this chapter does give some details of his later childhood, which fall into the category of the misspent youth. He experienced a conversion vision at age eighteen. He writes:

> When at last the years of his boyhood had gone by, and he had come to mature age, on one occasion his mind was illumined as cannot be described, so that, in some way wholly absorbed in the spirit, he was filled with exceeding delight ... so that the direction of his gaze and the love of his heart could not any longer be changed or distracted.[50]

It should be noted that this vision described here as marking his entry into mature spirituality is clearly an intellectual vision, that which Augustine designates as the superior level of vision which cannot be misapprehended because it eschews the senses. It is significant that Suso, who usually experienced spiritual visions, should emphasise the intellectual nature of his conversion experience. He subsequently embraced a life of great asceticism, developing ingenious methods of self-mortification, including carving the initials IHS (*Iesus hominum salvator*) into his chest with a slate pencil.[51]

Richard Rolle was an English visionary of the early fourteenth century (d. 1349). The chief source of information about his life is the *Officium et miracula* probably composed in the 1380s, possibly in the hope of furthering the process of his canonisation.[52] His childhood is barely alluded to in either the *Officium* or any of his visionary narratives. In a manner which we have seen to be characteristic of male visionaries, to all intents his life began with a radical break from previous secular preoccupations, in this case when he fled the university at Oxford to embrace a holy life. He embarked on the life of a hermit, borrowing two dresses from his sister which he cobbled together with one of his father's rainhoods to make an appropriate outfit.[53] After this dramatic separation from the outside world, Rolle experienced visions marked by *fervor, dulcor, canor* (heat, sweetness, song), clearly the spiritual vision of Augustine's typology. He wrote prolific accounts of his visions and meditations, apparently without the benefit of official ecclesiastical standing or authorisation.

Suso, Rolle, and, perhaps less obviously, Robert of Uzès and John of Rupecissa, modelled themselves according to the pattern established first by Augustine of Hippo (354–430) in his *Confessions,* and later replicated in the *Legenda Maior* of Francis of Assisi (1181/2–1226), written by his companion, the noted theologian Bonaventure

(1217–74). As a boy and young man, actually into his thirties, Augustine presents himself as deliberately heedless of God's ways and intent upon sensual pleasures. Though aware of the sinful nature of his life, he resisted God's intentions for him for many years, famously saying, 'Give me chastity and continency, only not yet'.[54] Similarly Francis, the son of a wealthy merchant, indulged his appetite for material pleasures, until, as a young man, a series of miraculous events brought about a dramatic conversion. According to the *Legenda*, he stripped himself naked before his father in a public square in Assisi, violently repudiating the avaricious tradition which he felt his father represented, before setting out to wander through the countryside and beg for his food.[55]

These two highly influential figures offered male visionaries a model, consciously or unconsciously, to follow for self construction. This model coincided with a cultural paradigm which emphasised the spiritual superiority of men because men were not seen to be essentially tainted by the legacy of Eve, by the lusts and deceptions of their bodily selves, as women were. Consequently, male visionaries could eschew representations of their childhood in favour of recounting radical conversion experiences which marked their transition from the immature spirituality traditionally associated with women and children, to a true and knowing dedication to God.

There are, of course, no hard and fast rules regarding the representations of childhood of medieval male and female visionaries. The childhood of some of the better-known women visionaries – including Julian of Norwich (d. *c.* 1416) and Margery Kempe (*c.* 1373 – *c.* 1433) – is never mentioned in any of the sources. Some male visionaries do include memories of their childhoods. The *Vita* of Auzias (Elzear) of Sabran (1286–1323), husband of Delphine of Puimichel, for example, gives copious examples of his precocious piety, compassion for poor children and disposition to virginity.[56] It is significant for the argument of this chapter, that, unlike the other male visionaries mentioned, Elzear never took orders. Because he remained within the secular world, he never achieved the authority to teach and preach except in his own household. As a layman he possessed a status vis-à-vis the church more like that of his female contemporaries and it may have been that the author of his *Vita* saw a need to stress his early exemplary piety. Nevertheless, by far the dominant tendency is for the *Vitae* and narratives of medieval visionaries to replicate and respond to the reigning gender paradigms. Male visionaries mark their separation from childhood; for them it is a time of worldly foolishness and immature spirituality. Their dramatic rejection of the world and of the flesh as a result of their conversion experience enhances their subsequent piety and helps to establish their reputation for holiness. Women, generally viewed as essentially tainted by the transgression of Eve, establish the roots of their spirituality in the innocence and purity of childhood. Whatever their conscious purpose, such accounts argued for their essential piety, in contrast to prevailing views of women as corporeal and prone to error. It is implied that these women never leave the state of childish innocence; their childhood visions illuminate their stories just as the great light irradiated the soul of the three-year-old Hildegard of Bingen.

Appendix

List of Sources: Women

Agnes of Montepulciano (d. 1317): *Vita auctore Raimundo de Capua*, ed. *AA.SS.* Apr. II, pp. 792–812.

Angela of Foligno (d. 1309): *Vita auctore Arnaldo ordinis S. Francisci*, ed. *AA.SS.* Ian, I. pp. 186–234.

Beatrice of Nazareth (d. 1268): L. Reypens (ed.), *Vita Beatricis*. (Ruusbroec-Genootschap, Antwerp, 1964).

Bridget of Sweden (d. 1373): Isak Collijn (ed.), *Vita beate Bridide prioris Petri et magistri Petri*, in *Acta et processus cononzationes beate Brigitte*, pp. 73–101; Margaret Tjader Harris (ed.), *Birgitta of Sweden: Life and Selected Revelations*, trans. Albert Ryle Kezel (Paulist Press, New York, 1990).

Catharine of Siena (d. 1380): *Vita auctore Raimundo Capuano*, ed. *AA.SS.* Apr. III, pp. 853–959; Raymond of Capua, *The Life of Catharine of Siena*, trans. Conleth Kearns, OP (Glazier, Wilmington, 1980).

Catherine of Sweden (d. 1381): *Vita*, ed. *AA.SS.* Mar. III, pp. 503–15.

Christina Mirabilis (d. 1224): Thomas de Cantimpré, *The Life of Chrisina Mirabilis*, trans. Margot H. King (Peregrina Publishing, Toronto, 1986).

Christina of Stommeln (d. 1312): André Billy, *Extases et Tortures: Vie de la Bienheureuse Christine de Stommeln* (Flammarion, Paris, 1957).

Clare of Montefalco (d. 1308): A. Semenza (ed.), *Vita S. Crarae de Cruce ex Codice Montefalconensi Saeculi XIV Desumpta*, Analecta Augustiniana, 18: 1 (1941).

Delphine of Puimichel (d. 1360): P. Jacques Campbell, OFM, *Vies Occitanes de Saint Auzias et de Sainte Dauphine* (Pontificium Athenaeum Antonianum, Rome, 1963).

Dorothy of Montau (d. 1394): Richard Stachnik and Anneliese Triller, *Dorothea von Montau: Eine preußische Heilege des 14. Jahrhunderts* (Münster, 1976).

Douceline of Marseilles (d. 1274): J.-H. Albanes, *La Vie de Sainte Douceline: Fondatrice des Béguines de Marseille* (Étienne Camoin, Marseilles, 1879).

Elizabeth of Hungary (d. 1231): Sarah McNamer (ed.), *The Two Middle English Translations of the Revelations of St. Elizabeth of Hungary* (Universitätsverlag C. Winter, Heidelberg, 1996).

Hildegard of Bingen (d. 1179): Sabina Flanagan, *Hildegard of Bingen: A Visionary Life* (Routledge, London, 1989).

Julian of Norwich (d. *c.* 1416): Julian of Norwich, *A Book of Showing to the Anchoress Julian of Norwich*, 2 vols, ed. Edmund Colledge and James Walsh (Pontifical Institute of Mediaeval Studies, Toronto, 1978).

Juliana of Mont Cornillon (d. 1258): *The Life of Juliana of Mont Cornillon*, trans. Barbara Newman (Peregrina Publishing, Toronto, n.d.).

Lutgard of Aywières (d. 1246): Thomas de Cantimpré, *The Life of Lutgard of Aywières*, trans. Margot H. King (Peregrina Publishing, Toronto, 1991).

Margaret Ebner (d. 1351): Margaret Ebner, *Major Works*, trans. and ed. Leonard P. Hindley (Paulist Press, New York, 1993).

Margaret of Roskilde (d. 1176): *Translatio*, ed. *AA.SS.* Oct. IX, pp. 717–18.

Margaret of Ypres (d. 1237): Thomas de Cantimpré, *The Life of Margaret of Ypres*, trans. Margot H. King (Peregrina Publishing, Toronto, 1990).

Margery Kempe (d. *c.* 1433): Margery Kempe, *The Book of Margery Kempe*, ed. Lynn Staley (TEAMS Middle English Texts Series, Kalamazoo, 1996).

Marguerite of Oingt (d. 1310): Antonin Duraffour, Pierre Gardette and Paulette Durdilly, *Les Œuvres de Marguerite d'Oingt* (Société d'Édition Les Belles Lettres, Paris, 1965); Renate Blumenfeld-Kosinski, *The Writings of Margaret of Oingt: Medieval Prioress and Mystic* (Focus Library of Medieval Women, n.p., 1990).

Marie of Oignies (d. 1213): Jacques de Vitry, *The Life of Marie d'Oignies*, trans. Margot H. King (Peregrina Publishing, Toronto, 1987).

Mechtild of Hackeborn (d. 1298/9): Theresa A. Halligan (ed.), *The Booke of Gostlye Grace of Mechtild of Hackeborn* (Pontifical Institute for Medieval Studies, Toronto, 1979).

Mechthild of Magdeburg (d. 1294): Mechthild of Magdeburg, *The Flowing Light of the Godhead*, trans. Frank Tobin (Paulist Press, New York, 1998).

Ursuline of Parma (d. 1408): *Vita*, ed. *AA.SS.* Apr. I, pp. 723–39.

Yvette of Huy (d. 1227): Hugh of Floreffe, *The Life of Yvette of Huy* (Peregrina, Toronto, 1999).

List of Sources: Men

Anthony of Padua (d. 1231): Fr. Thoma de Papia, *Dialogus de Gestis Santorum Fratrum Minorum*, 1923.

Benevenuto de Eugubio (d. 1232): Fr. Thoma de Papia, *Dialogus de Gestis Santorum Fratrum Minorum*, 1923.

Charles of Flanders (d. 1127): *Vita Karoli comitis Flandrensis*, by Galbert of Bruges, ed. *AA.SS.* Mar. I, pp. 163–79.

Elzear of Sabran (d. 1323): P. Jacques Campbell, OFM, *Vies Occitanes de Saint Auzias et de Sainte Dauphine* (Pontificium Athneaum Antonianum, Rome, 1963).

Francis of Assisi (d. 1226): Bonaventure, *The Soul's Journey into God: The Tree of Life: The Life of St Francis*, trans. Ewert Cousins (Paulist Press, New York, 1978).

Henry Suso (d. 1366): *Wisdom's Watch Upon the Hours*, trans. Edmund Colledge (Catholic University of America Press, Washington, DC, 1994).

Johannes de Rupecissa (d. *c.* 1364): Robert E. Lerner and Christine Morerod-Fattebert (ed. and trans.), *Liber Secretorum Eventuum* (Éditions Universitaires Fribourg Suisse, Fribourg, 1994).

John of La Verna (d. 1322): *Vita*, ed. *AA.SS.* Aug. II, pp. 459–69.

John Pelingotto of Urbino (d. 1304): *Vita*, ed. *AA.SS.* Iun. I, pp. 145–51.

Peter Crisci of Foligno (d. 1323): *Vita*, by John Gorini, OP, ed. *AA.SS.* Iul. IV, pp. 665–8.

Peter of Luxemburg (d. 1387): *Vita antiquissima*, ed. *AA.SS.* Iul. I, pp. 436–7.

Richard Rolle (d. 1349): Hope Emily Allen (ed.), *English Writings of Richard Rolle, Hermit of Hampole* (Allen Sutton, Gloucester, 1988).

Robert d'Uzès (d. 1296): Jeanne Bignami-Odier, 'Les Visions de Robert d'Uzès O. P.', *Archivum Fratrum Praedicatorum*, 24 (1954).

Torello of Poppi (d. 1282): *Vita*, ed. *AA.SS.* Mar. II, pp. 499–505.

Notes

We would like to thank Arizona State University for a grant to support research for this chapter.

1. Hannah Arendt, *Men in Dark Times* (Harcourt, Brace and World, New York, 1968), p. 104.

2. Margaret Tjader Harris (ed.), *Birgitta of Sweden: Life and Selected Revelations*, trans. Albert Ryle Kezel (Paulist Press, New York, 1990), pp. 72–4.

3. Henry Suso, *Wisdom's Watch Upon the Hours*, trans. Edmund Colledge (Catholic University of America Press, Washington, DC, 1994), p. 65.

4. Suso, *Wisdom*, p. 65. Although Suso himself wrote this, he used the third person, which was a common stylistic device in medieval religious writing.

5. Suso, *Wisdom*, p. 72.

6. Paul helped to establish the paradigmatic perception of women when he stated, 'And Adam was not deceived, but the woman being deceived was in the transgression' (1 Timothy 2:14).

7. Tertullian's 'On the Veiling of Virgins' argued that virgins, if they must go out in public, should be thickly veiled lest they generate lust in men who behold them, thereby imperilling both their own souls and those of the beholders. See A. Roberts and J. Donaldson (eds), *A Select Library of the Ante-Nicene Fathers of the Christian Church* (Eerdmans, Grand Rapids, 1951), vol. 4, *Tertullian*, p. 37. Later, in the middle ages, Thomas Aquinas, the highly influential thirteenth-century Scholastic theologian, endorsed Paul's injunction in 1 Corinthians 14:34 against women preaching and teaching in public in his *Summa Theologiae*. Women may speak privately, in familiar conversation, but because women are by nature and sex subject to men, because their beauty can inspire lust in men's minds, and because they lack sufficient wisdom, public speaking is strictly forbidden. See Thomas Aquinas, *Summa Theologiae*, 2a2ae, ed. and trans. R. Potter (O.P., London, 1970), vol. 45, *Quaestiones 171–8*, pp. 133–5.

8. Our own society tends to conflate vision and mysticism, and to consider it in the narrow sense of mystical union with God. In the middle ages, however, visions could vary widely in function and form. Many visions were prophecies, usually understood as divinely communicated revelations of things previously hidden or sometimes as predictions of future events. Other visions were apocalyptic, depicting the end of time frequently with the intent of criticising the corruption and abuses of the church and the evils of lay society. Many of these visions, like those of Bridget of Sweden, enjoined the visionary to prescribe reformist ideologies. Often, however, visions of this type tended to be dismissed or condemned by the church as unorthodox. Lastly, some visions directly revealed God's wisdom to the devotee. Such revelatory visions, for example those of Julian of Norwich, could provide an apt mode for women to speculate upon and express insights into theology or doctrine in a more public forum than they were usually permitted.

9. Note the particular use in this context of 'spiritual', here to be understood as imaginary, that is, employing sensory images to represent ideas.

10. J. Quasten, W. J. Burghardt and T. C. Lawler (eds), *Ancient Christian Writers: The Works of the Fathers in Translation*, (Newman Press, New York, 1982), vol. 42, Augustine, *The Literal Meaning of Genesis: Books 7–12*, trans. J. H. Taylor, SJ, p. 186.

11. Augustine, *Literal Meaning*, p. 213.

12. Augustine, *Literal Meaning*, p. 216.

13. This topic is examined in detail in Rosalynn Voaden, *God's Words, Women's Voices: The Discernment of Spirits in the Writing of Late-Medieval Women Visionaries* (York Medieval Press, York, 1999), pp. 34–40.

14. Jean Gerson, *Oeuvres Complètes*, ed. Palamon Glorieux (10 vols, Desclée, Paris, 1960–73), vol. 9, p. 468; translation R. V.

15. While there were no exact consistent delineations as to when it began or ended, in general, medieval conceptions of childhood are not unlike our own. Shulamith Shahar has pointed out that a variety of medieval theologians and physicians addressed and attempted to define the topic. In late medieval Europe, two or three stages of childhood were identified: *Infantia*, *Pueritia*, and *Adolescentia*. Depending on the authority, *Infantia* lasted from birth to about age seven, the age at which children are able to express themselves verbally and to begin their education. *Pueritia* spanned age seven to age twelve for girls and age fourteen for boys. At this time, with the onset of puberty, children were able to marry. *Adolescentia* appears to be an exclusively male phenomenon and can last until marriage or much longer. For a detailed study of medieval childhood see Shulamith Shahar, *Childhood in the Middle Ages* (Routledge, London, 1990).

16. Our interest in this chapter is in demonstrating the impact of gender on the writings of medieval visionaries, and our research took the form of a random survey of visionary narratives and *Vitae*. There was no attempt to balance the ratio of male to female, monastic to lay, or to control the representation from various time periods or regions. We chose to include both first- and second-hand accounts of childhood, believing that taken together they indicate a cultural attitude towards the function of childhood in the formation of, and the perception of, adult sanctity. Sources vary: some were written by the visionary, some by contemporaries, some at a later date. All sources exist in edited form, but not all are translated into English. See the 'List of Sources' in the Appendix for bibliographical details of all visionaries who featured in this study.

17. It is important to acknowledge that references to childhood sanctity do exist in *Vitae* of male saints – enough so that a *puer-senex* motif (a phenomenon in which special children, usually male, possess the wisdom of a learned and experienced elder) forms in early hagiography. Neither are instances of sudden conversion wholly foreign to the *Vitae* of women; for example Mary the Egyptian, who converted from a life of prostitution to an ascetic dedication to God. However, few of these saints had visionary experiences and almost all lived before the eleventh century, the starting point for our study. For Mary of Egypt's *Vita*, see Jacobus de Voragine, *The Golden Legend of Jacobus de Voragine*, trans. Helmut Ripperger and Ryan Granger (Arno Press, New York, 1969).

18. Augustine, *Confessions*, Book I, chs 7 and 19, trans. R. S. Pine-Coffin (Penguin Books, New York, 1961), pp. 27–8 and 40.
19. Oliver Davies, *God Within: The Mystical Tradition of Northern Europe* (Darton, Longman and Todd, London, 1988), pp. 21–2.
20. Sabina Flanagan, *Hildegard of Bingen: A Visionary Life* (Routledge, London, 1989), p. 25.
21. Flanagan, *Hildegard*, p. 25.
22. Thomas de Cantimpré, *The Life of Margaret of Ypres*, trans. Margot H. King (Peregrina Publishing, Toronto, 1990), p. 28.
23. André Billy, *Extases et Tortures: Vie de la Bienheureuse Christine de Stommeln* (Flammarion, Paris, 1957), p. 25.
24. Raymond of Capua, *The Life of Catharine of Siena*, trans. Conleth Kearns, OP (Glazier, Wilmington, 1980), p. 29.
25. Tjader Harris, *Birgitta*, p. 74.
26. P. Jacques Campbell, OFM, *Vies Occitanes de Saint Auzias et de Sainte Dauphine* (Pontificium Atheneaum Antonianum, Rome, 1963), p. 133; translation R.V.
27. Campbell, *Vies Occitanes*, p. 139.
28. Raymond of Capua, *Life*, pp. 45–6.
29. Raymond of Capua, *Life*, pp. 63–4.
30. Theresa A. Halligan (ed.), *The Booke of Gostlye Grace of Mechtild of Hackeborn* (Pontifical Institute for Medieval Studies, Toronto, 1979), pp. 71–2. translation R.V.
31. Thomas de Cantimpré, *The Life of Lutgard of Aywières*, trans. Margot H. King (Peregrina Publishing, Toronto, 1991), pp. 21–2.
32. Richard Kieckhefer, *Unquiet Souls: Fourteenth-Century Saints and their Religious Milieu* (University of Chicago Press, Chicago, 1984), p. 22.
33. This very apt phrase was coined by Richard Kieckhefer, see *Unquiet Souls*, p. 26.
34. Raymond of Capua, *Life*, pp. 121–2.
35. Tjader Harris, *Birgitta*, pp. 73–4.
36. Jacques de Vitry, *The Life of Marie d'Oignies*, trans. Margot H. King (Peregrina Publishing, Toronto, 1987), p. 27.
37. Raymond of Capua, *Life*, pp. 30–32.
38. J.-H. Albanes, *La Vie de Sainte Douceline: Fondatrice des Béguines de Marseille* (Étienne Camoin, Marseilles, 1879), p. 5; translation R.V.
39. Jacques de Vitry, *Marie*, p. 27.
40. *The Life of Juliana of Mont Cornillon*, trans. Barbara Newman (Peregrina Publishing, Toronto, n.d.), p. 27.
41. Albanes, *Douceline*, p. 5.
42. Thomas de Cantimpré, *Lutgard*, p. 22.
43. For further discussion of this topic, see Michael Goodich, 'Childhood and Adolescence Among the Thirteenth-Century Saints', *History of Childhood Quarterly: The Journal of Psychohistory*, 1 (1973), pp. 285–309.
44. Johannes de Rupecissa, *Liber Secretorum Eventuum*, ed. and trans. Robert E. Lerner and Christine Morerod-Fattebert (Éditions Universitaires Fribourg Suisse, Fribourg, 1994), p. 23.
45. Rupecissa, *Liber*, pp. 31–2.
46. Rupecissa, *Liber*, pp. 15–23.
47. Robert's writings had a significant influence on John of Rupecissa. See Kathryn Kerby-Fulton, *Reformist Apocalypticism and Piers Plowman* (Cambridge University Press, Cambridge, 1990), p. 101.
48. Jeanne Bignami-Odier, 'Les Visions de Robert d'Uzès O. P.', *Archivum Fratrum Praedicatorum*, 24 (1954), pp. 283–4.
49. Bignami-Odier, 'Robert', pp. 261–2, 273 and 283.
50. Suso, *Wisdom*, p. 73.
51. Davies, *God Within*, p. 100.

52. Nicholas Watson, *Richard Rolle and the Invention of Authority* (Cambridge University Press, Cambridge, 1991), p. 32.

53. Hope Emily Allen (ed.), *English Writings of Richard Rolle, Hermit of Hampole* (Allen Sutton, Gloucester, 1988), pp. xiv–xvii.

54. Augustine, *Confessions*, trans. Edward B. Pusey (Collier, London, 1961), pp. 124–5.

55. Bonaventure, *The Soul's Journey into God: The Tree of Life: The Life of St Francis*, trans. Ewert Cousins (Paulist Press, New York, 1978), pp. 185–94.

56. Campbell, *Vies Occitanes*, pp. 45–50.

8

Female Petitioners in the Papal Penitentiary

Ludwig Schmugge

Historians probably do not consider the Vatican Archives of major interest for gender studies, especially for the history of women. Consisting as it did of men dominating and excluding women from ecclesiastical careers, at least as concerned the sacred orders, the medieval Church did not produce the most likely of sources for gender studies. For most of the Archivio Segreto Vaticano this is certainly true; not so, however, for the registers of the papal Penitentiary, the central office of the medieval Church in charge of licences, dispensations and absolution for lay people, clerics, monks and nuns alike. In this chapter, I shall demonstrate that the tens of thousands of supplications registered by the Penitentiary provide totally unknown sources for gender studies and the history of women in the later middle ages.[1]

In the course of the thirteenth century, the papal administration expanded at a rapid pace, and the apostolic successor created the office of the Penitentiary, entitled to grant dispensations from a great number of ecclesiastical restrictions. In the centuries that followed, a considerable part of the tasks involving the dispensation of grace fell into the competence of this office.[2] As Pope Leo X (1513–21) put it, the Penitentiary was the place in which the correction of behaviour and the salvation of souls were daily business.[3] In terms of canon law, the Penitentiary granted three types of grace: dispensations, absolutions, and licences; only some of these will be discussed here. For example, the office gave dispensations to future clerics who would otherwise have been prevented from being ordained because of some

legal impediment such as illegitimate birth, a physical defect or failure
to fulfil an age requirement. Other clerics had to turn to the papacy
because they had violated certain ecclesiastical canons and thereby in-
curred a so-called 'inability and irregularity' (*inhabilitas et irregularitas*),
a legal status which prevented them from being ordained or taking up
benefices. Only the papal Penitentiary could restore the culprit to his
legitimate status. After the killing of a cleric or participation in violent
warfare, the same kind of rehabilitation became necessary also for
lay people. By the same token, laymen had to seek dispensation from
the papal Penitentiary if they were married, or wished to get married,
to someone too closely related to them. In certain cases, the
Penitentiary absolved people from ecclesiastical sanctions which the
pope had exclusively reserved to himself. In order to be freed from
excommunication, many people of either sex flocked to the papal
court for an absolution. The third type of grace consisted of special
permits or licences. These included dispensations from fasting (such
as letters allowing the use of butter instead of oil during Lent and
other fasts), the permission to have contact with Muslims and other
non-believers, which was particularly important for pilgrims on their
way to Jerusalem, or the privilege for nuns or monks to change from
one monastery or monastic order to another. The Penitentiary could
also loosen the bond tying every Christian to his parish priest by
granting the right to seek a personal confessor. Besides touching on
a number of canonistic issues, the emergence of a well-defined dis-
pensatory system in the late medieval period is of equal interest from
a social historian's viewpoint. Seen from this angle, the phenomenon
may appear as evidence for the 'gradual juridification of social needs'
(Klaus Schreiner).[4]

Dating back to the pontificate of Eugene IV (1431–47), the
registers of supplications submitted to the pope are preserved in
the archives of the Penitentiary. Since 1983 they have been accessible
to historical research on special request. The registers are exploited
for information on the late medieval German empire presented in
the *Repertorium Poenitentiariae Germanicum* (*RPG*) published by
the German Historical Institute in Rome. Up to now three volumes
have appeared; three more, covering the times of Calixtus III, Paul II
and Sixtus IV, are in preparation. As our research is still in progress, it is impossible to provide comprehensive statistical figures
for the share of women requesting the different graces from the
pope discussed here.

In this chapter I shall concentrate on supplications which are of specific interest for gender studies. Since women were excluded from priestly functions, female petitioners do not show up in the category of petitions concerning the sacred orders. Men and women alike, however, received dispensations in cases of illegitimate birth, asked for absolution for leaving a monastery or convent without permission, or when they wished to leave a monastery where they had been put against their will. And, of course, men and women can be found as supplicants for matrimonial dispensations. But 'gendering' this material is rather difficult. The same is true for dispensations to attend mass during interdict and requests for a 'private' confessor. Only a thorough statistical analysis of the thousands of supplications will bring further results.

The first sample to be considered here – illegitimate birth (*de defectu natalium*) – seems to underline the relative unimportance of ecclesiastical sources in general, even the Penitentiary registers, for gender studies and the history of women. Of a total number of 37,916 petitioners registered as requesting a dispensation in cases of illegitimate birth during the years 1449 to 1533, only 516 (1.4 per cent) are female.[5] These figures do not accord with the sex-ratio, which swings between 104:100 and 109/120:100,[6] nor do they reflect the fact that women were in the majority in some late medieval towns.[7] Why were there so few supplications from women?

The reason cannot be the notorious infant mortality, which hit boys and girls in the same way. Probably as many male children as female ones were born out of wedlock. It seems that for female petitioners the chances of being granted a dispensation in the case of illegitimate birth was much lower than for men. Women may also have been less interested in these dispensations. The reason is that women, who had no access either to the service of the altar or to benefices, were barred from the whole sector of pastoral care (*cura animarum*). The few female monastic communities with prebends for (mostly noble) women do not really count. According to canon law, it was (in theory) possible also for the illegitimate to enter a monastic or religious convent, but many religious orders and monasteries excluded illegitimate people by statutes and did not let bastards became abbots or priors. These (basically uncanonical) regulations then had to be overruled by papal letter (see for example the petitions from female supplicants in *RPG* II, 1102, 1334, 1539, 2282, 2416, 2540, and IV, 2509, 2546, 2856). This even applied to bastards of noble origin (see *RPG* II,

2216: Nesa, the daughter of the duke of Jülich; 2592: Katherina de Bavaria; and 2517: Egidius, the illegitimate son of a count of Ortenberg).

The 516 supplications from female petitioners are distributed evenly over time and amount to between one and seventeen petitions per year, statistically speaking an average of 6.4. Not even the Holy Years with their enormous influx of pilgrims and increased number of supplications pushed up the number of female petitioners. Regarding the social status of these 516 women, the preponderance of 301 religious persons is striking; among them several abbesses (like Violante, an Augustinian nun, who became abbess of the convent of S. Anna in Coimbra without mentioning her illegitimate birth). Of the orders represented, the Benedictines come first with 95 supplicants, followed by the Cistercians (94), the Clarisses and the Augustinians (33), while there were only 9 Dominican nuns. The others are simply called girls, *puellae* (131), and wives, *mulieres* (59), and there are just 2 widows, *viduae*, the most disadvantaged of women in the middle ages,[8] while 23 were of unknown social status.

Once again, why did these women address the papal Penitentiary? The answer is: they either wanted a papal letter of dispensation for entering a convent, which was denied to them because of their illegitimate birth, or (already being nuns) they wanted to take up leading functions in their religious communities, called *officia vel dignitates*. Entering a monastery during the middle ages meant to choose one of the few available lifestyles apart from getting married. As a consequence, urban female convents were particularly crowded and developed a policy of 'closed shop'. Religious women sometimes accounted for between one and three per cent of the urban population; that is, between a dozen and some hundred people, depending on the number of inhabitants of a city. In Florence 1,700 religious women were registered according to the *catasto* of 1427,[9] a phenomenon which has rightly been called 'la féminisation de la population religieuse' (Herlihy and Klapisch-Zuber).[10] This trend did not stop until the early sixteenth century.

In many of the 516 cases, the papal letter of dispensation became an important act in the strategy of families to obtain a place in a monastery or convent for one of their female members (notwithstanding the statutes of the order which had to be 'derogated'). Such places were often hard to get, let alone for illegitimate offspring.[11] It was legally impossible for a person of illegitimate birth to occupy a leading position in a monastery without papal dispensation. We can follow all the essential parts of such a supplication in the request submitted to the Penitentiary in 1524 by three nieces of the Spanish curial procurator Magister Johannes de Lerma, Catherina, Johanna and Anna de Lerma from Burgos, or in the petition registered in 1449 for Agnes Arnulfine, a Clariss novice of St Marceaux in Paris.[12] For someone who had had a good understanding of canon law and legal procedure, it was not difficult to 'overcome the prohibitive statutes' (*derogatio statutorum*) with the help of a papal letter.

The profile of our female petitioners becomes sharper if we look at their parents and their geographical distribution. Among the 516 fathers, there were 215 unmarried men, 80 married men (only two noblemen), and 216 clerics (including 4 bishops, 7 abbots and 143 priests). The bulk of the mothers were 430 *solutae*, unattached women, while there were only 34 married wives, 45 nuns (with 2 abbesses) and 6 widows (and in one case the mother is missing). As 74 of the 516 supplicants (14 per cent) were siblings, we can assume that the respective relationships from which they originated had been of some duration. Unfortunately, we cannot trace the careers of illegitimate children of clerics and nuns in this chapter.[13] The geographical distribution (188 cases from the Iberian peninsula, 129 from the German empire, 111 from France, 58 from Italy, and 29 from England (mostly Irish petitioners), just one from eastern Europe) highlights the social consequences of the system of 'barragania' in Spain, where as many as 75 petitioners asked for access to leading positions in their community.[14]

Compared to the 37,400 men of illegitimate birth who show up in the registers of the Penitentiary, 516 female petitioners are a tiny minority. But they belonged to a well-informed elite, which, with the help of canon law, managed to place their daughters in an ecclesiastical environment into which even people of legitimate birth could scarcely enter. But this also tells us that the fate of illegitimate women was very seldom influenced by papal dispensation. Just occasionally a dramatic story is told in the registers, like the case of a Humiliate nun from Bimio in the diocese of Milan, which was brought before the Penitentiary by her confessor in 1452.[15] The woman became pregnant by an unmarried young man, who obviously would not marry her. The nun delivered a boy, baptised the child herself, killed and buried it within the walls of her monastery 'ashamed of the world', as her confessor reported to Rome, when he asked for a licence to absolve her. To protect the seal of confession, the name of the woman and of the convent were not mentioned in the registers. There may have been many such stories that did not find their way into the registers!

Although monastic life, at least in its Benedictine form, included the commitment never to leave the monastery, numerous monks and nuns did in fact leave their monasteries or convents in the later middle ages, thus committing the crime of *apostasia*. Occasionally, the various reasons for *apostasia* are explicitly written down for us.[16] In the registers of the Penitentiary, many supplications can be found under the rubric called *De diversis formis*, where monks or nuns speak about problems within their order and why they left their monasteries. In some of the texts the petitioners explained their reasons for running away and why it was impossible to remain in the monastic community *sana conscientia*. Leaving a convent or monastery resulted in automatic excommunication, from which the guilty person could only be absolved by the pope.

The basic canonistic preconditions for 'changing orders' (*transitus ad aliam religionem*) were defined in Innocent III's constitution *Licet*.[17] A century later, Pope Boniface VIII declared that 'leaving a monastery' (*apostasia a religione*) resulted in 'automatic excommunication' (*excommunicatio ipso facto*) of the religious person.[18] And Pope Martin V did not allow mendicants to change their order without papal approval.[19] Thus, a religious person wanting to leave his or her flock (*ovile*), as the terminology of the formularies goes, always had to ask for papal permission prior to the act; otherwise he or she was automatically excommunicated.

Let us now have a look at some of the texts in which religious women speak about their fate. All of the material is taken from the *RPG*; that is, from German-speaking areas, but for other countries the stories do not differ all that much. Almost every nun registered here left her community without permission of the superior, leaving behind the monastic garb and living a secular life often including relationships with men by whom they bore children. In quite a few cases, the nun entered a relationship with a secular cleric or a runaway monk. Barbara Barchabechin, a member of the third order of Saint Dominic, who left her order, declared in her petition that 'she stayed with a secular cleric for many years, slept with him and had children by him' (*aliquot annis cum clerico quodam seculari soluto conversando pluries ab eodem carnaliter cognita fuit ac prolem ab eodem suscepit*).[20]

One would like to hear more about the specific circumstances of such a way of life, but here the registers are moot.[21] We also have to keep in mind that all the petitions registered by the Penitentiary come from repentant sinners. As for Barbara Barchabechin, the procurator expressed her 'Damascus-experience' in the following words: 'As she (Barbara) has returned to her heart repenting thoroughly and wishing to live a better life in the future' (*cum autem dicta oratrice ad cor rediens, de premissis intime condoleat cupiatque vitam suam in melius emendare*). Many of these women wanted to be reintegrated into their orders, sometimes even to return to their former convents. In some cases the women went straight to the Roman curia in person to obtain a papal absolution.[22] Sometimes, different reasons for running away were given: war and disorder,[23] bad air in the convent(!),[24] imprisonment,[25] going to visit baths.[26]

Indeed, some of the supplications tell us that the nuns who turned away from their communities felt compelled to do so because of reforms imposed on their monasteries.[27] During the fifteenth century the monastic reform movement was one of the major forces within the late medieval church, promoted by secular powers as well as ecclesiastical institutions. Reforming a convent or monastery could create major problems for its members.[28] Even the opposite happened: a nun devoted to a strict monastic life left her community in protest, because the 'proper rules' (*stricta observantia*) were no longer observed there.[29]

How violently a conflict could explode within a convent that was about to be reformed is vividly expressed in the complaints which a Roman procurator dramatically condensed for his client, the fifty-six-year-old Cistercian nun Mechtild de Mülhofen from the abbey Pons Salutis near Edenkoben in the diocese of Speyer.[30] For more than forty years she had served God in her monastery, when some nuns *de observantia* entered the community to carry out the reforms. Many of her fellow sisters left; not so Mechtild, who, according to her own words, tried very hard 'to live up to the new rules' (*strictum huiusmodi observantie ordinem*) for more then twelve months. When she finally realised that she could not endure the severe new community life, she asked her abbess for permission to leave. As this was denied to her, she left the abbey without permission to stay with her relatives. After six weeks, her family persuaded Mechtild 'to return to the monastery and try harder' (*monasterium causa se melius probandi reintravit*). But when she went back, she suffered even more. The abbess herself tore her veil from her head and 'gave her an indecent scolding' (*ignobili castigatione*). The noblewoman Mechtild, not willing to endure such humiliating treatment, left the monastery again without the abbess's consent, always retaining her monastic garb. The Penitentiary absolved her from the excommunication she had automatically suffered and, 'with the explicit consent' (*fiat de speciali et expresso*) of Pope Sixtus IV, allowed her to transfer to another order, even a Benedictine house.

In contrast to these nuns, some women were forcibly kept inside the monastery, although they would have loved to leave. They were compelled to enter a religious house at a juvenile age and stay there against their will, even to take the monastic profession (*professio*), that is, to remain in the monastery for a lifetime. In many cases, the parents or relatives of the petitioners were responsible for what in Italian is duly called 'monacazione forzata'. When the nuns reached adulthood, they proceeded to obtain a dispensation from the Penitentiary that entitled them to return to a secular life. Let us have a look at some examples.

Magdalena Payrerin came from a noble family in the diocese of Constance.[31] At the age of seven, as we learn from her supplication, her father put her against her will in the convent of the female Augustinian canons at Münsterlingen on Lake Constance. It was his intention to disinherit her in favour of her brother. When she learned this (probably years later), she protested, claiming that she never wanted to become a nun, and when the time of her *professio* arrived (probably not before the age of fourteen), she refused to take the veil. As soon as her father was informed of her refusal, he came to the convent, beating her and threatening to put her in jail; if she dared to leave the monastery, she would be killed. With tears in her eyes Magdalena assured some of her fellow sisters that she would never take the *professio* of her own will, and that if she ever took it, it must be 'by force and in fear of death' (*per vim et metum mortis*). Under such pressure she finally took the *professio*, but she left Münsterlingen at the first opportunity, leaving behind her monastic garb with the intention of marrying and having children. The great penitentiary ordered the bishop of Constance to inquire into the case and, if the facts turned out to be correct, declare that there were no ties to prevent Magdalena from living a secular life.

The question of inheritance was not involved in all cases. Ida Wynkens, from the diocese of Utrecht, was ten years old when her relatives and friends forced her to enter the Augustinian convent in Bronope to take the habit of a lay nun, a *conversa*; she stayed there for several years as a professed member. As she saw no alternative but to give in to her relatives' will, she resigned herself to her fate. But, at the first opportunity she saw, she left the convent with the intention of living a secular life and marrying. According to the 'papal decision' (*signatura*) the bishop of Utrecht was instructed to verify her statements, especially that 'she acted under such force and fear as could overcome even the strongest' (*per talem vim et metum quod cadere poterat in constantem*), before declaring her to be no longer tied to monastic life.[32]

As a young girl (*iuvenis*), Gertrud Doven was given by her mother to a convent of religious women of the third order of Saint Francis de Penitentia in Wesel, diocese of Cologne. After staying at the convent for some time against her will, Gertrud left and married a certain Stephan de Walle in a clandestine ceremony. Because the convent could claim that she was still a Franciscan nun, she asked the Penitentiary for a letter allowing her to remain in her marriage with Stephan and their children to be legitimate offspring.[33]

Our next example comes once again from the diocese of Utrecht. By a variety of persuasions and threats (*diversis persuasonibus et minis*), Alheydis Wynandi was, at a juvenile age, talked into entering the house of the Beguines in the town of Dotinckhem by her mother. She lived with the religious women for several years. After her mother's death, she left the Beguines and their garb, wishing to live a secular life and marry. Again, the bishop was commissioned to declare her to be no longer bound to the Beguine house.[34]

The experience of the noblewoman Ursula Schenkin de Erbach from the diocese of Mainz was more complex. Like the other women in our sample, she was forced by a relative, a certain Bernard de Knersteyngast, to enter a monastery at a juvenile age, this time the Benedictine house of Frauenalb in the diocese of Speyer, and she was compelled to take profession within a year of arriving at Frauenalb. She only did this under pressure and protested against this treatment, which contradicted the regulations set up by canon law. She finally managed to leave the abbey, declaring that she would never return there, but was once more brought back by Bernhard and her relatives, who even threatened to kill her. After a while, the relatives transferred her to the Benedictine abbey of Fraumünster in Zürich, once again without her consent. Altogether she remained with the Benedictine nuns for about four years. She also escaped from Zürich, leaving her monastic garb behind, and lived with a cleric from Constance named Johannes Zacz, by whom she had children and whom she intended to marry.[35]

These supplications were granted because the women claimed they had been put in their religious houses before coming of age and against their will 'under pressure and in fear' (*per vim et metum*, as the Latin formula goes). Anything done *per vim et metum* was regarded to be null and void in medieval canon law. Therefore, even the monastic professions of these women could be declared invalid by the Penitentiary.

Until Martin Luther declared marriage to be a worldly matter, the regulation of marriages was entirely within the realm of the Church. The most important marital impediments in canon law, which, according to the Fourth Lateran Council (1215), only the pope could give dispensation from, were kinship bonds defined as being too close, such as certain blood ties (*consanguinitas*), ties between in-laws (*affinitas*), and spiritual ties (*cognatio spiritualis*) existing, for example, between baptised children and their godfathers. At the same time, clandestine marriages were forbidden. During the pontificate of Pius II (1458–64) alone, the Penitentiary registered 4,040 requests of this kind from all over Europe, which clearly indicates how much significance contemporaries attached to the matter.[36] Leading in this kind of dispensation was Italy, where by far the most of this type of request came from.

On the diocesan level, the informality of the wedding ceremonies, which the Church continued to tolerate until 1563, led to much litigation. Many petitions arriving at the Penitentiary resulted from previous proceedings held before local officials, as is evident from the numerous well-documented cases preserved in the European archives. In many cases, the couple asked for a papal dispensation after having been separated by their local bishop on the basis of a canon law ruling. Thus Johannes Ripoldi and his wife Elizabeth from Worms, who were related to each other in the third degree of consanguinity, asked Pope Calixtus for dispensation to stay together, although they had been separated by the bishop's official. This, they declared, would create a scandal in their family, and so they obtained an absolution together with the legitimisation of their children.[37]

In the German church provinces, the impediments described above seem to have played a rather subordinate role. Under Pius II, 518 requests from 38 dioceses dealt with them, which amounts to 86 per year, or an annual 2 to 3 per diocese. Not so in France. Around 1500, kinship represented the most common reason for marriage annulments. The local ecclesiastical judges imposed compensatory payments on couples who were related in the third or fourth degree and ordered them to obtain dispensations from the papal delegate. In 1462, the Penitentiary registered more than 120 of these petitions coming in from France. In England, however, only a very small number of marriages were declared null and void on similar grounds. The examination of all marital dispensations registered in 1462 yielded the following results: of a total of 678 requests, only 4 were of English origin. Twenty-nine arrived from Scotland (especially Glasgow and St Andrews), another 38 from Ireland.

The request points to yet another late medieval reality. We learn that many of the interested couples had been living together unmarried for a long time and often had numerous children. The latter were regularly included in the petitions in the hope that the dispensation would at the same time raise them to legitimate status. In some of the entries it is further mentioned that the marriage had been contracted clandestinely. This shows that informal relationships continued to exist, despite the contrary provisions of the Fourth Lateran Council. Couples were all the more prepared to enter into a clandestine marriage if they knew about their being related too closely, by blood or spiritually. It is equally obvious that the Penitentiary proceeded against people with intervening spiritual ties much more harshly than against those who needed a dispensation from other types of marital impediments. In a few cases, the spiritually related couples were required to live separately for a certain amount of time, from one to four months, including, in one case, fasting as well.

For the petitioners, marriage dispensations could turn into a very costly affair, especially because of the compositions (*compositiones*), a sort of fine that had to be paid to the pope. On 113 occasions (making up 17 per cent of the total of all cases under Pius II), we hear that the Penitentiary left it to a papal officer called *datarius* to fix the amount that was due, without giving any precise figures. Among them, 59 petitions for dispensations concerned affinity in the third degree, 18 concerned consanguinity in the fourth degree, and 17 consanguinity in the third degree. Four entries concerned illicit degrees of spiritual affinity. Under Paul II (when the Introitus Registers enable us to check the exact amount of a *compositio*) the expenses ranged

from four to thirty ducati, a heavy sum roughly equal to the annual
income of an artisan.

A special case, which could have been taken from a medieval
tabloid newspaper had such a thing existed at the time, is registered
during the pontificate of Calixtus III. It concerns a certain George de
Burge from the diocese of Freising and his wife Elizabeth, a former
prostitute. George had met her 'in a public house' (*in publico lupanare*)
in Padua, Italy, 'took her out of this brothel into the city' (*eam de
dicto lupanare in civitate extraxit*) and married her. He later learned
that his brother had also frequented the brothel and slept with Elizabeth. This created, after their marriage, an obstacle to a canonically
valid marriage, called *impedimentum publice honestatis*. Because no
third party knew about this impediment, the pope himself decided to
ask the bishop of Padua, where the couple resided, to grant them
absolution, ordering the respective letter to be sent without a fee.[38]

The registers also reveal many cases of other matrimonial impediments that seem to have been fairly frequent, as well as cases where a
woman proceeded against a man with whom she had had a relationship. Caspar an der Thayr from the parish of Matrei in the diocese of
Brixen, who had slept with a certain Barbara, had been tried by
the official of the bishop of Brixen and his relationship with Barbara
was made a valid marriage. Caspar then appealed to the archbishop of
Salzburg as the superior appeal judge, claiming to have had a relationship with her sister Agnes as well. The vicar of the archbishop sent the
case to Rome for adjudication, because the impediment of incest was
involved.[39]

The 'impediment of a crime' (*impedimentum criminis*), a canonical
obstacle to a legitimate marriage since the time of Pope Alexander III,
prevented Hermann Reychenberger and Barbara from the diocese
of Mainz from getting legally married without the pope's consent.
Hermann had had intercourse with Barbara when she was still married
to a certain Osvald Baumgartner, thus committing adultery. They
also promised each other to marry after Osvald's death. When Osvald
finally died, they married, having now lived together for more than
twelve years. They declared that they had played no part in the death
of Osvald, neither he nor she asking for absolution and legitimisation
of their existing marriage.[40]

For future research the enormous number of matrimonial dispensations in the registers of the Penitentiary must be linked up with
the legal records in diocesan archives or in notary registers. In the

sixteen years of the reigns of Calixtus III, Pius II, and Paul II (1455–71) no less than 13,974 dispensations for matrimonial cases were registered. Because, in the Vatican registers, the names of husband and wife are both given together with their home diocese, identification ought to be relatively easy. As the texts are rather formalised, they are also very well suited to computerised evaluation.

According to the prevailing patriarchal tradition of medieval family structures, many girls were either forced to enter a religious house, or were married off by their parents even against their express will. Canon law in principle recognised the freedom for both men and women to choose their marriage partners or to live a celibate life. Thus the medieval Church demanded the partners' freedom of choice for a legally valid marriage, and enforced it as a legal norm in the decisions of ecclesiastical matrimonial courts. We can hear the echo of this principle in some of the petitions submitted to the Penitentiary by female supplicants. Those texts in fact prove that the story of Romeo and Juliet was not an invention of some novelist but was taken from real life.

Nicolas Calciator and Fides, the daughter of a certain mister Glavelder from Strasbourg, had contracted their marriage secretly, that is, 'by giving clandestine consent' (*per verba de presenti clandestine*) and slept together, but they did not dare tell their parents (who would obviously not have agreed).[41] The parents of Fides later married their daughter to a certain Jacob Obrethenselen and the couple had children. As rumours went about town concerning the children's father, Nicolas, the first lover, acted as godfather 'in order to counteract wild suspicions' (*ad tollendum suspiciones vehentissime exortas*). This was meant to demonstrate that he was not the father of Fides's children. Fortunately (for Fides and Nicolas) Jacob, who probably was much older than Nicolas, died soon after. Many men remarried, and their second and third spouses were often much younger than they themselves.[42] Now Fides and Nicolas started living together once more and Fides became pregnant again, this time – no doubt – by Nicolas. They asked the Penitentiary for an absolution and dispensation to be able to continue their marriage, which was granted by the great penitentiary.

The next case tells a tale that seems to be the opposite of a Romeo-and-Juliet-type love-story. It shows another fact of female life, the fate of women who were seduced without this leading to marriage. A certain Ludovicus, called Loze Wogener, from the diocese of Mainz, had been taken to the court of the bishop or the local governor by

Ahelide Veyndulden 'for having slept with her' (*actu fornicario illam cognovisset*) without at least promising to take her as his future wife.[43] It seems that the court found him guilty and ordered that he be put in jail. Some days later he was taken to the church (normally in front of the portal, called 'marriage-portal'), under custody as it seems, by Ahelide's relatives, so that he should marry her. Loze protested vigorously, but was threatened to be hanged by Ahelide's family if he did not consent. This was too much for Loze, who said in his supplication that 'he was quite young at that time' (*cum etiam satis puerilis esset*) and that 'he took Ahelide as his wife' (*cum Ahelide matrimonium contraxit*) against his own will. To escape consummation of the marriage, Loze 'abandoned the woman without having slept with her' (*in fugam se convertit muliere penitus incognita*), as he stressed. It was only under these circumstances that he could hope to be separated.

The rest of the story is not included in his supplication and is therefore unknown to us. Loze may have tried to get a separation from the local official's court, though unfortunately the official's matrimonial registers from Mainz have not survived. But because he had already been condemned to stay with Ahelide, he might have appealed directly to the papal court. The decision by the Penitentiary, alas, was not in favour of Loze, as we can gather from the registered text: Filippo Calandrini, the great penitentiary, decided 'as in the formulary' (*ut in forma*) and ordered the case to be transferred to the archbishop of Mainz, who was told to inquire into the matter once more. Considering his previous experience, there was probably little hope for Loze to escape marriage with Ahelide. As a rule, the papal Penitentiary was not a court to agree easily to a separation.

Throughout the medieval period, excommunication and interdict were two of the papacy's most powerful weapons against its real or supposed enemies.[44] Worn out by indiscriminate use, these weapons gradually lost their force. During the Great Schism, when the rival pontiffs kept brandishing excommunication and interdict against each other and their respective hangers-on, few people felt threatened any longer by these weapons. With church unity re-established after the Council of Constance, both excommunication and interdict regained some of their previous effectiveness, for instance in local conflicts between ecclesiastical and secular powers. During the period of interdict, the faithful were deprived of regular church services, which created confusion for many conscientious Christians. One way out of this dilemma was a papal licence to attend mass and other church services even during the time of interdict. This apostolic favour was requested by many female petitioners as well as married couples. Such a licence was regularly granted by the Penitentiary under the condition that the interdict was not imposed or confirmed by the Holy See and that the petitioner her- or himself was not the reason for taking this measure.[45]

Another grace frequently requested by men and women was the right to make confession to a private confessor. Again, it was the Fourth Lateran Council (1215) which decreed, in one of its canons concerning the major principles of pastoral care, that every Christian was to approach his parish priest for confession at least once a year.[46] But individuals who had obtained letters of confession were free to choose a different confessor. These letters functioned as privileges that allowed the holders to circumnavigate the general rule tying all believers to confession within their parish.

In their regular form, these letters of confession simply granted the recipient the right to choose a personal confessor, either for the next five years or for a lifetime. A grant 'in a wider form' further conferred special powers to the confessor, permitting him to absolve the holder from sins usually reserved for the higher clergy. If the holder was in possession of a 'plenary indulgence' (*absolutio plenaria*), a confessor could absolve him or her from all sins committed and all sanctions imposed. The 543 petitions for a simple letter of confession in which Germans, including 51 single women and 177 couples, asked to choose their confessor at will, during the pontificate of Pius II, accounted for 21 per cent of the total of 2,580 pertinent requests. Here the words of Hermann Heimpel come to life; he wrote: 'Late medieval piety had a tendency towards the private, the personal, and the peculiar. People felt comfortable only in their chapel, and invoked the aid of the heavenly protector together with their brothers and sisters at their own altar'.[47] The registers of the Penitentiary underline this trend. If we add the 373 letters that ended up in the registers of the Chancery, and therefore appear in the *Repertorium Germanicum*[48] the total runs to more than 900 German entries during the six years of Pius's pontificate. German petitioners making this type of request were, however, outnumbered by the French from whom some 4,109 supplications for an individual confessor were registered in the Penitentiary between 1455 and 1471.

Generally speaking, women received the same privileges, absolutions, dispensations and licences from the papal Penitentiary as did men. In handling the incoming petitions, the office did not treat the sexes differently. As we have just noted, women obtained licences for a personal confessor, and these were not only noblewomen like Catherina, duchess of Austria,[49] or other members of the medieval nobility, but also citizens and town-dwellers.[50] Women can be found in the crowds that went on pilgrimage either to local shrines or the great sanctuaries of Rome[51] and (sometimes, like the famous wife of Bath), even Jerusalem, by Venetian galley via Acre as did Barbara Sleghelin from Breslau in 1472.[52] We should not be astonished that women were as interested in relics as men. On a pilgrimage to Cologne, Margareta Timermans from Utrecht stole some stone relics from the Dominican church, thus committing a 'sacrilege' (*sacrilegium*).[53] Women could also be counted among the increasing number of petitioners from north of the Alps who asked for the licence to use butter and dairy products instead of olive oil during Lent and other fasts.[54] Women were even capable of 'murdering clerics' (*presbitericidium*), as we can see in several supplications throughout all the pontificates.[55] Two collective supplications from women, which occur very rarely, are also of great interest: in 1450 the women of two towns in northern Germany, Ellrich and Einbeck, asked for the privilege to bury pregnant women who died in labour without having given birth to their children.[56]

Penitentiary sources indeed make a contribution to gender studies and the history of women in the middle ages in general. This kind of source material also gives us new insights into the living conditions, the religious and social situations, and the conscience of women in the later middle ages. But research in this field has barely started and may produce surprising results in the future. If it is true that the majority of women in the Renaissance experienced strong constraints within their personal and social spheres (which I doubt),[57] the 'well of grace', as the Penitentiary was called at the time, offered a major possibility for women to obtain their rights.

Were the female petitioners who appear in these petitions less literate and did they have less knowledge of canon law than male petitioners? Did the papal administration adopt a more condescending tone towards women than men? Judging from the registered texts, there is no difference between the petitions submitted by female and male supplicants in these matters. Nor did the procurators, who normally determined the wording of the petitions, use a more condescending tone towards the women. There is no real gender difference with regard to the professionalism, style and canonistic expertise of the texts. Neither canon law nor the personnel of the papal Penitentiary treated men and women differently. For an in-depth study, the bulk of registered supplications presented to the pope by men and women would have to be taken into consideration. Certainly, the marriage dispensations, for example, do not seem to be gendered at all. At least there are no indications who actually submitted a petition, whether the wife or the husband took the initiative in soliciting a papal letter. The same is true in the case of dispensations for runaway monks and clerics. Nevertheless, for the fifteenth century, the registers of the papal Penitentiary represent an unexpectedly rich source for gender studies.

....

Notes

1. As to the theoretical connotations of 'gender', I follow Joan W. Scott, 'Gender: A Useful Category of Historical Analysis', *American Historical Review*, 91 (1986) pp. 1053–75, esp. pp. 1067–8.
2. For the general bibliography see the works of E. Goeller and F. Tamburini cited in L. Schmugge, *Kirche, Kinder, Karrieren* (Zürich, 1995), pp. 425–53.
3. ASV Reg. Vat. 1200 fol. 428r.
4. K. Schreiner, 'Dispens vom Gelübde der Keuschheit', in *Proceedings of the 9th International Congress of Medieval Canon Law, Munich 13–18 Juli 1992* (Vatican City, 1997), pp. 1079–100.
5. See especially Schmugge, *Kirche*, ch. 4.
6. See D. Herlihy, 'Life Expectancies for Women in Medieval Society', in *The Role of Women in the Middle Ages*, ed. R. T. Morewedge (London, 1975), pp. 6, 13–14, 22.
7. See Herlihy, 'Life Expectancies', pp. 11ff. For Augsburg, see R. Kiessling, *Bürgerliche Gesellschaft und Kirche in Augsburg im Spätmittelalter* (Abhandlungen zur Geschichte der Stadt Augsburg 19; Augsburg, 1971), p. 239; E. D. Jones, 'Going round in Circles: Some New Evidence for Population in the Later Middle Ages', *Journal of Medieval History*, 15 (1989), pp. 338–45. Concerning the 'majority of women' in late medieval towns see K. Wesoly, 'Der weibliche Bevölkerungsanteil in den spätmittelalterlichen und frühneuzeitlichen Städten und die Betätigung von Frauen im zünftigen Handwerk (insbesondere am Mittel- und Oberrhein)', *Zeitschrift für die Geschichte des Oberrheins*, 128 (1980), pp. 69–117.
8. See for example S. Heißler and P. Blastenbrei, *Frauen in der italienischen Renaissance: Heilige – Kriegerinnen – Opfer* (Frauen in Geschichte und Gesellschaft 13; Pfaffenweiler, 1990), pp. 139–40; M. Parisse (ed.), *Veuves et veuvage dans le haut moyen âge* (Paris, 1993); S. Sheridan Walker (ed.), *Wife and Widow in the Middle Ages: Essays in Memory of Michael Sheehan* (Ann Arbor, 1994).
9. Vgl. E. Koch, 'Entry into Convents and the Position on the Marriage Market of Noble Women in the Late Middle Ages, in *Marriage and Social Mobility*, ed. W. Prevenier (Studia Historica Gandensia 274; Gent, 1987), p. 50.
10. D. Herlihy and C. Klapisch-Zuber, *Les Toscans et leurs familles* (Paris, 1978), pp. 156–8.
11. See for example for Augsburg, Kiessling, *Bürgerliche Gesellschaft*, p. 239.
12. Schmugge, *Kirche*, p. 149; ANTRNR 32247, 32248, 32249. ANTRNR 33317, 1449: 'quatenus ipsa in dictis monasterio et ordine votum professionis emittere et monialis esse desiderat, sed obstante sibi constitutionibus et ordinationibus dictorum monasteriorum

ordinis, quod nulla mulier defectum natalium patiens inibi ad professionem recipiatur, supplicat ...'

13. For some examples, see Schmugge, *Kirche*, pp. 209–41.

14. F. Aznar Gil, 'Mujeres de la peninsula iberica dispensadas *super defectu natalium* durante la baja edad media (siglos XV–XVI)', *Anuario Juridico y Economico Escurialense*, 26 (1993), pp. 373–401, has used our data base for this study.

15. ASV SP 3 fol. 223v, Rome anno quinto III Id. Julii.

16. For England see F. Donald Logan, *Runaway Religious in Medieval England (c.1240–1540)* (Cambridge, 1996). For the canonistic aspect, see Orazio Condorelli, *Clerici peregrini: Aspetti giuridici della mobilità clericale nei secoli XII–XIV* (Rome, 1995).

17. X 3.31.18, Friedberg 2 col. 575 sq.

18. VI 4.24.2, Friedberg 2 col. 1065 sq.

19. Extravagantes comm. 3.8.1, Friedberg 2 col. 1277 sq.

20. *RPG* VI, PA 30 fol. 21v (1481).

21. The following are examples of runaway nuns who bore children. *RPG* III, 298: Barbara Kespenbach, Cistercian nun from the diocese of Constance (1456), whose case was handed over to the bishop of Constance; *RPG* III, 431: Dorothea Biczlin, from Augsburg (1457); *RPG* III, 217: Margaretha Horim from Saint Gall, diocese of Constance (1456); *RPG* IV, 1633: Margarita Gorne from Augsburg (1463); *RPG* III, 86: Margarita Homoden from the diocese of Mainz, who got pregnant while she was still in her convent, and then left (1456).

22. Rome: *RPG* III, 222 and 355: Barbara Seckendorferin, a Premonstratensian nun from Sulz, diocese of Würzburg; *RPG* III, 498: Elizabeth van Gheinen from the diocese of Cologne (1457); *RPG* II, 773 Meckelingna de Bobarden, Fia de Cultz et Elsa de Lonbuselle from the diocese of Mainz (1450); *RPG* III, 558: Margreta Colerin from Vienna (1458).

23. *RPG* IV, 1155: Barbara Voegtin from Katharinental, diocese of Constance (1460).

24. *RPG* I, 388: Elizabeth de Blonden from Olmütz (1442).

25. *RPG* IV, 1235: Katherina Assenmechers from Cologne (1460); *RPG* V, PA 13 fol. 192v: Magdalena Moserin from Constance (incarcerata fuit).

26. *RPG* III, 456: ad balnea.

27. For leaving the monastery in protest against the reforms, see *RPG* II, 392.

28. For a case where the reformer was accused of having slept with the abbess of the Cistercian abbey he was ordered to reform, see L. Schmugge, 'Johann von Ytstein und die Äbtissin von Tiefenthal, oder: Wie man einen Zisterziensermönch um seinen guten Ruf bringt', in *Vita religiosa im Mittelalter Festschrift Kaspar Elm*, ed. F. J. Felten und N. Jaspert (Berlin, 1999), pp. 249–57.

29. See for example *RPG* IV, 1730, the petition from Barbara Lengin (1464); *RPG* II, 716, Kunegunda Smarmin, who wanted to stay with her parents, because of the bad moral life in her former community.

30. *RPG* VI, PA 22 fol. 136rs, 1473.

31. *RPG* I, 1 (1438).

32. *RPG* V, PA 14 fol. 101r (1466).

33. *RPG* V, PA 20 fol. 135r (1472).

34. *RPG* V, PA 20 fol. 135rs (1472).

35. *RPG* VI, PA 21 fol. 146r (1472).

36. See L. Schmugge, P. Hersperger and B. Wiggenhauser, *Die Supplikenregister der päpstlichen Pönitentiarie aus der Zeit Pius' II*. (Bibliothek des DHI in Rom Band 84, Tübingen, 1996), pp. 68–95.

37. *RPG* III, 1660 (1455): '... in eorum sic contracto matrimonio remanere non possunt dispensatione apostolica desuper non obtenta et si divortium inter eos sequeretur diversa scandala inter se et eorum parentes exoriri possent'.

38. *RPG* III, 251 (1457).

39. *RPG* III, 1775 (1456).

40. *RPG* III, 1812 (1456).

41. *RPG* II, 943 (1452).
42. See Arthur E. Imhof, 'Wiederverheiratung in Deutschland zwischen dem 16. und dem Beginn des 20. Jahrhunderts', in *Studien zur deutschsprachigen Leichenpredigt der frühen Neuzeit*, ed. Rudolf Lenz (Marburg, 1981), pp. 185–222.
43. *RPG* IV, 110 (1459).
44. E. Vodola, *Excommunication in the Middle Ages* (Berkeley, 1986). Peter Clarke (Cambridge) is preparing a book on the interdict.
45. See for example, *RPG* II, 232, 274, 305, 308, 337, 714, 1010, 1012, 1013; *RPG* III, 20, 115, 122, 136, 170, 186, 193, 323, 423.
46. Canon 21, X 5.38.12. See M. Ohst, *Pflichtbeichte* (Beiträge zur historischen Theologie 89, Tübingen, 1995), as well as J. Goering, *The Internal Forum and the Literature of Penance and Confession*, History of Medieval Canon Law (Washington DC, 1999), forthcoming.
47. Hermann Heimpel, 'Das fünfzehnte Jahrhundert in Krise und Beharrung', in *Die Alpen in der europäischen Geschichte des Mittelalters* (Vorträge und Forschungen 9, Konstanz, 1965), pp. 9–29, here p. 20.
48. *Repertorium Germanicum: Verzeichnis der in den päpstlichen Registern und Kameralakten vorkommenden Personen, Kirchen und Orte des Deutschen Reiches, seiner Diözesen und Territorien vom Beginn des Schismas bis zur Reformation*, vol. 8, *Pius II. 1455–1458*, bearb. von Dieter Brosius und Ulrich Scheschkewitz, Index bearb. von Karl Borchardt (Tübingen, 1993).
49. *RPG* I, 48 (1439).
50. See for example *RPG* I, 76, 163; *RPG* III, 604, 606, 609, 512, 622, 629, 631, 649, 654, 655, 675, 706, 711, 719, 746, 772, 778, 779, 798, 813, 815, 826, 830, 845, 846, 851, 857, 858, 863, 867, 871, 878, 879, 895, 898, 905, 910, 911, 918, 921, 931, 962, 964, 969, 976, 979, 980, 983, 994.
51. Rome: *RPG* II, 766 and *RPG* II, 814
52. *RPG* VI, PA 20 fol. 217r.
53. *RPG* VI, PA 21 fol. 96v (1472).
54. Only one example of the many may be given here: *RPG* III, 376.
55. See *RPG* II, 260, 323, 364, 370, 372, 517; *RPG* V, PA 12 fol. 81r (1465): Margareta Ziglerin from Strasbourg; *RPG* VI, PA 22 fol. 157v (1474): Margareta Nicolai from Bamberg, who went to Rome to do penance.
56. See L. Schmugge, 'Im Kindbett verstorben', in *Festschrift Peter Landau* (forthcoming).
57. See Joan Kelly-Gadol, 'Gab es eine Renaissance für Frauen?', in *Männer Mythos Wissenschaft: Grundlagentexte zur feministischen Wissenschaftskritik*, ed. Barbara Schaeffer-Hegel and Barbara Watson-Franke (Feministische Theorie und Politik 1, Pfaffenweiler, 1989), pp. 33–65.

9

Gendering Princely Dynasties: Some Notes on Family Structure, Social Networks, and Communication at the Courts of the Margraves of Brandenburg-Ansbach around 1500

Cordula Nolte

In 1990 Werner Affeldt, a pioneer of German medieval women's history and gender studies, commented sceptically on the state of research in Germany.[1] Summarising his experiences as a speaker at an interdisciplinary project on women in late antiquity and the early middle ages, he observed a widespread reluctance among German scholars to accept a gendered perspective on the middle ages and to support the academic institutionalisation of women's and gender studies. At any rate, in his opinion German scholars of modern history were ahead of the more conservative medievalists.[2]

In recent years new professorships and research centres have provided the necessary institutional establishment of gender studies at
German universities. The gendered approach has lost its exotic touch
and made its way into many areas of German medieval and modern
historiography. In fact, even those historians who still do not consciously conceive gender as an essential analytical category have at least
extended their perspective on the past and added some new questions
to their catalogues.

The success of gender history is connected with the rise of other
concepts and approaches which share some of its topics. Some of
them are part of the science of history itself, some are influential by way
of interdisciplinary cooperation: in the first place cultural anthropology,
but also ethnology and sociology, cultural science, history of mental-
ities and of daily life, micro-history, history of the family, psychohistory, body-history, linguistic turn and so forth. The category of
gender being employed by these approaches, which often fuse, thus
became common property and accordingly gained multiplied impact.

The history of the family, a classical branch of social history,
is a field particularly suited to interdisciplinary work and to the
application of combined gender-orientated approaches.[3] Actually,
none of its topics can be examined in a gender-neutral way: neither
demography nor questions of, for example, individual life-course,
family life cycle, familial relations and communication, social roles
and norms, individual and collective self-perception. This is also
true in regard to medieval aristocratic families and dynasties which
in several respects differed from families of other social strata, in the
first place by their political dimension. Aristocratic dynasties being
political and constitutional elements, the actions and relations of their
members always had political implications. The realm of family life
was thus not 'private' but related to the realm of politics and power.[4]
Dynastic strategies, family dynamics, as well as personal relations,
were shaped by the need to keep and extend power and prestige and
to maintain property.

This political embedding of dynastic and familial networks is the
point of departure of my present project, which centres on the socially,
politically and constitutionally leading group of the late medieval
German empire, the territorial princes and their 'houses', with special
attention to the electors and margraves of Brandenburg-Ansbach.
This dynasty is particularly worth studying because of the frequent
correspondence of its members, some of whom resided in Franconia

in southern Germany, others in the Mark Brandenburg in north-eastern Germany. Thus, long distances had to be bridged by letters. These letters are the basic data of any study on the margraves' family network.[5]

This essay sketches some of the main points of the project, which is still a work in progress.[6] It seeks to present princely dynasties and families as complex subjects of historical and anthropological research by gendering them. Throughout, the margraves of Brandenburg-Ansbach will serve as a main point of reference in order to introduce individual persons and configurations which help to illustrate abstract statements. It should be noted, though, that most of the observations can be generalised mutatis mutandis to the other dynasties and families.

The chapter is divided into five parts. First some basic character-istics of aristocratic families and their structure, their networks of relations and communication, will be presented. The next part will deal with the dynamics of family networks in connection with life course and family life cycle. It centres on the consequences of aging and age within the family and within the wider unit of the dynasty. Then a topic which has received rather little attention from historians of the medieval family will be examined: the situation of married women among their families-in-law. The perspective then widens to the court. Its architecture and its personnel, in particular the female entourage, will be discussed in relation to members of the princely families. Finally, the main points will be summarised in connection with some remarks on the present situation of research on the social history of the medieval aristocracy.

Aristocratic dynasties and families in the middle ages pursued two basic aims which were difficult to reconcile: on the one hand their members strove for biological continuity by begetting as many chil-dren as possible. On the other hand they tried to prevent the family property on which their power and prestige were based from being split up. Yet, a crowd of children who had to be adequately provided for with dowries, allowances and dominions threatened the coher-ence of property. As Heinz Reif and Karl-Heinz Spieß observed, this dilemma could be solved by imposing a rigid system of ranking and behaviour on all family members. Reif and Spieß called this regulation, a kind of unwritten law of the family, 'Familienordnung' (family regu-lation).[7] According to this system a certain position, rank and career (succession as ruler, marriage, ecclesiastic or monastic career) were assigned to each female and male member, the individual life courses thus being determined with regard to one's gender and place in the succession of siblings and to the number of children.[8] Consequently, social norms and roles, familial relations, individual ranges of action and emotions, were also shaped by this system.[9] The principle of inequality prevailed but included the complementarity or reciprocity of roles.[10]

According to the patriarchal, authoritarian family structure, the head of the family, the ruling prince, represented and executed the family regulation. Like his kin, he was obliged to observe it himself but his initiative was still by far the largest. His wife, the princess, supported his handling of the family order with regard to their children. Being principally subordinate to her husband, she sometimes nevertheless enjoyed a wide range of action. She participated in decisions on family politics and often functioned as an intermediary between the prince and their children. As a member of two families, her family of origin and her family of arrival, she was supposed to act as a link between these groups. In terms of inheritance, though, she belonged to neither of them. Princely women who received a dowry from their family at their marriage dispensed with any further claim to their parental property. Neither could they inherit part of the property of their family-in-law. Not competing with their next of kin, they were thus particularly suited for the role of an intermediary. The position of daughters and sons in the family-network can be characterised by just one word: obedience. They were expected to submit to their parents' will and accept the career assigned to them. Conflicts between the generations were often a matter of struggle between the father and that son who had been designated as future ruler and who because of this was educated with particular severity.

The ruler thus dominated the family network, holding all its threads in his hand. This is reflected in the family communication via letters, which proves him to have been the central person of the communicative net as well. His relations to his wife, his siblings, his children and other relatives are well-documented, whereas during his lifetime comparatively little is known about the communication between other family members. Their attitudes towards each other must have been considerably influenced by him, given their orientation towards him and his frequent interventions in their contacts. This is suggested for instance by letters of elector Albrecht of Brandenburg (1414–86) in which he reminded his next of kin of their mutual obligations.[11] Only after the prince's death did direct communication between his next of kin intensify in connection with a change of roles. The father's central position was adopted by his son, the successor and new head of the family, who from now on was supposed to function as a father to his brothers and sisters. In view of his new responsibilities, he demanded to be respected by them, in particular by his unmarried sisters who hoped for an adequate dowry. His sisters sometimes even appealed to him as to their 'father' in order to make sure of his solidarity by such a rhetoric of subordination.[12] Occasionally the dead prince's widow functioned as another, informal, head of the family next to her son, provided that the relationship between mother and son was good. Princess Anna of Brandenburg (1437–1512) for instance, after the death of her husband in 1486, played an active part in the solution of family conflicts, in marrying her daughters and in bringing up her grandchildren.[13] Retiring from the family's main residence to her widow's seat did not mean isolation or lack of communication to her. Whereas some other widows complained to their sons of getting too little information,[14] Anna stayed in close contact, both by letters and by visits, in particular to her son Friedrich the Elder (1460–1536) who ruled Franconia.

The communication by letters which reflects some if not all aspects of the social network tells much about the family hierarchy. Letters were stylised in accordance with writing instructions, *artes dictaminis*, which regulated how to address persons of higher, equal and lower rank, how to compose letters in view of their function (greetings, transmission of news, supplication, etc.) and which elements a letter should contain in order to be complete.[15] Thus, as already mentioned, a woman could signal subordination to her brother by calling him her father and using certain prescribed formulas. Another means of expressing respect was writing a letter in one's own hand instead of having it written in the chancery as was customary at princely courts. Around 1500, writing in one's own hand was still considered hard work among the high aristocracy. Princely persons seized a pen only when the correspondence seemed very important to them. Autographs thus were sent preferably to persons of higher rank and very often served to emphasise a supplication.

Characteristically, the family correspondence of the margraves of Brandenburg included autographs of wives to their husbands, of sons and daughters to their fathers and less often to their mothers, as well as autographs of sisters to their brothers.[16] Among brothers the younger ones were more inclined to write in their own hand to the elder ones than vice versa. Fathers do not seem to have sent autographs to any of their children, neither did brothers send autographs to their sisters. Autographs of husbands to their wives are rare until the 1520s when writing in one's own hand had become more usual.

This unequal distribution underlines the hierarchical difference of the correspondents in relation to gender, generation and age. Proportions could change, though, when in the course of the family cycle persons changed their status. Women for instance could expect autographs from their sons as well as from their daughters as long as they were married to the ruler. When at the prince's death his wife changed to the status of a widow whereas the son became ruler, mother and son entered into a different relation. Now the mother would express her subordination to the new ruler by means of autographs, while the son had letters to her written in the chancery.

These changes of the social and communicative network at the death of the head of the family indicate a flexible aspect of the family structure. At first sight, the family regulation with its assigning of roles seems to imply static structures. However, in the light of the collective and individual life cycle, the dynamics of the network and its permanent changes of configurations become visible. With regard to birth, marriage of family members and thus the origin of new families, changing composition and size of households, transmission of government, transition to widowhood, aging and death, the family appears as a process.[17] In premodern times this process was accelerated by phenomena such as the high mortality rate of infants, the frequent death of women in childbirth and the short duration of marriages. As marriages of aristocratic partners lasted only about fifteen or sixteen years on average, many men and some women remarried once or twice.[18] These dynamics of the family life cycle and its implications for the family network have hardly been studied by medievalists, let alone from a gender and anthropological perspective. To give just one example, aging and age is still a neglected topic in comparison with historical and anthropological research on modern times. We still know little about medieval perceptions of old age, which began to be discussed in written documents only in the middle of the fifteenth century.[19] Definition and individual experience of aging and age were gender-related.[20] Elector Albrecht of Brandenburg and his second wife, Anna, for example, both considered Anna to be old when she was in her late thirties and would still give birth to further children.[21] However, Albrecht began to refer to himself being old only when he was beyond his fifties.[22] Accordingly, Ludwig of Diesbach (1452–*c.* 1527) in his autobiography called himself young at the age of thirty-four.[23]

Like many other aristocratic couples, Anna and Albrecht were of unequal age. Albrecht was twenty-three years older than Anna, whom he had married in 1458 after the death of his first wife. 'Unequal couples' as a result of remarrying were to be found in other social strata as well and became the subject of critique and satire in art and literature around 1500.[24] Family relations were of course influenced by the difference of age. In particular, marital relationships may have been affected by infirmity as a result of old age. Elector Albrecht for instance complained in his seventies that at times he was as helpless as a baby and had to be fed and carried.[25] His wife who nursed him was a good doctor to him, as she herself once mentioned.[26] Some years before, when Albrecht was still in his sixties, he had sometimes felt full of physical energy and sexually lustful like a young man, as he wrote proudly to his friend, count Eberhard of Württemberg (1445–96). However, he explained at the same time, with his tongue in his cheek, that he had better not exhaust himself too much sexually.[27] He also indulged in erotic fantasies and jokes in letters sent to his wife and other women.[28] Remarkably, such sex-talk can only be found in letters he wrote as an elderly man when he perhaps devoted more thought to potency than before.

Old age of the prince could also cause problems in regard to his children. If for instance the prince died leaving behind a young widow with minor children, these had to be provided for and to be put under tutelage. A period of tutelage, though, often brought about a weakening of power and was considered a critical situation for each dynasty. Further, a generational problem lurked behind the principle of life-long rulership. In spite of old age and infirmity, the princes kept hold of the reins as long as they lived, and were not willing to transmit power to their grown-up sons. Instead they kept them in a state of dependence and expected them to obey. This reinforced generational conflicts between fathers and sons and led to political and dynastic crises which in some cases ended up in the old prince being deposed on the grounds of his alleged mental weakness. His sons then had him put under tutelage and imprisoned. To give examples, this was the fate in 1515 of both Margrave Christoph of Baden (1453–1527) and Margrave Friedrich the Elder of Brandenburg-Ansbach.[29] As the principle of aging fathers retaining power and control over the property 'is a fundamental rule of behaviour in patriarchal households' (David Herlihy), other social strata knew such conflicts as well though with less dramatic consequences.[30] When in the first half of the sixteenth century the motif of the life-stairs came into use it may have been intended as an admonition to elderly people to withdraw in favour of younger generations.[31]

Remarkably, aging princes who did not have sons to succeed them were more ready to retire. Elector Friedrich II of Brandenburg (1413–71) for example, who had lost two small sons, felt old and sick at the age of fifty-five. In 1470 he resigned in favour of his brother Albrecht. He commended his wife Katharina (1421–76) and his daughter Margarethe (c. 1450–89) to Albrecht who by contract promised to care for them in accordance with princely rank and to provide Margarethe with a dowry.[32] Leaving Katharina and Margarethe behind in the Mark Brandenburg at the court of Albrecht's son Johann (1455–99) at Berlin, Friedrich then moved as a pensioner to a castle in Franconia. For Katharina, her husband's resignation meant losing her former status as the wife of the ruler. Further, as a result of separation she changed to a strange, somewhat precarious position. Being separated from her husband but not yet widow, she was not entitled to take possession of her future dower but had to be maintained by her brother-in-law and by his son who ruled the Mark Brandenburg as his father's representative. Both she and her daughter became dependent on the good will of Friedrich's family to fulfil the contracts.

Katharina's and Margarethe's situation illustrates the tight connections between dynastic politics and family relations. In this case the relations between elector Albrecht and his son Johann were strained by the question of the women's maintenance.[33] Albrecht who by contract was obliged to support his sister-in-law and his niece actually put this burden on Johann's shoulders. Staying far away in Franconia, he expected his son to manage the situation in Berlin in spite of Johann's chronic financial trouble which often enough annoyed the father. When Johann, in view of his financial problems, spent little money on his cousin, Margarethe sent letters of complaint to her uncle. Albrecht promptly reminded his son of his duties towards Margarethe: 'She has nobody but us and you in our place'.[34] Katharina was obviously better off than her daughter. After being widowed in 1471, she sealed a contract with Albrecht according to which she gave her dower to him and in return received adequate maintenance and residence for herself and her staff of twenty persons at Johann's court.[35] She nevertheless lamented over being a stranger there and asked for Albrecht's help and advice concerning marriage-projects for Margarethe.[36]

This lament of being a stranger among the family of one's husband is a common theme in letters written by women to those men from whom they expected support: usually their own fathers or brothers or whoever was the head of the family. It was a topos used exclusively by women in order to emphasise an appeal. This rhetorical strategy was certainly related to the writer's actual perception of her situation and should not be dismissed as an empty phrase. Being a stranger among one's relatives-in-law seems to have been an experience shared by many women. In fact, a certain kind of permanent strangeness originated from the aristocratic law of property and inheritance which did not aim at the integration of women marrying into a family. Both her own family and the family of her husband provided for a woman in case she should be left a widow but, as mentioned above, she was excluded from the property of her family-in-law. On the contrary, this property had to be guarded from being alienated in the event that the widow remarried and gave birth to further children. One effect of this law has already been mentioned: married women were particularly qualified to mediate between their husband and their children. On the other hand, it may be assumed that the emotional ties between spouses were influenced by caution on the part of the husband and his family. Thus, in a way, a woman was considered a lifelong guest or even a stranger among her family-in-law. This was expressed by elector Albrecht of Brandenburg who advised his daughter Elisabeth (1451–1524) not to get involved in conflicts between her husband and his relatives: 'You are an alien woman and you will remain alien all your life'.[37] This status did not necessarily prevent women from sharing the interests of their families-in-law and from perceiving themselves as family members. The daughter of elector Friedrich II of Brandenburg, Margarethe, for instance, was married to prince Bogislaw X of Pomerania (1454–1523) in 1477 after spending some years at the court of her cousin Johann in Berlin (see above). In spite of her good relations with her uncle, elector Albrecht of Brandenburg, she then sided with her husband against her own relatives in the conflict over Pomerania's feudal independence from Brandenburg.[38]

In the first years of marriage a woman's position in the network of her family-in-law was often affected by the principle of lifelong rule which has already been discussed. As a consequence of this practice, most men at the date of their marriage were not yet rulers but still dependent on their fathers. Usually the son lived together with his wife at his father's court unless the prince gave them a modest household elsewhere. Naturally, under these circumstances the father-in-law proved to be a central figure for the young woman. It was of great importance to her whether she and her husband were on good terms with him and whether her husband's rank in the family system was undisputed. She herself could try to establish harmony by behaving obediently, decently and politely, but the influence of her individual attitude was limited. Childlessness, delay of payment of her dowry by her own family, conflicts between her husband and his family could lead to tensions at court and endanger the young couple's position. Quite often women were drawn into conflicts which already existed among their family-in-law. Princess Amalie of Pfalz-Zweibrücken-Veldenz (1461–81) for instance, a daughter of elector Albrecht of Brandenburg, in letters to her father urgently complained about being treated contemptuously by her parents-in-law who even refused to eat and drink at the same table with her.[39] This resulted from a quarrel between her husband and his parents, who had formerly designated him to be the single heir but then changed their minds. Amalie, who had been married to her husband on the condition that he would be the future ruler, was as little willing to accept this new decision as her husband was. Amalie's sister Elisabeth, who was married to count Eberhard the Younger of Württemberg (1447–1504), also suffered from conflicts in her husband's family and turned to her father for support. Though on the one hand her situation was aggravated by marital tensions she was on the other hand luckier than her sister because her father-in-law, and, after his death, another relative as the head of the Württemberg-dynasty, sided with her. This was not just a question of individual attachment to her, as Elisabeth was quite aware. She wrote to her father that she profited by his being on good political and personal terms with her father-in-law: 'Whatever you do for the benefit of my master and father-in-law, you do for the benefit of me, because he treats me in a friendly way for the sake of you'.[40] Characteristically, neither Amalie nor Elisabeth had children with their husbands. Otherwise their integration might have been easier and the position of the couples would have been strengthened. Such problematic constellations were probably not the rule. However, they are better documented than harmonious relations which, just as nowadays, were less often an explicit subject of correspondence and other written evidence.

The courts of princes and kings have been studied from a multiplicity of perspectives in recent years: architecture, representation, ceremony, culture, festivals, daily life, offices and composition of personnel and so forth. A gendered history of the courtly world, though, has not yet been written.[41] Neither have the networks of dynasties been examined in relation to the courts which formed their personal and physical framework. As Norbert Elias observed, the court's 'Wohnstrukturen' (structures of living) reflected the structure of the social net.[42] The court shaped familial relations both by documenting and by defining the ranks of the family members. Admittedly, it is very difficult to draw conclusions concerning daily family life at court from written and architectural evidence. According to letters and itineraries, the princes still ruled by travelling ('Reiseherrschaft') at the end of the middle ages, though residences became more permanent. Thus the princes and their families were often separated. Furthermore, staying together at court did not necessarily mean spending much time together and being close to each other. The prince, the princess and their kin each had their own staff whose size was related to their gender and familial rank. They were surrounded by different circles of persons and spent most of their time within these groups. They resided in different apartments, some of them having 'a room of one's own', which was considered an indication of high status.[43] As the spatial location of individuals reflected the hierarchical structure, it was taken very seriously. Decisions were reserved for the prince himself. He even had to agree on temporary changes if for instance somebody needed a more comfortable room in order to recover from an illness or if guests crowded the court.

At German courts the system of placement implied that women and men were segregated for the greatest part of the day. Apart from festivals, the 'women's court' (Frauenhof) seldom appeared in the public area of the court. The princess and her maids of honour stayed in the 'Frauenzimmer' (women's room) which consisted of living-rooms and bedrooms. It was situated near the apartment of the princess or constituted an architectural unit within it. The women's rooms were usually placed in a controllable part of the castle, preferably under the roof or on an upper floor.[44] The 'Frauenzimmer' used to be well-guarded or even locked day and night. With the exception of the prince, who enjoyed special rights, male visitors were allowed at certain hours only. The stewardess as the head of the women's court was advised to watch the visitors' communication with the maids of honour. At some courts the women did not even share the meals with the men but had their own dining-room, the princess thus dining separately from her husband.

Under these circumstances close relationships seem to have developed between some princesses and members of their entourage, in particular if the maids of honour had served the lady since her childhood and accompanied her when she got married. However, at some courts women marrying into the family were not allowed to keep their familiar staff. They had to send back their maids of honour and accept those given to them by husbands or fathers-in-law. This may have served a woman's integration at court in the long run even though at first the feeling of being a stranger probably increased. From the perspective of the prince it meant better control of his wife or his daughter-in-law.

In general, friendly relations were tolerated as long as the hierarchical distance between a princess and the maids of honour was observed in public. At the command of prince Ludwig the Rich of Bavaria (1417–79), for instance, his wife's stewardess had to prevent the maids of honour from publicly treating the princess as a friend rather than as their lady. As long as they were by themselves, the women were allowed to amuse themselves together as they wished, though in a decent way.[45] In the case of Albrecht and Anna of Brandenburg, both the prince and the princess seem to have been on good terms with the maids of honour. Albrecht sent his wife some letters containing sexual joking which were obviously intended to be read and talked about in the 'Frauenzimmer' at Ansbach in Franconia.[46] Using obscene metaphors, the prince alluded to erotic practices he wished to perform with Anna and her maids after returning home. He also asked his wife to entertain him with similarly amusing letters. Anna then answered in a correspondingly humorous fashion after discussing the matter within the group.[47]

This quite unusual correspondence can be interpreted from several perspectives. As evidence of erotic communication and burlesque humour at court it reveals a little-known facet of the social network. Further, the special position of the ruler is underlined by his erotic claims on the whole group of women. His communication with the princess and her maids of honour proves him to be present in their relations among each other. Obviously, there did not exist an exclusively female sphere at court in spite of the separation of the '*Frauenzimmer*'.[48] Neither is the marriage of the princely couple an exclusive, 'private' relationship between two individuals which takes place in an intimate, outwardly secluded realm. In view of the talk in the '*Frauenzimmer*', marriage is a 'public' affair and part of a wider network.

Such crossovers of networks and interactions between members of different groups within a larger collective certainly deserve further analysis in order to reconstruct important aspects of the daily life of aristocratic families at court. They point last but not least to the categories of 'public' and 'private' which in recent years have been redefined and differentiated. Former associations of 'the public' and 'the private' with gender have been rethought, too, in order to reassess women's and men's ranges of action. The premodern court as a centre of power in terms of politics, culture, social relations, and communication proves to be a proper field for further reflections on these basic categories within the project of gendering the middle ages.

I would like to conclude by summarising the main points of this study and indicating the direction of further research. The chapter has discussed some basic characteristics of a certain social group, the aristocratic or, to be even more precise, the princely dynasty. The margraves of Brandenburg-Ansbach functioned as representatives of this group which in some regards differed from family and kinship in other social strata (for example, the political aspect of family-related decisions and actions, the lack of a 'private sphere') while in others it shared common features, above all the patriarchal, authoritarian structure with a male head. In aristocratic families this structure was enforced by a system of regulations to which all family members had to submit for the benefit of the group. Two results of this family regulation have been underlined in the present study: the central role of the patriarch in the family network and communication, and the order of precedence among family members which determined their comportment and, as an analysis of letters showed, was carefully expressed towards each other. It has been stressed that in spite of this firm hierarchy with its distribution of roles and attitudes, the family network was far from static but proved to be dynamic in accordance with transitions and caesurae of the individual and collective life cycle. Aging and old age of the father served as an example to show the interlacing of the individual life course, individual experiences and relations within the group. Not only did age affect the individual, but it brought about change of status and reversal of positions for other members of the family as well. Both individual biographies and relationships between single individuals should thus always be studied within an analysis of the wider social network. This also became apparent considering the situation of married women, in particular newly married women. Starting from the lament of some women at being a stranger among their relatives-in-law, their status has been examined in relation to the status of the husband. As long as the husband was not yet ruler but dependent on his father, his relations with his parents deeply influenced his marriage. Thus, for his wife the father-in-law or the parents-in-law turned out to be as important as the husband himself. Accordingly it does not make sense to examine marital relations without paying sufficient attention to further relations, for example, between husband and father or between wife and father-in-law. On a certain level this, of course, concerns families of other social strata as well. Once again, however, the aspect of politics and power distinguishes the aristocratic family. It is noted, for instance, that family conflicts could ruin the younger generation's prospects of ever receiving the reins of power.

The need not just to examine a group from within but to extend the perspective to other groups in its immediate surroundings has been demonstrated by looking at the circles at court which shared daily life with the members of princely families. Princesses and their female entourage are shown to constitute a group secluded from the men at court but under the control of the ruler and in close communication with him. Marital relations of the prince and the princess unfolded in this sphere and were influenced by it as indicated by the example of the prince who addressed both his wife and her maids with erotic promises.

This essay has applied modern questions and approaches developed by gender studies and historico-anthropological family studies to a social group that has only recently been discovered as a subject of social history. Traditionally, rulers and their families belonged to the domain of genealogists and scholars of political and constitutional history, in spite of the fact that the *Kulturgeschichte* (cultural history) of the nineteenth century had already begun to be interested in aristocratic family life, 'private' correspondence of princes and daily life at courts. The modern history of the family which sprang up in the 1960s has so far taken little notice of aristocratic dynasties (for exceptions see the literature given in the endnotes). This is now about to change with the blending of family history, gender studies, cultural anthropology, 'classical' studies on courts and residences, and other approaches. Needless to say, given the politically and culturally important role of the medieval aristocracy, new studies are necessary in order to learn more about the linkage between individuals, groups, institutions, society and political development. This is especially true in regard to the territorial princes and their 'houses' who played a decisive role in the origin of the early modern state. In view of the rich sources which have hardly been exploited from modern perspectives, further research in this field seems to be a particularly promising enterprise.

Notes

1. Werner Affeldt, Preface, in *Frauen in Spätantike und Frühmittelalter: Lebensbedingungen – Lebensformen – Lebensformen*, ed. Werner Affeldt (Thorbecke, Sigmaringen, 1990), p. 7; Werner Affeldt, Preface, in *Frauen im Frühmittelalter: Eine ausgewählte, kommentierte Bibliographie*, ed. Werner Affeldt, Cordula Nolte, Sabine Reiter, and Ursula Vorwerk (Lang, Frankfurt/Main, Bern, New York, Paris, 1990), p. ix.

2. To Merry E. Wiesner, though, in 1994 the political history of the German Empire in early modern times still seemed to be a 'backwater in terms of gender scholarship'. 'Gender and Power in Early Modern Europe: The Empire Strikes Back', in *The Graph of Sex and the German Text: Gendered Culture in Early Modern Germany 1500–1700*, ed. Lynne Tatlock (*Chloe: Beihefte zum Daphnis*, vol. 19; Rodopi, Amsterdam, Atlanta, 1994), pp. 201–23, here p. 202.

3. Tamara K. Hareven, 'The History of the Family as an Interdisciplinary Field', *Journal of Interdisciplinary History*, 2 (1971), pp. 399–414. On a historical-anthropological gender history with regard to the family, cf. Rebekka Habermas, 'Geschlechtergeschichte and "anthropology of gender": Geschichte einer Begegnung', *Historische Anthropologie*, 1 (1993), pp. 485–509, here pp. 505–9.

4. For a case-study, see Ebba Severidt, 'Familie und Politik. Barbara von Brandenburg, Markgräfin von Mantua (30 September 1422 – 7 November 1481)', *Innsbrucker Historische Studien*, 16/17 (1997), pp. 213–38. See also Ebba Severidt, *Struktur und Entfaltung von Verwandtschaft im Spätmittelalter: Die Beziehungen der Gonzaga, Markgrafen von Mantua, zu den mit ihnen verwandten deutschen Fürsten (1444–1519)* (phil. diss. manuscript, Freiburg i. Br., 1998).

5. Only parts of the correspondence have been published. Cf. in the first line Felix Priebatsch (ed.), *Politische Correspondenz des Kurfürsten Albrecht Achilles*, 3 vols (Publicationen aus den K. Preußischen Staatsarchiven, vols 59, 67, 71; Hirzel, Leipzig, 1894–1898); Georg Steinhausen (ed.), *Deutsche Privatbriefe des Mittelalters*, vol. 1, *Fürsten und Magnaten, Edle und Ritter* (Denkmäler der deutschen Kulturgeschichte, 1. Abteilung: Briefe, 1. Bd.) (Gaertner, Berlin, 1899). The materials are deposited at the Geheimes Staatsarchiv Preußischer Kulturbesitz Berlin, Staatsarchiv Nürnberg, Staatsarchiv Bamberg.

6. For a more detailed catalogue of topics, see Cordula Nolte, '"Ir seyt ein frembs weib, das solt ir pleiben, dieweil ihr lebt": Beziehungsgeflechte in fürstlichen Familien des Spätmittelalters', in *Geschlechterstudien im interdisziplinären Gespräch*, ed. Doris Ruhe (Königshausen & Neumann, Würzburg, 1998), pp. 11–41. The present contribution is based on that paper and on a short sketch of the project; see Cordula Nolte, 'Projektskizze: Studien zum familialen und verwandtschaftlichen Beziehungsnetz der Markgrafen von Brandenburg (Arbeitstitel)', *Mitteilungen der Residenzen-Kommission der Akademie der Wissenschaften zu Göttingen*, 8 (1998), pp. 59–64.

7. Heinz Reif, *Westfälischer Adel 1770–1860: Vom Herrschaftsstand zur regionalen Elite* (Kritische Studien zur Geschichtswissenschaft, vol. 35; Vandenhoeck & Ruprecht, Göttingen, 1979), pp. 78–122. Karl-Heinz Spieß, *Familie und Verwandtschaft im deutschen Hochadel des Spätmittelalters. 13. bis Anfang des 16. Jahrhunderts* (Vierteljahrschrift für Sozial- und Wirtschaftsgeschichte, Beihefte 111; Steiner, Stuttgart, 1993), in particular pp. 454–93.

8. With regard to succession it should be noted that the principle of primogeniture was not yet applied by all of the dynasties.

9. Roger Sablonier, 'Die aragonesische Königsfamilie um 1300', in *Emotionen und materielle Interessen: Sozialanthropologische und historische Beiträge zur Familienforschung*, ed. Hans Medick and David Sabean (Veröffentlichungen des Max-Planck-Instituts für Geschichte, vol. 75; Vandenhoeck & Ruprecht, Göttingen, 1984), pp. 282–317; Dorothea A. Christ, *Zwischen Kooperation und Konkurrenz: Die Grafen von Thierstein, ihre Standesgenossen und die Eidgenossenschaft im Spätmittelalter* (Chronos, Zürich, 1998), pp. 51–6.

10. Otto Gerhard Oexle, 'Soziale Gruppen in der Ständegesellschaft: Lebensformen des Mittelalters und ihre historischen Wirkungen', in *Die Repräsentation der Gruppen: Texte – Bilder – Objekte*, ed. Otto Gerhard Oexle and Andrea von Hülsen-Esch (Veröffentlichungen des Max-Planck-Instituts für Geschichte, vol. 141; Vandenhoeck & Ruprecht, Göttingen, 1998), pp. 9–44, here p. 15.

11. Cf. note 34.

12. Cf. for instance a letter of Dorothea of Brandenburg (1471–1520) who in 1503 addressed her brother Margrave Friedrich the Elder of Brandenburg as her most beloved brother and faithful father ('mein hercz allerlibster pruder vnd getrewer vater', Geheimes Staatsarchiv Berlin, BPH Rep. 27 W 54.

13. Reinhard Seyboth, 'Neustadt an der Aisch als Residenz der Kurfürstenwitwe Anna von Brandenburg 1486–1512', *Streiflichter aus der Heimatgeschichte* (1990), pp. 9–35; Reinhard Seyboth, 'Das Testament der Kurfürstenwitwe Anna von Brandenburg (1436–1512)', in *Tradition und Geschichte in Frankens Mitte. Festschrift für Günther Schuhmann* (Jahrbuch des Historischen Vereins für Mittelfranken, vol. 95; Selbstverlag des Historischen Vereins für Mittelfranken, Ansbach, 1991), pp. 103–12.

14. Jörg Rogge, 'Muterliche liebe mit ganzen truwen allecit: Wettinische Familienkorrespondenz in der zweiten Hälfte des 15. Jahrhunderts', in *Adelige Welt und familiäre Beziehung: Aspekte der 'privaten Welt' des Adels in böhmischen, polnischen und deutschen Beispielen vom 14. bis zum 16. Jahrhundert*, ed. Heinz-Dieter Heimann (Verlag für Berlin-Brandenburg, Potsdam, 2000), pp. 203–39.

15. In continuation of Latin *artes dictaminis*, Friedrich of Nürnberg finished the first instruction on writing letters in the German language ('Deutsche Rhetorik') in 1468, Franz Josef Worstbrock, 'Friedrich von Nürnberg', *Die deutsche Literatur des Mittelalters: Verfasserlexikon*, 2 (1980) col. 953–7.

16. Cordula Nolte, '*Pey eytler finster in einem weichen pet geschrieben*: Eigenhändige Briefe in der Familienkorrespondenz der Markgrafen von Brandenburg (1470–1530)', in *Adelige Welt und familiäre Beziehung: Aspekte der 'privaten Welt' des Adels in böhmischen, polnischen und deutschen Beispielen vom 14. bis zum 16. Jahrhundert*, ed. Heinz-Dieter Heimann (Verlag für Berlin-Brandenburg, Potsdam, 2000), pp. 177–202. The autographical correspondence of other dynasties has not yet been examined.

17. The 'family as process' is the subject of the numerous studies of Tamara K. Hareven. For a bibliography of her work, see Josef Ehmer, Tamara K. Hareven, Richard Wall (eds), *Historische Familienforschung: Ergebnisse und Kontroversen: Michael Mitterauer zum 60. Geburtstag* (Campus, Frankfurt, New York, 1997), pp. 405–7.

18. On the average duration of aristocratic marriages, see Spieß, *Familie und Verwandtschaft*, p. 421.

19. Luke Demaitre, 'The Care and Extension of Old Age in Medieval Medicine', in *Aging and the Aged in Medieval Europe*, ed. Michael M. Sheehan (Papers in Medieval Studies, vol. 11; Pontifical Institute of Medieval Studies, Toronto, 1990), pp. 3–22.

20. On the sixteenth and seventeenth centuries, see Heide Wunder, '*Er ist die Sonn*', *sie ist der Mond*': *Frauen in der Frühen Neuzeit* (Beck, München, 1992), p. 34.

21. Cf. the contract of 1476 on Anna's provision in case of becoming widowed; Adolph Friedrich Riedel (ed.), *Codex diplomaticus Brandenburgensis. Sammlung der Urkunden, Chroniken und sonstigen Quellenschriften für die Geschichte der Mark Brandenburg und ihrer Regenten*, vol. C 2 (Morin, Berlin, 1860), no. 148, pp. 178–9.

22. Cf. for instance a letter to his brother written in 1468 at the age of fifty-four, Riedel, *Codex*, vol. C 1 (1859), no. 333, p. 475.

23. Urs Martin Zahnd (ed.), *Die autobiographischen Aufzeichnungen Ludwig von Diesbachs: Studien zur spätmittelalterlichen Selbstdarstellung im oberdeutschen und schweizerischen Raume* (Berner Burgerbibliothek, Bern, 1986), p. 97.

24. Erhard Chvojka, '"Nu ist sie junk, so ist er alt": Zur sozialen und kulturellen Bedeutung des Motives des Ungleichen Paares" vom 15.–17. Jh.', *Medium Aevum Quotidianum*, 35 (1996), pp. 35–52; Ursula Rautenberg, 'Altersungleiche Paare in Bild und Text', *Aus dem Antiquariat, ed. Arbeitsgemeinschaft Antiquariar im Börsenverein*, 4, 7, 12 (1997), pp. A 185–8, A 367–72, A 661–5.

25. Julius von Minutoli (ed.), *Das Kaiserliche Buch des Markgrafen Albrecht Achilles. Kurfürstliche Periode von 1470–1486* (Schneider, Berlin, 1850), no. 87, p. 103.

26. Priebatsch, *Correspondenz*, vol. 3, no. 769, p. 78.

27. Steinhausen, *Privatbriefe*, no. 217, p. 153.

28. Steinhausen, *Privatbriefe*, e. g. no. 164, p. 117, no. 181, pp. 128–9, no. 183, p. 129, no. 193, pp. 136–7, no. 202, p. 144.

29. Friedrich Wielandt, 'Markgraf Christoph I. von Baden 1473–1515 und das Badische Territorium', *Zeitschrift für die Geschichte des Oberrheins*, 85 (1932/3), pp. 527–611; Reinhard Seyboth, *Die Markgraftümer Ansbach und Kulmbach unter der Regierung Markgraf Friedrichs des Älteren (1486–1515)* (Schriftenreihe der Historischen Kommission bei der Bayerischen Akademie der Wissenschaften, vol. 24; Vandenhoeck & Ruprecht, Göttingen, 1985), pp. 405–34.

30. David Herlihy, 'Age, Property, and Career in Medieval Society', in *Aging*, ed. Sheehan, pp. 143–58, here p. 143. Cf. in the same volume Joel T. Rosenthal, 'Retirement and the Life Cycle in Fifteenth-Century England', pp. 173–88.

31. Josef Ehmer, 'The "Life Stairs": Aging, Generational Relations, and Small Commodity Production in Central Europe', in *Aging and Generational Relations over the Life Course: A Historical and Cross Cultural Perspective*, ed. Tamara K. Hareven (de Gruyter, Berlin, 1996), pp. 53–74, here p. 59.

32. Riedel, *Codex*, vol. C 1 (1859), no. 369, pp. 518–21, no. 371, pp. 523–5 (declaration of resignation).

33. Cf. Nolte, 'Frembs weib', pp. 22–3.

34. '*Sie hat doch nymants dann vns vnd an vnser stat euch*', Riedel, vol. C 2 (1860), no. 162, p. 199.

35. Riedel, *Codex*, vol. C 2 (1860), no. 55, pp. 54–6. Margarethe is not mentioned in the contract.

36. Riedel, *Codex*, vol. C 2 (1860), no. 162, p. 199.

37. '*Ir seyt ein frembs weib, das solt ir pleiben, dieweil ihr lebt*', Steinhausen, *Privatbriefe*, no. 391, p. 269.

38. Hannelore Böcker, 'Margaretha, Markgräfin von Brandenburg, Herzogin von Pommern und Fürstin von Rügen', in *Fürstinnen und Städterinnen: Frauen im Mittelalter*, ed. Gerald Beyreuther, Barbara Pätzold, and Erika Uitz (Herder, Freiburg, Basel, Wien, 1993), pp. 190–211, here p. 200.

39. Steinhausen, *Privatbriefe*, no. 309, p. 210.

40. '*Und was ir meinem hern und schweer guz tünd, das tund ir mir selbß, wan er mir freuntlich tud von euren wegen*', Steinhausen, *Privatbriefe*, no. 213, p. 151.

41. Ute Daniel, 'Die Fürstin als höfische Zentralperson: Das Beispiel der Kurfürstin Sophie von Hannover', in *Geschichte als Argument. 41. Deutscher Historikertag in München 1996* (Oldenbourg, München, 1997), p. 113.

42. Norbert Elias, *Die höfische Gesellschaft: Untersuchungen zur Soziologie des Königtums und der höfischen Aristokratie mit einer Einleitung: Soziologie und Geschichtswissenschaft* (Luchterhand, Darmstadt, 1977), p. 81.

43. On the system of apartments, see Stephan Hoppe, *Die funktionale und räumliche Struktur des frühen Schloßbaus in Mitteldeutschland: Untersucht an Beispielen landesherrlicher Bauten der Zeit zwischen 1470 und 1570* (62. Veröffentlichung der Abteilung Architekturgeschichte des Kunsthistorischen Instituts der Universität zu Köln, Köln, 1996), pp. 365–412.

44. Hoppe, *Struktur*, pp. 387–92.

45. Joseph Baader (ed.), 'Haus- und Hofhaltungsordnungen Herzogs Ludwig des Reichen von Niederbayern für das Residenzschloß Burghausen, während des Aufenthalts seiner Gemahlin Herzogin Amalie dortselbst', *Oberbayerisches Archiv für vaterländische Geschichte*, 36 (1877), pp. 25–54, here p. 31.

46. See note 28. On this correspondence see also Cordula Nolte, 'Verbalerotische Kommunikation, gut schwenck oder: Worüber lachte man bei Hofe? Einige Thesen zum Briefwechsel des Kurfürstenpaares Albrecht und Anna von Brandenburg-Ansbach 1474/ 1475', in *Das Frauenzimmer: Die Frau bei Hofe in Spätmittelalter und Früher Neuzeit*, ed. Werner Paravicini (in press).

47. Steinhausen, *Privatbriefe*, no. 196, pp. 139–40.

48. On the omnipresence of men in relationships among women, see Hedwig Röckelein and Hans-Werner Goetz, 'Frauen-Beziehungsgeflechte – eine Forschungsaufgabe', in *Frauen-Beziehungsgeflechte im Mittelalter*, ed. Hedwig Röckelein and Hans-Werner Goetz, also published as *Das Mittelalter. Perspektiven mediävistischer Forschung. Zeitschrift des Mediävistenverbandes*, 1 (1996), pp. 3–10, in particular p. 9.

10

THEMATIC REVIEWS

Gender, Memory and Social Power

Janet L. Nelson

Elisabeth van Houts, *Memory and Gender in Medieval Europe 900–1200* (Macmillan, London, 1999).
Lynda Garland, *Byzantine Empresses: Women and Power in Byzantium AD 527–1204* (Routledge, London, 1999).

Earlier medieval patriarchy, like its modern variant, presupposed a world of little patriarchs. Every *paterfamilias*, Charlemagne said, must acknowledge his responsibility for carrying out within his own *familia*, that is, his household, the moral precepts endorsed by state and church.[1] Yet in Charlemagne's great enterprise of social correction, mothers as well as fathers were mobilised; and mothers, then as later, thus colluded in patriarchy. To some extent, Charlemagne and other moral advisers of that period invented new roles for women as guides and educators of the young and of social dependents (the duties of godmotherhood were in effect a new theme, for instance);[2] but the essential materials were already to hand. Women, at every social level, were the primary teachers of young children. Thus cultural reproduction was always the business of women as well as of men.

Elisabeth van Houts, in *Memory and Gender in Medieval Europe 900–1200*, shows that one important reason why this was so was women's participation in the construction of social memory.[3] In Part I, 'Gender and the Authority of Oral Witnesses', van Houts argues that while the writing of chronicles and annals and saints' lives was largely the work of men, a few highborn women also wrote about the past, or commissioned writing about it, in these genres; and, more important still, women were frequently responsible for the orally transmitted information contained within such texts.[4] What was recorded was therefore the result of joint efforts by men and women. Indirect evidence for such collaboration survives in the prologue of the later tenth-century Anglo-Saxon chronicler Æthelweard, addressing his cousin, Abbess Matilda of Essen in Germany: his work, he said, was the response to a request from her to record 'what is known of our common family and the migration of our people' (the Anglo-Saxons were believed, correctly, to have come from north Germany), but he now had to ask her to supply him with information about the German branch of the family, 'since you have not only the family connection but the capacity'.[5] Van Houts stresses the importance of women's 'commemorative activity' in tenth-century Germany, linking this with another kind of remembering through liturgy. In this, as in many other cultures, widows were by custom their husbands' remembrancers, but it might be said that women as such commemorated kin in general, by way of extending the care they gave the dead.[6] Patrick Geary has offered telling evidence, iconographic as well as textual, for the role of women in the commemoration of the dead in the tenth century. He argued that this ended, however, when monasteries took over, or rather were entrusted by the laity with, these essential social tasks.[7] Van Houts, taking the story through the eleventh and twelfth centuries, convincingly rebuts this: rather, women and monasteries cooperated, as when, for example, a widow endowed masses and commemorative feasts at a particular monastic house in her husband's memory. More broadly, there was 'continuous collaboration between monastery and lay world'.[8]

In the eleventh and twelfth centuries, too, women's 'remembrance of the past' continued to be embodied in both histories and hagiographies. This is the theme of Part II. Thus Dudo of St Quentin in his *History of the Normans* (*c*. 1010) praises the 'capacious memory' of the countess Gunnor, whose husband and son had commissioned Dudo to write; and 'it is tempting to see this remark as an indication of her, presumably oral, contribution to Dudo's work'.[9] Edward the Confessor's widow Edith was surely a prime source of oral information for the author of Edward's Life.[10] This was hagiography with a strong historical component. The Life of St Margaret of Scotland presents more of a contrast than a parallel, however. It was commissioned by Margaret's daughter Queen Matilda, wife of Henry I of England and Normandy, to publicise her own descent from Anglo-Saxon kings. But since Matilda had hardly known her own mother, she could only have gained, rather than supplied, information about her; and this Life is, in fact, thin on history.[11] Van Houts points to a parallel between the commemorative work of an aunt and a niece: another of Margaret's daughters, Mary, wife of the count of Boulogne, had a daughter named Matilda (she married Count Stephen of Blois, future king of England), who commissioned a Life of her grandmother, Countess Ida. Three further generations of women in the Boulogne family showed some concern with 'memorial guardianship': 'Their example shows that literary images of women sitting together and telling each other tales about the past must bear relation to what happened in real life'.[12] But it has to be admitted that the genres and forms of commemoration were as diverse as the pasts revealed in them were hazy and restricted. Claims to descent from Charlemagne were a recurrent feature that, as van Houts recognises, was hardly gender-specific. She is on firmer ground with a late eleventh-century Durham memorandum concerning six estates claimed by the cathedral community: the lands passed down through four generations of the descendants of Bishop Ealdhun (died *c.* 1013), all of them women, whose counter-claims were pursued in court by their husbands. Here, as often, a woman's position as heiress gave not only her but also her husband and offspring an excellent reason for remembering one very particular past. Van Houts is surely right in this case to point to oral transmission by women (as well as by men) of hard information. Another kind of knowledge well attested for noblewomen in this period is awareness of their own nobility, hence revulsion at the idea of marriage to a man of lower rank. Such *mésalliances* did happen, as van Houts shows. In many cases, this was because lords and kings wanted to reward their followers of lesser rank with high-status women, and the followers knew that a woman of noble lineage on both sides would give them noble offspring. In some cases, though, the noblewoman herself so chose. There was some sense that a woman's nobility rubbed off on her husband – even, that a suitable pairing was of male *potentia* and female *nobilitas*.[13] Van Houts quotes a literary depiction of a noble girl showing off her family heirlooms to a poor suitor: 'Up to now I have kept their heirlooms, always the most treasured among my great-grandfather's, grandfather's and father's things, so that I could present them to my bridegroom. Now I favour you above all men for your bravery and courageous spirit'.

To be truly confident of a noble lineage, then, you had to know your ancestry in the female if not in the male line, and van Houts ends her chapter on 'Female Traditions' by discussing some cases where genealogical information, though recorded by a male chronicler, was supplied by women. Long-lived widows were likely to be the best sources of knowledge on this score. Lambert of Wattrelos is an example made famous by Georges Duby, of an author dependent on oral information transmitted via women, especially his own mother, Gisla. Some authors wrote to colleagues to seek written genealogical information, and several letters survive providing just that. The surviving evidence privileges the concerns of churchmen who, in the eleventh century, were extending the degrees of relationship within which people were forbidden to marry. The notion that serious efforts were made, at any rate by kings and magnates, to avoid marrying within the prohibited degrees, can't really be very firmly supported.[14] But the ideal, or social goal, was there, and there is no doubt either about the widespread interest in genealogy or about the increased recourse to writing for recording it.

Part II ends with the transmission of memory through sites and through objects. Examples of places of memory for individuals and family groups were the tombs made for dead kin, or the rune-stones erected by Scandinavian women to commemorate fathers, brothers, husbands and children, and at the same time to mark property inherited from the dead (mothers inherited from children who predeceased them). Examples of objects were very varied indeed.[15] The dedication page of the gospel-book presented to Brunswick cathedral by Duke Henry the Lion of Saxony and his wife Matilda, daughter of Henry II of England, is both work of art and memorial, and a photo of it makes an apt choice for the cover of van Houts's book. Henry's mother and grandmother, and Matilda's grandmother, are prominently named here, alongside their spouses, but Matilda's mother is absent – unless, as van Houts persuasively suggests, the unidentified woman 'tucked away in a corner … disguised as an insignificant lay woman' is indeed Eleanor of Aquitaine.[16] If so, it's perhaps unnecessary to infer, with van Houts, that 'something clearly went wrong' in the relationship between mother and daughter, and that Eleanor was thus deliberately consigned to oblivion: those in the know would appreciate that a family dispute (Eleanor's support for her sons' revolt against their father, and her consequent imprisonment) required a tactful anonymity in what was a more or less public document. Treasures made of precious materials were the stuff of commemorative gifts that conveyed something of the giver's past: that same Eleanor gave her first husband, Louis VII of France, a carved rock-crystal bottle inherited from her grandfather, the heroic Duke William IX of Aquitaine, who had received it as a gift from a famous Muslim companion-in-arms back in 1120 in the days before the Spanish Reconquest had been assimilated to a crusade. Eleanor made sure to tell Louis and his friend the abbot of St Denis about the object's history.[17] Queens as well as kings bequeathed bits of their regalia as *quid pro quo* for commemoration. Tapestries and vestments embroidered by women were commissioned by men as well as by women to commemorate not only the deeds of the living and the dead, but also the donor's charity. Late Anglo-Saxon women's wills include bequests of clothing, jewellery, household linen, to daughters and granddaughters. Yet van Houts observes that women evidently distinguished between such bequests and the luxury objects used for display, such as tableware or the liturgical vessels of a noble chapel, which were left to churches. Van Houts infers 'a reluctance … to see their belongings being depersonalised': 'why give your grandmother's precious necklace to a monastery if it is being used as yet another string of beads around one of their saints' relics?' And she goes on to suggest an important correlation between 'men's and women's options' and the public and private spheres: men did not feel the need to have their private roles remembered, but women, 'leading private lives to a much greater extent, perpetuated their private lives through oral bequests of their potential memorials to their daughters and granddaughters who simply perpetuated this tradition'.[18] Gendered giving thus reflected in precise ways the gendering of both consciousness and being.

Part III examines the Norman Conquest through the lens of contemporaries' memories. Here van Houts is on the Anglo-Norman historiographical territory she has made her own.[19] She argues convincingly that whatever the Benedictine Rule in principle required of monks in the way of detachment from family ties, in practice the monks who wrote up the history of the Conquest remained firmly attached, hence could draw on much oral material from both lay men and lay women. Since they were of Anglo-Saxon ancestry on both sides or on one, part of their very purpose in writing was to counteract the 'trauma' which they and their families had suffered. As ever, van Houts has new suggestions to make about the contribution of women's testimony to the authors of written sources. It is not just a question of noting a woman, Constance fitzGilbert, as patron of the historian Gaimar, but of intelligently surmising the impact on the monk-historians Orderic and William of their Anglo-Saxon mothers, and, more controversially and intriguingly, of the wife of the mid twelfth-century archdeacon Henry of Huntingdon (since, in van Houts's view, Henry was 'almost certainly married') on her husband's 'down-to-earth tone' and 'attention to the practical side of life'.[20] Thus histories incorporated women's as well as men's memories. A different and very specific kind of recollection is that involved in the oral transmission of property claims. If many claims recorded in the late twelfth and early thirteenth centuries pertained to lands that had passed through the female line, it seems entirely legitimate to ask 'whether such claims were kept alive because they were associated with strong feelings about the loss of land and kin', even if, since contentious claims through women are characteristic of much medieval documentation,[21] an equally pertinent question would focus on the interests of husbands and sons and daughters. As with Bishop Ealdhun's female descendants, in a world where legal transactions were frequently unrecorded, and where what we would call infant and early primary education was normally mothers' department, property rights gave people of both sexes a strong motive to remember. But van Houts has been able to make a good case for women's remembering over five or even six generations of genealogical time, whereas 'the oral male line often runs out after the (paternal) grandparents are mentioned'.[22] This difference can be attributed, quite plausibly, to demographic factors: girls married at a lower age, perhaps by as much as a decade, than did young men, hence women were more likely to remember their grandmothers, and even great-grandmothers, than men were their grandfathers. Van Houts is much too experienced a historian to overstate women's contribution to the memorialising of the medieval past: what she rightly insists on, and what gives this book its cutting edge, is that women's contribution be recognised as important and distinctive.

For its implications are considerable. They concentrate our minds on the importance of the spoken (and the sung?) as well as the written word; and once that's appreciated, Georges Duby's linking of the appearance of genea-logical literature *c.* 1000 with a change to primogeniture in the transmission of family property at this same time has to be called into question. In other words, families had memories before the early eleventh century, but for the most part they transmitted them orally, though just enough written evidence survives to indicate that they did so. The systematic use of quite detailed charters, and the systematic keeping of large charter collections, from *c.* 1000 onwards, signalled what Dominique Barthélemy and Pauline Stafford have termed a documentary mutation, rather than a tenurial or familial one.[23] That change had its own dynamic, but it should not be confused with a change of lay perceptions about the family's shape and identity over time. Given these continuities, it's perhaps to be regretted that van Houts did not extend her purview back a little to the Carolingian period or say more, too, about the tenth century.[24] Between Charlemagne and the period on which van Houts concentrates, the Carolingian world changed and diversified. Régine Le Jan has recently claimed that 'at the very heart of the atom of kinship constituted by the conjugal family, a fundamental shift produced a new definition of the role of the woman and of the maternal line within the family'.[25] On the other hand, there were continuities: one of the most interesting bits of evidence for women's part in transmitting knowledge of the past in the earlier middle ages is Bishop Hildegar of Meaux's claim, in the mid-ninth century, that the women of Meaux danced in a ring while they sang of the deeds of Bishop Faro back in the seventh century.[26] True or false, this story assumes the normality of women's singing and dancing the past as well as telling of it. But to complain that Elisabeth van Houts has not covered more chrono-logical ground is unfair, given her brief to produce a compact, student-friendly book. Within those constraints, not only has she covered a great deal, but she has produced a book that's timely, path-breaking, and emphatically more than the sum of its parts.

One of the writers briefly discussed by van Houts is Anna Comnena (known to Byzantinists as Komnene), whom she uses to exemplify a woman writing history – in fact a biography of her father the emperor Alexios Comnenos – in the central medieval period. She comments on Anna's use of a good deal of oral testimony, especially on military matters, though no woman informant is ever mentioned. Further, she notes with some surprise that Anna was her own prime informant, 'the ultimate witness on which the story of her father is based'. In an endnote, van Houts adds that a recent important paper by James Howard-Johnson argues for 'close co-operation' between Anna and her husband in the production of the Alexiad.[27] It's also worth pointing out that Anna and her husband were disappointed claimants to the imperial throne after Alexios's death, and that this has a bearing on the stance Anna assumed as her father's confidante and eye-witness reporter of his reign. Further, Anna needs to be set within the historiographical tradition of her cultural world, that is, of Byzantium. Her model was Thucydides, a historian well known in the Greek-speaking east but quite unknown, and unknowable, to any others among the writers considered by van Houts.

Before returning to the question of difference between the Latin-speaking west and Byzantium, I turn now, more briefly, to Lynda Garland's *Byzantine Empresses: Women and Power in Byzantium AD 527–1204.* Garland has written within a tradition, as she acknowledges in her preface: Charles Diehl's two-volume *Figures byzantines,* cited here in the second edition of 1937–8, but originally published in 1906–8, was translated in 1964 as *Byzantine Empresses.* It too was a series of vivid biographical sketches. Donald Nicol's *The Byzantine Lady: Ten Portraits, 1250–1500* (1994) is another set of essays in the same belle-lettristic mould. Garland says that while she could not hope to compete with Diehl in readability, she has attempted to supply the documentation Diehl omitted, and also to take account of 'the interpretations of modern scholars'. What she has produced is a useful book for Byzantinists, but one that makes few concessions to the rest of us. It assumes an insider's knowledge; and the limited amount of contextualisation offered in the excellent seven-page Introduction is simply not enough to acclimatise non-specialists. Documentation, in the sense of the rehearsal of the series of events recorded by Byzantine chroniclers, is thorough, indeed unremitting. Though some chapters, notably the first, on Theodora,[28] attempt analysis, in others narrative is the dominant mode. The twists and turns of Constantinopolitan politics do not make for easy reading.

Two chapters in particular offer material of potential interest to historians of the Latin west. One is chapter 11, 'The Empresses of Alexios I Komnenos'. Alexios is the emperor who welcomed, then broke with, the leaders of the First Crusade; and crusade historiography has recently given his role the attention it deserves.[29] But Garland in this chapter has nothing to say about the crusaders, presumably because no source assigns any role in their reception to Alexios's wife, Irene, or his mother, Anna Dalassene. Garland thinks the senior Anna, influential in the early years of Alexios's reign, had been sidelined, at last, sometime between 1095 and 1100, not by her daughter-in-law, but by her own son: 'two determined women in the palace may have been one too many for Alexios to cope with, and it was certainly easier to get rid of his mother than his wife, if one had to go'.[30] Anna Komnene first mentions the political influence of her mother Irene anent the events of 1102. Garland indicates that Anna's view of her parents' marriage is rose-tinted, and suggests that Alexios's real motive for wanting Irene with him when he was away on campaign was to prevent her from intriguing in Constantinople in his absence. Anna gives a touching account of Alexios's deathbed and Irene's grief. Anna's near-contemporary, Zonaras, revealingly says that 'there was no-one to ritually bathe the emperor's corpse nor any imperial dress to clothe it'. Though there seems to be no direct evidence that imperial women were responsible for laying out the emperor's corpse and preparing it for funeral, could Zonaras's allegation be a veiled attack on Irene and Anna? Garland does not raise the question. What is lacking in this book is any introduction to, or sustained critique of, the sources, or any synoptic treatment of the empress's office or function. The Introduction mentions all too briefly the prescribed rituals for an imperial marriage, and for an empress's coronation, but there is no systematic discussion of the liturgical texts. Did Byzantine treatises on emperorship also cover empress-ship? Perhaps any such concept was simply not at home in Byzantium, but, if so, the contrast with the west should be noted. What must disappoint a medieval historian of the western sort is the complete absence here of any comparative take. Garland's bibliography contains not a single reference to any of the recent rich crop of historiography on medieval queenship or empress-ship in the west; and this is especially regrettable since some of that work is well informed by gender theory.[31]

One other chapter that cries out for linked, or at least comparative, treatment of east and west is that on the empress Irene, Charlemagne's contemporary and – according to the contemporary Byzantine chronicler, Theophanes – hoped-for marriage-partner. Irene, widow of the emperor Leo IV, had ruled first as regent for her son; then as co-ruler with him; then, after his blinding and murder at her behest, as his successor. Between 796 and 802 she ruled in her own right, with the support of the army and a team of eunuch advisers. Charlemagne became emperor in the west on Christmas Day 800. His proposal of marriage to Irene followed in 802. Theophanes comments that the objective was 'to unite east and west', and that Irene would have agreed, but for the opposition of the eunuch Aetios 'who ruled by her side and was trying to seize imperial power on behalf of his brother'. In Garland's view, Irene now faced united opposition from the high officials opposed to Aetios. The marriage-proposal 'could only fill a Byzantine bureaucrat with dread', Garland comments,[32] without giving reasons, and without explaining why, in that case, Irene favoured a policy that could never have won acceptance in Constantinople. Perhaps she had completely lost her grip – but, if so, it would seem hard to justify Garland's response to her own question, 'Irene: a successful ruler?': 'it was her misfortune that she felt it incumbent on herself, for whatever reason, to rely where possible on eunuchs, even for military expeditions'.[33] The western historian will hope for some clarification here, but all that is offered is a brief endnote: '[eunuchs] dominated the personal activity of the imperial couple as wardrobe officials, chamberlains and treasurers'.[34] But doesn't Garland miss the crucial point about Irene's reliance on eunuchs? They were, despite Theophanes's coruscating comments on their ambitions for their own relatives, safe counsellors for an empress and unable to pose any dynastic threat. As Justinian had calculated with Narses in the sixth century, a eunuch could be counted on as military commander to win campaigns without then bidding to usurp the imperial throne. In other words, Irene's reliance on eunuchs was part of, rather than in contradiction with, what Garland recognises as her political skill.

Too often, Garland is satisfied with explaining her empresses's activities in terms of naked lust for power. Is this not to swallow whole the gender-stereotyping of Byzantine male writers? Certainly it leaves open the nature of the power in question. Byzantine imperial power needs to be, not assumed, in reductionist or positivist fashion, but clearly specified, perhaps in terms of contrast to the medieval west, where even the feistiest royal women were not vilified as usurpers of control over central institutions, an army and a bureaucracy. If the power of rulers was familial in both east and west, it was so in different ways and to differing degrees. In the east, all politics were *not* family politics. An approach that disregards structural or cultural change through seven centuries does its subject no favours. It can make Byzantium seem, oddly, at once weirdly exotic and dull.

Eunuchs of course played no comparable political role in the west. Their institutionalised position in the Byzantine court points, therefore, towards critical differences between attitudes towards gender and power in east and west. The only functionally similar groups in western courts might be the palatine clergy, or, contemporary with Irene, the unmarried daughters of Charlemagne who served him as his eyes and ears at court but never posed a dynastic risk or threat.[35] Two further points about gender and power can round off this review-chapter by comparing and contrasting west and east. Social power is in part about control of communications. Van Houts shows how large and diffused a role women played in transmitting oral traditions about family and property in a western world where political power was to a great extent privatised in and by noble families. It is symptomatic of the east that local, oral, traditions are relatively harder to track, and that, with the single exception of Anna Komnene, Byzantine historians operated within a rarefied written culture descending directly from Greek antiquity.[36] My second point is about the gendering of political space. Just as Byzantine historians focused their attention on Constantinople, the queen city, and the doings of emperors, so politics and ritual were concentrated in the capital, controlled from and by the imperial court. Within Constantinople, the imperial palace occupied a huge area, and the *gynaikonitis*, the women's quarters, housed a staff of some 1,000 to 2,000, mostly women and eunuchs.[37] Again, only in the reigns of Charlemagne and his successor did anything like a capital exist in the earlier medieval west, and the numbers at Aachen were certainly far smaller than those in the great palace and city of Constantinople. 'The wives of [the emperor's] counsellors' mentioned in a western source in 834[38] may have been on the way to forming an institutionalised group, but, if so, that experiment was discontinued and, instead, with courts again itinerant, royal entourages reverted to smaller numbers. The concentration of women in the *gynaikonitis* evoked 'a quality of mystery and intrigue' reflecting the political skulduggery that was sometimes plotted there.[39] In the west, a plurality of little courts, lordly and royal, don't seem to have afforded such separate spaces for male and female socialising. At any rate, for serious entertainments mixed company seems to have been usual. Here, by the twelfth century if not sooner, Norbert Elias dimly discerned the origins of a civilising process which would eventually produce modern manners in Renaissance courts.[40] Here, indeed, women's social power was displayed in conjunction with that of men. Could this not be said of Byzantium too? While there will always be plenty of room for thematic studies that illuminate aspects of either west or east (and van Houts's is one that does so brilliantly), what's also needed, especially when themes require theoretically informed treatment as gender does, is a more comprehensive, and comparative, European cultural history that takes in east and west.[41] Both, after all, were heirs of classical and Christian traditions, they were in fairly frequent contact throughout the earlier medieval period, and those who wrote within them were aware, more often than not, of much in common. The history of gender has always been able to transcend disciplinary sectionalism and the arbitrary divides of academe. In its wide embrace, memory and social power, Europe-wide, are clearly well worth the enfolding.

....

Notes

1. Capitulary no. 121, *Missi cuiusdam admonitio*, in *Monumenta Germaniae Historica, Capitularia regum Francorum*, ed. A. Boretius (vol. I, Hannover, 1883), pp. 238–40. There is a good translation in P. E. Dutton, *Carolingian Civilization* (Peterborough, Ontario, 1993), pp. 81–3. Cf. also Capit. nos. 64, cc. 7, 17, p. 153: 'De ebrietate, ut primum omnium seniores semetipsos exinde vetent et eorum iuniores exemplum bonae sobrietatis ostendant'; c. 17: 'De vulgari populo, ut unusquisque suos iuniores distringat, ut melius ac melius oboediant et consentiant mandatis et praeceptis imperialibus' ('Concerning drunkenness, first of all lords of everyone shall forbid that for themselves and show their juniors the example of good sobriety'; 'Concerning the common people, let everyone keep control of his juniors so that they obey and agree better and better to imperial orders and commands'); and, in a nutshell, no. 65, c. 5, p. 154: 'De semetipso et sua familia unusquisque corrigendum' ('Each man must be responsible for correcting himself and his household'). Every man's *familia* was his own little realm.

2. See K. Heene, *The Legacy of Paradise: Marriage, Motherhood and Woman in Carolingian Edifying Literature* (P. Lang, Frankfurt am Main, 1997); J. Smith, 'Gender and Ideology in the Early Middle Ages', *Studies in Church History*, 34 (1998), pp. 51–74.

3. Cf. J. Fentress and C. Wickham, *Social Memory* (Blackwell, Oxford, 1992), p. 7: 'When we remember, we represent ourselves to ourselves and to those around us. To the extent that our "nature" – that which we truly are – can be revealed in articulation, we are what

we remember'; and pp. 137–43, on the problems of capturing the memory, and the social memory, of women, whose 'life stories give less, or different, space to "public" history than men's do'. The latter quotation refers particularly to evidence about working-class women. Elite women in the central middle ages may have perceived themselves as more active participants in 'public' history, but surely did so, none the less, differently from the way elite males did.

4. As memorable as van Houts's vignettes of women storytellers is the picture evoked in the preface, of the author herself, and her general editor Miri Rubin, discussing the shape of this book 'with our children at our feet'. History-writing and gender are connected, re-currently, in our time as well as in the past; cf. N. Z. Davies, 'Gender and Genre: Women as Historical Writers, 1400–1820', in *Beyond their Sex: Learned Women of the European Past*, ed. P. Labalme (New York University Press, New York, 1980), pp. 153–82. Davies's title is echoed (with due acknowledgement) by J. L. Nelson, 'Gender and Genre in Women Historians of the Early Middle Ages', in *L'Historiographie médiévale en Europe*, ed. J.-P. Genet (Éditions du CNRS, Paris, 1991), pp. 149–63, repr. in Nelson, *The Frankish World, 750–900* (Hambledon Press, London, 1996), pp. 183–99; and by S. Gaunt, *Gender and Genre in Medieval French Literature* (Cambridge University Press, Cambridge, 1995).

5. Æthelweard's prologue is translated in van Houts, *Memory and Gender*, Appendix 1, pp. 151–2.

6. See M. Bloch and J. Parry (eds), *Death and the Regeneration of Life* (Cambridge University Press, Cambridge, 1982), especially the editors' Introduction, and Bloch's chapter, 'Death, women and power', pp. 1–44, 211–30.

7. P. Geary, *Phantoms of Remembrance: Memory and Oblivion at the End of the First Millennium* (Princeton University Press, Princeton, 1994).

8. Van Houts, *Memory and Gender*, p. 13.

9. Van Houts, *Memory and Gender*, p. 72, but not citing E. Searle, 'Fact and Pattern in Heroic History: Dudo of St Quentin', *Viator*, 15 (1984), pp. 75–85. E. Christiansen, *Dudo of St Quentin, History of the Normans, Translation with Introduction and Notes* (Boydell Press, Woodbridge, 1998), p. xxvii, dismisses the possibility of Gunnor's input a little too briskly, I think, though he's certainly right to stress Dudo's wish to impress Bishop Adalbero of Laon, and Count Richard of Normandy, Gunnor's son. The important issue here is the sources of Dudo's information about the tenth century, and here Christiansen, p. 224, n. 460, seems nearer to van Houts. His fine translation evidently appeared too late for van Houts to use it.

10. Van Houts, *Memory and Gender*, p. 72. See now P. Stafford, *Queen Emma and Queen Edith. Queenship and Women's Power in Eleventh-Century England* (Blackwell, Oxford, 1997).

11. D. Baker, '"A Nursery of Saints": St Margaret of Scotland Reconsidered', in *Medieval Women: Studies in Church History, Subsidia 1*, ed. D. Baker (Blackwell, Oxford, 1978), pp. 119–42.

12. Van Houts, *Memory and Gender*, p. 76.

13. R. Le Jan, *Famille et pouvoir dans le monde franc (VIIe–Xe siècle): Essai d'anthropologie sociale* (Publications de la Sorbonne, Paris, 1995), p. 231 and n. 35.

14. The case was elegantly put by C. Bouchard, 'Consanguinity and Noble Marriages in the Tenth and Eleventh Centuries', *Speculum*, 56 (1981), pp. 268–87; but the evidence is not conclusive. For the eleventh-century extension of prohibited degrees, see J. Goody, *The Development of the Family and Marriage in Europe* (Cambridge University Press, Cambridge, 1983), and the thoughtful review by M. Bloch, *London Review of Books*, 5–19 July 1984, pp. 19–20.

15. In addition to the excellent paper of Remensnyder cited by van Houts, *Memory and Gender*, p. 10, see P. Buc, 'Conversion of Objects', *Viator*, 28 (1997), pp. 99–143.

16. Van Houts, *Memory and Gender*, p. 96.

17. Van Houts, *Memory and Gender*, p. 107.

18. Van Houts, *Memory and Gender*, pp. 118–19. Cf. n. 3, above.

19. Van Houts, *History and Family Traditions in England and the Continent, 1000–1200* (Ashgate, Aldershot, 1999).
20. Van Houts, *Memory and Gender*, p. 132.
21. P. Stafford, 'La Mutation familiale: A Suitable Case for Caution', in *The Community, the Family, and the Saint, Patterns of Power in Early Medieval Europe, International Medieval Research*, 4, ed. J. Hill and M. Swann (Turnhout, 1998), pp. 103–26.
22. Van Houts, *Memory and Gender*, p. 149.
23. D. Barthélemy, *La Société dans le comté de Vendôme de l'an mil au XIVe siècle* (Fayard, Paris, 1993), pp. 19–116; Stafford, 'La Mutation familiale'.
24. C. Bouchard, 'Family Structure and Family Consciousness among the Aristocracy in the Ninth to Eleventh Centuries', *Francia*, 14 (1986), pp. 639–58, and 'The Bosonids: Rising to Power in the Carolingian Age', *French Historical Studies*, 15 (1988), pp. 407–31; Le Jan, *Famille et pouvoir*, esp. ch. X and XI.
25. Le Jan, *Famille et pouvoir*, p. 434: 'Il y eut alors, au coeur même de l'atome de parenté que constitue la famille conjugale, un basculement fondamental qui s'est traduit par une nouvelle définition du rôle de la femme et de la lignée maternelle au sein de la famille'.
26. Nelson, *Frankish World*, pp. xix, 185.
27. *Memory and Gender*, p. 167, n. 59. Cf. n. 30, below.
28. C. Pazdernik, '"Our most pious consort given us by God": Dissident Reactions to the Partnership of Justinian and Theodora, A.D. 525–548', *Classical Antiquity*, 13 (1994), pp. 256–81, and M. Angold, 'Procopius's Portrait of Theodora', in *Philhellen: Studies in Honour of Robert Browning*, ed. C. Constantinides (Istituto ellenico di studi bizantini e postbizantini di Venezia, Venice, 1996), pp. 21–34, are worth taking account of in addition to the works Garland cites. I am very grateful to my colleague Judith Herrin for putting me on the track of Pazdernik's paper.
29. J. France, *Victory in the East: A Military History of the First Crusade* (Cambridge University Press, Cambridge, 1994); J. Phillips (ed.), *The First Crusade: Origins and Impact* (Manchester University Press, Manchester, 1997).
30. Garland, *Byzantine Empresses*, p. 193. Garland does not cite J. Howard-Johnson, 'Anna Komnena and the *Alexiad*', in *Alexios I. Komnenos*, ed. M. Mullett and D. Smythe (Queen's University of Belfast, Belfast, 1996), pp. 260–302.
31. See J. C. Parsons (ed.), *Medieval Queenship* (St Martins Press, New York, 1993); A. Duggan (ed.), *Queens and Queenship in Medieval Europe* (Boydell Press, Woodbridge, 1997); P. Stafford, *Queen Emma and Queen Edith*; and also Stafford's earlier fundamental work, now reprinted, *Queens, Concubines and Dowagers: The King's Wife in the Early Middle Ages* (Batsford, London, 1983; repr. Leicester University Press, London, 1998).
32. Garland, *Byzantine Empresses*, p. 89.
33. Garland, *Byzantine Empresses*, p. 92.
34. Garland, *Byzantine Empresses*, p. 261, n. 83, quoting J. Herrin, 'In Search of Byzantine Women', in *Images of Women in Antiquity*, ed. A. Cameron and A. Kuhrt (Routledge, London, 1983), pp. 167–89. Garland does not cite S. Tougher, 'Byzantine Eunuchs', in *Women, Men and Eunuchs: Gender in Byzantium*, ed. L. James (Routledge, London, 1997), pp. 168–84, nor K. Hopkins, *Conquerors and Slaves* (Cambridge University Press, Cambridge, 1977), pp. 172–96, on eunuchs in imperial government in late antiquity.
35. Nelson, 'Women at the Court of Charlemagne: A Case of Monstrous Regiment?', in *Medieval Queenship*, ed. Parsons, pp. 43–61, reprinted and slightly revised in Nelson, *Frankish World*, pp. 223–42.
36. R. Beaton, 'Byzantine Historiography and Modern Greek Oral Poetry', *Byzantine and Modern Greek Studies*, 10 (1986), pp. 41–50.
37. Garland, *Byzantine Empresses*, p. 5, following A. Kazhdan and M. McCormick, 'The Social World of the Byzantine Court', in *Byzantine Court Culture from 829 to 1204*, ed. H. Maguire (Dumbarton Oaks Research Library and Collection, Washington DC, 1997), pp. 167–97. Compare the 10,000 that had Versailles bursting at the seams in 1744: N. Elias, *The Court Society* (Blackwell, Oxford, 1983), p. 80.

38. Thegan, *Gesta Hludowici Imperatoris*, c. 52, ed. E. Tremp, *Monumenta Germaniae Historica, Scriptores rerum germanicarum in usum scholarum* (Hannover, 1995), p. 244. The context is Lothar's entourage at Chalon but he had recently been forced to withdraw from Aachen.

39. Garland, *Byzantine Empresses*, p. 5.

40. Elias, *The Civilizing Process* (Blackwell, Oxford, 1994), pp. 68–70. J. Gillingham, *The English in the Twelfth Century* (Boydell Press, Woodbridge, 2000), p. xvii, observes that Elias 'recognised, but did not give enough weight to, eleventh- and twelfth-century developments'. Cf. Gillingham's thought-provoking analysis at pp. 233–58.

41. For an inspiring essay in this sense, see C. Wickham, 'Ninth-century Byzantium through Western Eyes', in *Byzantium in the Ninth Century: Dead or Alive?*, ed. L. Brubaker (Aldershot, Ashgate, 1998), pp. 245–56.

11

Gender and Sanctity
in the Middle Ages

Katherine J. Lewis

John Kitchen, *Saints' Lives and the Rhetoric of Gender: Male and Female in Merovingian Hagiography* (Oxford University Press, New York and Oxford, 1998).
Catherine M. Mooney (ed.), *Gendered Voices: Medieval Saints and their Interpreters* (University of Pennsylvania Press, Philadelphia, 1999).

The last few decades of the twentieth century witnessed a flourishing growth in scholarship revolving around hagiography and the cult of saints.[1] Ironically, a phenomenon that had traditionally been perceived of as largely indicative of medieval credulity and superstition, and of very limited use to the historian, has been successfully mined by a wide variety of scholars to uncover and explore aspects of religious, social, political, and cultural history.[2] The extent to which sanctity is socially constructed continues to be an important focus of much research. As a result the current trend in scholarship is to locate and attempt to understand hagiographic texts within the wider social and devotional contexts in which they were written and disseminated.[3] This approach has led scholars to ask questions about the practices of saints' cults and the function of saints and hagiography: for example, exploring the ways in which concepts of sanctity and the popularity of different saints change over time and from place to place, and the ways in which individual and group devotion to particular saints is governed by such factors as location, profession, age, experience and gender.

The burgeoning of scholarly interest in saints has, to some extent, grown up alongside a growing preoccupation with questions of gender, generally held to signify the social construction of biological difference between the sexes. Scholars have begun to explore the ways in which the meaning and function of both sanctity and gender are contingent on the various religious and social locations in which they operate, rather than having innate, universal meanings.[4] The study of gender and sanctity developed in the first instance as a branch of women's history, as part of ongoing attempts to uncover and understand the roles and experiences of women in the past and the influence that patriarchal structures and gender ideology had on these. This sort of approach generally involves the selection of documentary evidence drawn from particular locations or within a specific chronological range and its interpretation in terms of the practices and perceptions of sanctity and related value systems which emerge from these.[5]

Another approach which has had a great influence upon the study of gender and sanctity is application of the theories and techniques of literary criticism to hagiographic texts. Studies taking a literary approach are particularly interested in the textual construction of forms of sanctity and gender roles in hagiographic texts, and have opened up questions about the ways that gender operates both within these texts, and without, in terms of audience response. This affects how and why saints' lives were written and rewritten, the ways in which men and women read and misread them, and the possibilities for gendered, or cross-gendered identification which they offer.[6]

Until recently studies exploring gender and sanctity have largely focused on women.[7] The Lives and writings of female saints and a concomitant consideration of the ways in which female devotees related to them comprises a considerable proportion of published work on sanctity and hagiography.[8] There has been much interest in what female saints' lives can tell us about the social and cultural construction of different versions of femininity in their relationship to the female life cycle and what they reveal about the gendered expectations and proscriptions placed upon women's status, activities and conduct.[9]

More recently, scholars have begun to recognise the importance of not drawing exclusive lines of affiliation between female saints and female devotees, or between male saints and male devotees. Gendered patterns of devotion to the saints were much more fluid than this and although some consideration has been given to male devotion to female saints,[10] much more work needs to be done on women's interest in male saints. More generally male saints and the whole issue of the gendered ways in which male sanctity was constructed and maintained have received very little attention, until quite recently, when the study of masculinity (or more properly masculinities) entered the realm of medieval studies.[11] The forthcoming interdisciplinary collection

Gender and Sanctity, edited by Sam Riches and Sarah Salih considers not only the means by which male and female sanctity is gendered, but the ways in which gender performance itself is affected by sanctity.[12]

Two studies published in the late 1990s illustrate some of these trends and concerns. Both works explore, in very different ways and for very different reasons, the ways in which male and female authors write about saints and sanctity and the operation or influence of gendered concerns in their texts. John Kitchen explicitly sets out to refute the findings of those scholars who have argued that female saints' lives 'reveal a distinctive form of female sanctity which only female hagiographers managed to properly articulate'.[13] From a literary perspective, Kitchen compares and analyses the lives of both male and female saints, written by men and women, in an attempt to restore them to their original hagiographic context and understand them on their own terms, rather than with reference to more recent concerns. The essays edited by Catherine M. Mooney all explore three overarching methodological concerns relating to sanctity and gender: how far is it possible to distinguish the voices of female saints from those of their interpreters? Are the voices which emerge from the texts under consideration gendered? To what extent are portrayals of sanctity influenced not so much by gender as by genre?[14] Like Kitchen, the essays all consider (in some form) both male and female authored texts and constructions of sanctity, but conversely this study has its roots very much within the tradition of scholarship on female sanctity against which Kitchen sets himself and his work.[15]

Kitchen positions his study of Merovingian hagiography[16] in opposition to those which have 'started with the question of the historical saint', as part of a social historical agenda to uncover a specifically female experience of sanctity, and instead seeks 'to investigate the hagiographic literature as hagiographic literature'.[17] His method is to compare the accounts of male saints written by male authors with the account of female saints written by the same authors, and then to compare these with the account of a female saint written by a female author.[18] This is how the book proceeds, examining first the male author Venantius Fortunatus's prose biographies of male saints, and the lives contained in Gregory of Tours's *Liber Vitae Patrem*, then turning to consider male-authored lives of female saints – Fortunatus's Life of St Monegund and Gregory's Life of St Radegund – before finally turning to the nun Baudonivia's Life of St Radegund. Through the medium of philology Kitchen questions how far these depictions of male and female saints are attributable to such factors as the kinds of rhetorical strategies which hagiographers of the period employed, rather than being purely governed by issues of gender.[19]

The burgeoning scholarly interest in masculinities recognises that representations of men need to be analysed and theorised. This prevents men/male remaining static, universal categories, and allows us to approach representations of women with a more nuanced sense of the ways in which binary gender identities are constituted and performed in opposition to each other. In this respect Kitchen's approach is quite valid, one that can explore claims about the essentially female/feminine nature of certain experiences or tropes within hagiography from an informed position, and avoid the accusation of special pleading. Indeed, Kitchen makes some interesting observations about Baudonivia's depiction of Radegund which question the alleged tendency for female authors to construct female saints largely within a register of maternal imagery, stressing their caring, nurturing and charitable traits.[20]

At the end of his detailed analysis of a wealth of hagiographic materials, Kitchen ultimately concludes that the depiction of female sanctity and the construction of sanctity more widely within these texts has very little to do with gender or gender concerns at all.[21] Hagiographic conventions undoubtedly play an important role in the ways in which both male and female saints are represented, but Kitchen privileges them to such an extent that he denies that gender has any significant role in the depictions of the saints under consideration. Part of the problem lies in his apparent understanding and use of the term 'gender'. It is used without definition or discussion throughout the book as if it had some intrinsic, self-evident meaning, within both a medieval and a modern critical context.[22] It becomes apparent that for Kitchen's purposes 'gender' relates exclusively to women, and a scholarly concern with gender/gender issues signifies an interest in women.[23] As has already been noted, the study of gender and history has often concerned itself almost exclusively with women, and to some extent Kitchen's approach here has presumably been determined in part by this emphasis in the scholarship which he critiques.

However, much more problematic is Kitchen's use of the term in relation to the ways in which the writers are seen to be bringing 'the issue of gender to the forefront of their writing'.[24] In this context gender appears to mean the authors merely drawing attention to the fact that their subjects are female; 'modifications due to gender' apparently only come into play in texts describing female saints.[25] Kitchen goes so far as to argue that having 'problematised gender'[26] in the prefaces to their respective lives of female saints, Fortunatus and Gregory never again 'dwell' on gender in these texts.[27] This conclusion is reached despite the fact that both the male and female lives discussed include descriptions of the young saints' childhood, the very life cycle stage in which their gender becomes enshrined in their differing upbringing.[28] These hagiographic narratives outline the frequently dichotomous modes of conduct, roles and accomplishments which were deemed appropriate to boys and girls in their preparation for adulthood and, ultimately, sanctity.[29]

Kitchen's attempt to erase the differences between male and female saints, to conceptualise both in terms of the non-gender-specific paradigm of 'the holy person',[30] rests on the premise that 'gender' was of no concern to the male and female authors under consideration, indeed, that it has been imposed on these texts by the subjective modern audience.[31] However, these saints, as well as the men and women who wrote and read their lives, lived within settings which did assign specific meanings (social, cultural, ideological and other) to male and female and to being man or woman. It is extremely important to understand saints' lives on their own terms within the context of hagio-literary trope and convention.[32] However, their composition was not simply a literary or rhetorical exercise, for these saints' lives may have been intended to provide an example of piety, or wider forms of social behaviour, to a particular audience, to further the agenda of a certain group or institution or structure monastic piety in specific ways. Hagiographic texts have no one stable meaning, then or now, and in order to uncover their specific agenda with respect to women, men and gender, it is often helpful to consider them in terms of the wider patterns and practices of belief and devotion within which they were composed and circulated.

Throughout his revisionist polemic, Kitchen attacks what he frequently refers to as 'the current scholarship', but the works against which he sets himself do not really merit this epithet, having being written in the 1980s and early 1990s.[33] Much more representative of the ways in which scholarship on female saints and sanctity more generally has developed and of actual current approaches and concerns is Mooney's collection *Gendered Voices: Medieval Saints and their Interpreters*.[34] The nuanced ways in which the essays making up the book approach the issues of female sanctity and its representation are drawn together in Mooney's lucid introduction, which provides a methodological frame for the collection as a whole.[35] Although none of the essays deals with Merovingian hagiography, the collection can be seen to answer many of the criticisms that Kitchen has for studies that seek to identify intrinsically female aspects to sanctity. Comparison between the two works in this respect is also appropriate because both are concerned with the issue of the different perceptions that female and male writers may have of female sanctity.[36] All of the essays deal with women who have left behind some 'vestiges of their voices or personal agency' in texts, either ones that they wrote themselves, or ones in which their words have been incorporated (or claimed to have been so) by male writers.[37] Although the focus is on female saints, the question of gender (in particular of gendered voices and identities) is explored with reference both to women and to the men who wrote about them.

Many common themes and concerns emerge from the collection as whole. Mooney draws these together in her introduction describing the ways in which the essays all seek to answer 'three interrelated methodological questions that face scholars of medieval sanctity', revolving around questions of gender, voice and genre.[38] The subjects in question are Hildegard of Bingen, Elisabeth of Schonau, Clare of Assisi, Beatrice of Nazareth, Christine of Stommeln, Henry Suso, Catherine of Siena and Dorothea of Montau. Several of these have already formed the basis for a great deal of scholarship, upon which these essays build by presenting studies which are focused on a very specific text or small corpus of texts. For example, in her comparison of the ways in which Hildegard of Bingen's voice and persona were textually transformed, Barbara Newman examines a first-person autobiographical memoir written by Hildegard, the *vitae* written by Gottfried of St Disibod and Theodoric of Echternach and two later medieval versions of her life. Taking into account the circumstances of each text's composition and concurrent developments in spirituality, Newman demonstrates the ways in which Hildegard's sanctity is remade by her male interpreters. The image of the seer/prophet which emerges from her own writings is deliberately played down by them; she is presented as a less formidable Mother of Mystics to the many other female visionaries who became active in the thirteenth century in particular.[39]

This sense of the male author's anxiety about his female subject and the need to circumscribe her textual subjectivity by rendering her a safe exemplar of feminine spirituality is a theme throughout the collection. Male authors frequently present themselves as mere translators, converting the words and lives of their female subjects into Latin. However, Raymond of Capua's *Vita* of Catherine of Siena frequently depicts quite a different figure from the Catherine who emerges from her own letters. Karen Scott's comparison of the two indicates the ways in which Raymond's hagiographic agenda and spiritual theology led him to emphasise her call to the apostolate and her mystical suffering rather than the practicalities of the apostolate itself, which is Catherine's own concern.[40] Thus Raymond's Catherine, like the later medieval Hildegard, loses some of her individuality and becomes a more generalised figure of feminine piety.

Dyan Elliott also traces a process of textual construction and reconstruction in her study of the writings about Dorothea of Montau produced by John Marienwerder in the 1390s.[41] John was concerned to establish Dorothea as a saint with texts in which she herself had collaborated and Elliott examines the ways in which his hagiographic agenda gave form to mystical experiences which had, until the intervention of the male author, lacked any kind of fixed meaning. Similarly Anne Clark explores the ways in which Elisabeth of Schonau's brother Ekbert recorded her visions as well as their circumstances and played a key role in locating his sister within the textual paradigm of the female visionary.[42]

Catherine Mooney's own essay compares the few extant writings of Clare of Assisi with the many written about her, both in the medieval period, to establish her sanctity, and the more recent scholarly corpus.[43] Mooney demonstrates the powerful influence that the accepted register of gendered language which was used to describe female saints continues to have over our interpretation of them and their experiences. Clare was presented in her *Vita* as a 'feminine' figure imitating Mary, fitting in with contemporary opinion about the interests of female visionaries and rendering her a convenient mirror image to St Francis who imitates Christ. This continues to be the way in which she is perceived by some more recent commentators, despite the evidence of her own writings which indicates that she too took Christ as her primary model. Despite the powerful influence exerted over the experiences of female saints and the ways in which they have been enshrined for us within hagiographic texts, there were instances in which these women could and did resist the forms of female religiosity and subjectivity prescribed for them.

In order to facilitate discussion about these and other dichotomies between self-perception, textual presentation and subsequent interpretation (both medieval and modern), the collection as a whole proceeds with a keen appreciation of the settings in which saints' lives, as well as related texts such as letters, poems, papal bulls and theological treatises were composed and circulated. In this respect, the collection shows the sort of sensitivity to the nature and demands of hagiographic literature that Kitchen highlights in his study.[44] But here this information is considered alongside the lives and experiences of both saints and their interpreters. This approach accounts for the understandings and constructions of sanctity which emerge in their writings. It also demonstrates in rigorously defined ways the influence of their own gender identity as men or women upon their texts, while taking other factors such as literary trope and shifts in the depiction of female sanctity into account as well. In this way it is possible for the eight contributors to consider the ways in which a wide range of influences underpin particular representations of female sanctity constructed by both men and women.

As a whole the collection presents a stimulating body of scholarship illuminating the fruitful potential which the study of saints offers to historians in general, and to historians interested in gender and gender identity in particular. By not regarding 'men' and 'women' purely as antithetical or dichotomous categories and recognising the vast 'common heritage shared by female saints with their male interpreters', this collection is able to demonstrate in precise terms the divergent emphases that do exist between male and female accounts of female sanctity.[45]

....

Notes

1. Hagiography is here used in a wide sense as the study of the entire corpus of hagiographic texts, encompassing the written/visual lives of saints, as well as materials relating to their relics, posthumous miracles, canonisation and so on.

2. Seminal works in the development of this scholarship are Peter Brown, *The Cult of the Saints: Its Rise and Function in Latin Christianity* (Chicago University Press, Chicago and London, 1981); Andrez Vauchez, *La Sainteté en Occident aux derniers siècles du moyen age d'après les procès de canonisation et les documents hagiographiques* (École

française de Rome, Rome, 1981; second edition 1987), now translated into English by Jean Birrell as *Sainthood in the Later Middle Ages* (Cambridge University Press, Cambridge, 1997); Donald Weinstein and Rudolph M. Bell, *Saints and Society: The Two Worlds of Western Christendom, 1000–1700* (University of Chicago Press, Chicago and London, 1982); Steven Wilson (ed.), *Saints and their Cults: Studies in Religious Sociology, Folklore and History* (Cambridge University Press, Cambridge, 1983); and the work of Caroline Walker Bynum, see below, note 4. There is no general survey published in English of the history, study and use of hagiography, but Thomas Head's online essays at http://orb.rhodes.edu/encyclop/religion/hagiography/hagindex.html provide an invaluable introductory guide to hagiographic scholarship and research.

3. Examples of this approach are provided by Kathleen Ashley and Pamela Sheingorn (eds), *Interpreting Cultural Symbols: Saint Anne in Late Medieval Society* (University of Georgia Press, Athens and London, 1990); Renate Blumenfeld-Kosinski and Timea Szell (eds), *Images of Sainthood in Medieval Europe* (Cornell University Press, Ithaca and London, 1991).

4. The work of Caroline Walker Bynum has been extremely influential in this field: *Holy Feast and Holy Fast: The Religious Significance of Food to Medieval Women* (University of California Press, Berkley, 1987); *Fragmentation and Redemption: Essays on Gender and the Human Body in Medieval Religion* (Zone, New York, 1992). For a critique of her approach in *Holy Feast and Holy Fast*, see Kathleen Biddick, 'Genders, Bodies, Borders: Technologies of the Invisible', in *Studying Medieval Women: Sex, Gender, Feminism*, ed. Nancy F. Partner (The Medieval Academy of America, Cambridge, MA, 1993), pp. 87–116.

5. Katherine J. Lewis, *The Cult of St Katherine of Alexandria in Late Medieval England* (Boydell and Brewer, Woodbridge, 2000) provides an example of this sort of approach.

6. Jocelyn Wogan-Browne's work on female saints' lives has led the field in this respect: 'Saints' Lives and the Female Reader', *Forum for Modern Language Studies* 37 (1991), pp. 314–32; 'The Virgin's Tale', in *Feminist Readings in Middle English Literature: The Wife of Bath and All Her Sect*, ed. Ruth Evans and Lesley Johnson (Routledge, London and New York, 1994).

7. This is true of the study of gender and history more widely.

8. For example Elizabeth Petroff (ed.), *Medieval Women's Visionary Literature* (Oxford University Press, Oxford, 1986); Bridget Cazelles, *The Lady as Saint: A Collection of French Hagiographic Romances of the Thirteenth Century* (University of Pennsylvania Press, Philadelphia, 1991); *Karen A. Winstead, Virgin Martyrs: Legends of Sainthood in Late Medieval England* (Cornell University Press, Ithaca and London, 1997); works by Bynum and Wogan-Browne already cited. Karen Winstead's online bibliography of recent work on Middle English hagiography illustrates this trend very well: http://www.cohums. ohio-state.edu/english/People/Winstead.2/hagiogbiblio.html.

9. Winstead, *Virgin Martyrs*, pp. 112–46; Katherine J. Lewis, 'Model girls? Virgin Martyrs and the Training of Young Women in Late Medieval England', in *Young Medieval Women*, ed Katherine J. Lewis, Noël James Menuge and Kim M. Phillips (Sutton Publishing, Stroud, 1999), pp. 25–46; Kim M. Phillips, 'Desiring Virgins: Maidens, Martyrs and Femininity in Late Medieval England', in *Youth in the Middle Ages*, ed. P. J. P. Goldberg and Felicity Riddy (Boydell and Brewer, Woodbridge, forthcoming).

10. Both Winstead and Lewis have considered male as well as female interest in and devotion to virgin martyr saints.

11. Claire Lees (ed.), *Medieval Masculinities: Regarding Men in the Middle Ages* (Garland, Minneapolis, 1995); Dawn Hadley, *Masculinity in Medieval Europe* (Routledge, London and New York, 1999).

12. Sam Riches and Sarah Salih, *Gender and Sanctity* (under negotiation).

13. John Kitchen, *Saints' Lives and the Rhetoric of Gender: Male and Female in Merovingian Hagiography* (Oxford University Press, New York and Oxford, 1998). Quote from dust-jacket.

14. Catherine M. Mooney (ed.), *Gendered Voices: Medieval Saints and their Interpreters* (University of Pennsylvania Press, Philadelphia, 1999), pp. 1–4.

15. The fact that Mooney's collection is prefaced by Caroline Walker Bynum, and the substance of the preface itself, makes this very clear, *Gendered Voices*, pp. ix–xi.

16. In fact, despite the range suggested by the book's title Kitchen focuses on a very specific selection from this large corpus, as will be seen. Joseph-Claude Poulin's review of the book expands on this criticism: *The Medieval Review* 5 April 1999: http://www.hti. umich.edu/b/bmr/tmr.html

17. Kitchen, *Saints' Lives*, p. 15. The whole of chapter 1 contains an articulation and justification of his methodology, pp. 1–22. While stating that 'a great debt' is owed to Suzanne Wemple and Jo Ann McNamara for bringing hitherto unknown texts to scholarly attention (*Saints' Lives*, p. 13), they are presented as representative of what Kitchen holds to be a flawed approach to Merovingian hagiography, and, by implication, to hagiography more widely.

18. *Saints' Lives*, p. 18.

19. *Saints' Lives*, p. 17.

20. *Saints' Lives*, pp. 150–52.

21. *Saints' Lives*, pp. 154–60 for his conclusion, in particular pp. 156–7.

22. It should be noted that Kitchen quite explicitly does not engage with what he refers to as 'the latest critical approaches', *Saints' Lives*, p. 16, see also p. 21.

23. For example, 'gender' as an index term refers only to those parts of the book which deal with representations of female saints. The term 'masculinity' is used only with reference to female saints displaying what Kitchen identifies as 'manly' traits; for example, *Saints' Lives*, pp. 125–6.

24. *Saints' Lives*, p. 101.

25. *Saints' Lives*, pp. 101–4, quote from p. 104.

26. *Saints' Lives*, p. 104, p. 113, here the phrase is used to mean simply that the authors make mention of the fact that their subjects are female.

27. *Saints' Lives*, p. 113, p. 122.

28. See pp. 26–31, 117 for discussion of passages relating to the childhood of saints. On p. 133, within the context of a brief discussion on cross-dressing and castrated saints, Kitchen does make reference to 'the conventional roles of gender as socially defined', but the social definition of gender roles does not feature in his analysis overall.

29. For a discussion of recent approaches to medieval childhood and youth, see Kim M. Phillips's introduction to Lewis, James Menuge and Phillips, *Young Medieval Women*, pp. xi–xiii. The collection as a whole considers the importance of gender ideology to the representation and experience of young women.

30. Having used this term in an apparently gender neutral way (*Saints' Lives*, p. 25), 'the holy person is, as a rule, not made, but born', Kitchen finishes the sentence 'sometimes even with a tonsure'.

31. See, for example, *Saints' Lives*, p. 151, p. 157.

32. A rather more nuanced literary gender analysis of Merovingian hagiography is provided by Giselle de Nie, '"Consciousness fecund through God": From Male Fighter to Spiritual Bride-Mother in Late Antique Female spirituality', in *Sanctity and Motherhood: Essays on Holy Mothers in the Middle Ages*, ed. Anneke B. Mulder-Bakker (Garland, New York, 1995), pp. 101–61

33. As noted above, Kitchen sets himself against the works of Wemple and McNamara – the most recent work by either cited in the bibliography is 1996, McNamara's *Sisters in Arms: Catholic Nuns through Two Millennia* (Harvard University Press, Cambridge, MA) the others listed represent the (in some cases much) earlier scholarship of both.

34. Bynum's foreword indicates the ways in which the book grows out of previous studies of and approaches to saints (*Gendered Voices*, pp. ix–xi).

35. *Gendered Voices*, pp. 1–15,

36. As Mooney notes, the collection explores 'whether holy women qua holy women per-
     ceived and represented their sanctity in ways significantly different from the ways their
     male contemporaries perceived and represented female sanctity', *Gendered Voices*, p. 2.

37. *Gendered Voices*, pp. 3–4.

38. *Gendered Voices*, pp. 2–3.

39. Barbara Newman, 'Hildegard and her hagiographers: The remaking of female sainthood',
     Gendered Voices, pp. 16–34.

40. Karen Scott, 'Mystical Death, Bodily Death: Catherine of Siena and Raymond of Capua
     on the Mystic's Encounter with God', *Gendered Voices*, pp. 136–67.

41. Dyan Elliott, 'Authorizing a Life: the Collaboration of Dorothea of Montau and John
     Marienwerder', *Gendered Voices*, pp. 168–91.

42. Anne L. Clark, 'Holy Woman or Unworthy Vessel? The Representations of Elisabeth of
     Schonau', *Gendered Voices*, pp. 35–51.

43. Catherine M. Mooney, '*Imitatio Christi or Imitatio Mariae?* Clare of Assisi and her Inter-
     preters', *Gendered Voices*, pp. 52–77.

44. *Gendered Voices*, pp. 6–9 for Mooney's discussion of the ways in which the essays examine
     textual factors in hagiographic accounts about medieval women.

45. *Gendered Voices*, pp. 9–15, quote from p. 9.

12

Gendering the Black Death: Women in Later Medieval England

S. H. Rigby

Mavis E. Mate, *Daughters, Wives and Widows after the Black Death: Women in Sussex, 1350–1535* (Boydell, Woodbridge, 1998).

A simplistic view of historical research would see it as a two-stage process in which the gathering of information is then followed by synthesis and generalisation. In fact, the study of medieval women over the last two decades has taken exactly the opposite path: from an initial handful of Europe-wide surveys of women of all classes, covering centuries of medieval history,[1] it has now burgeoned into a multiplicity of empirically based, local case-studies. Nevertheless, despite all the important work now appearing on medieval women, it is a salutary reminder of just how much still remains to be done that Mavis E. Mate's *Daughters, Wives and Widows after the Black Death: Women in Sussex, 1350–1535* is the first detailed study of how 'economic and legal changes in the post-Black Death period affected women in rural, southern England' (p. 1). Mate's earlier research on England in the fourteenth and fifteenth centuries has put her in the front rank of medieval economic historians and her latest work has much to offer to specialists in the field. However, in order to understand and assess her work, we need first to examine the prior debate about the condition of women in the later middle ages, a debate to which her views are, in many ways, a response.

It has been said that the problem of balancing structure and agency lies at the heart of all historical and sociological writing[2] and, undoubtedly, this issue has been central to many of the debates about the social position of women in the middle ages. Thus, whilst some historians have emphasised the restrictions imposed on women by the patriarchal structure of medieval social relations,[3] others, perhaps in reaction to historians' traditional neglect of women's contribution to medieval life, have tended to stress women's agency, initiative and achievements.[4] For instance, in her pioneering work, Eileen Power argued that there was an inverse correlation between, on the one hand, medieval women's class position and, on the other, the degree of freedom they enjoyed as women, so that peasant women enjoyed 'greater equality and perhaps even greater self-respect' than women of higher estate.[5] Yet, more recently, Jennifer Ward has shown how even women of the nobility could themselves enjoy authority and responsibility despite the social restrictions which confronted them.[6]

Historians are, by training, inclined to look for historical specificity, a predisposition which encourages them to search for historical change. Thus, whereas the accusations made against women by medieval misogynists were repeated over and over, for century after century (as in the case of the *topoi* employed in Chaucer's satire of the Wife of Bath[7]), a number of historians have argued that the real opportunities open to women altered over the course of the medieval period under the pressure of demographic, economic, social, political, legal, religious and cultural change. Whereas some literary critics have been tempted to see a congruence between women's social position and their representation in misogynist intellectual and literary discourses,[8] historians are more likely to identify a divergence between the relatively unchanging dominant intellectual discourses about women and the development of women's actual social position, a divergence similar to that found in other areas of medieval social life.[9]

In particular, recent studies have tended to argue that the post-plague period was one in which the social 'exclusion'[10] experienced by Englishwomen was to some degree moderated and their social and economic opportunities increased. The plague first arrived in England in the summer of 1348 and may have killed off 45 per cent of the population within a year. By the time of the poll tax of 1377, England's population, at around 2.75 million, was only about half of its pre-plague level. The continued high mortality of the late medieval period meant that by the 1520s, England's population may have been 2.25 million or less.[11] Such high mortality rates resulted in individual social mobility, as people were able to acquire the land, jobs and social positions of those who had died.[12] More generally, population decline meant a social redistribution of wealth, as labourers benefited from high wages and low food prices, whilst peasants had access to land at a low rent and were able to use the shortage of tenants to bring an end to manorial impositions and restrictions associated with villeinage.[13]

For many historians, most notably Jeremy Goldberg, women's gains were particularly marked in this period. As tenants, women were, in an age of high mortality and low male replacement rates, now more likely to acquire land as heiresses and by their widow's right of dower. As labourers, women shared in the general rise in real wages and, given the types of work in which they were most likely to be employed, should have benefited from the disproportionate rise in the wages of the unskilled and the reduction in wage differentials. With skilled labour in short supply, women could find employment in jobs which had once been the preserve of men, as smiths, tanners, carpenters, tilers and so on. In the post-plague age of labour mobility, women may have been particularly attracted to the towns as servants and as workers in the expanding textile industry and in the industries whose products were, in an age of high wages and cheap food, in increasing demand. The evidence of the poll taxes suggests a ratio of 90–95 men per 100 women in the towns. In an age of labour shortage, householders may have attempted to guarantee themselves a supply of labour by the practice, familiar from the sixteenth century, of using resident 'servants', often young unmarried men and women. It is possible that the effect of these trends was to produce deferred marriage for women and a reduction in marriage and fertility rates.[14] Furthermore, if women have been seen as enjoying 'a remarkably high degree of economic independence'[15] in this period, their status may also have improved in other spheres of late medieval life. For instance, in the realm of popular piety, K. L. French has argued that the development of lay activity within the parish in the later middle ages inadvertently enlarged the space for women's social agency.[16] We are accustomed to think of the later middle ages as the 'golden age of the bacillus' or, because of the consequent labour shortage, as the 'golden age of the labourer'. Now, we are encouraged to think of this period as, in the words of Caroline Barron's study of late medieval London, a 'golden age' for women.[17]

This new approach to late medieval economic change has turned the received wisdom of Malthusian demographic theory on its head. Malthusians have traditionally assumed an automatic correlation between living standards and levels of fertility, with high living standards leading to earlier marriage, higher fertility rates and population growth. By contrast, those who argue that high wages resulted in deferred marriage would see the late medieval period as one in which, in addition to high mortality rates, there was actually a decline in the fertility rate. Humans do not necessarily respond in some mechanical Pavlovian fashion to a particular situation: subjective agency must also be allowed a role, an agency which means that late medieval people could perhaps have adopted what was, by Malthusian standards, a 'perverse' response to rising living standards. Late medieval England may therefore have possessed Hajnal's 'Western European' marriage pattern,[18] one characterised by relatively low fertility produced by late marriage (as in sixteenth-century England, when the average age of marriage was 27–28 for men and 25–26 for women) and by a high proportion of women never marrying (about 10 per cent in the sixteenth century).[19]

The problem for late medieval women was that, since the social position of any particular individual is the product of the meeting point of many different axes or dimensions of inequality,[20] there was no reason why a reduction of the exclusion they experienced in one dimension of social inequality (such as economic opportunities) would necessarily result in corresponding gains in other spheres of their lives (such as political power). As in other pre-industrial societies, it becomes extremely difficult to speak of '*the* status of women' in medieval England when women's status was characterised by a unevenness and inconsistency between the different areas of social life.[21] Thus, when women's position came under threat once more, whether through economic recession and a slump in demand in the mid to late fifteenth century or through an increase in the supply of labour in the late fifteenth or sixteenth century, the fact that their economic gains had not been accompanied by a growth of their legal rights or political power meant that they were singularly ill-equipped to defend themselves. Any optimism about women's gains in the later middle ages must therefore be strictly qualified since, as Goldberg puts it, in the long term, society became 'more polarised' and 'more patriarchal' as 'women were more clearly subordinated to men'.[22] Thus, rather than presenting pre-industrial society in terms of a unilinear growth or decline of women's social exclusion, this new approach emphasises how women's wealth, status and power could fluctuate between and within the late medieval and early modern periods.

The great attraction of this perspective is that instead of simply providing us with yet more descriptive (although extremely valuable) information about female work, it provides a coherent model in which women's changing social position and agency come to have a key role in *explaining* change within the economy as a whole. Nevertheless, despite its attractions, this model of late medieval social change faces a number of challenges. The first comes from those such as Mark Bailey who remind us how problematic any deductions about changes in the age of marriage and in fertility rates must be in the era before the introduction of parish registers of births, marriages and deaths.[23] The second comes from Judith Bennett, who offers a rather different interpretation of women's social history, one which emphasises long-term continuity, rather than change, within late medieval and early modern society. Whilst a number of social, intellectual and cultural historians have pessimistically seen the early modern period as one of worsening social status and opportunities for women,[24] Bennett offers a 'neo-pessimistic' interpretation of the late medieval period itself, one which stresses that, even during the late medieval labour shortage, women 'tended to work in low-skilled, low-status, low-paid jobs, and they also tended to be intermittent workers, jumping from job to job or juggling several tasks at once. This was true in 1300, and it remained true in 1700'.[25]

Mate's study of women within the aristocracy, gentry, peasant and labouring classes, and urban society of late medieval Sussex is the latest instalment of this debate. Her work begins by emphasising the specificities of her subject. Firstly, she divides the late medieval period into three separate sub-periods: the immediate post-Black Death population decline; a mid fifteenth-century agricultural, commercial, industrial and monetary recession; and a late fifteenth-century economic revival. Secondly, she stresses the local peculiarities, even within sub-regions of Sussex, which could affect women's social opportunities. Economic trends could have a very different impact on long-settled coastal Sussex, where agriculture was carried out in severalty, from that on the sheep-rearing and common-field agriculture of the South Downs chalklands (where land was inherited by the youngest son or daughter, rather than being passed on through primogeniture or division between heiresses) or on the woodland economy of the High Weald, with its active land market and low entry-fines.

Mate cautions against any 'simple tale of benefit or loss' for women in this period: 'conditions that helped some women, hurt others' (p. 9). Nevertheless, overall, her analysis lends weighty support to the 'pessimistic', rather than the 'golden age', view of late medieval women's history. Whilst Goldberg has seen women as choosing to remain single because of the employment opportunities open to them, Mate cautions against an inflated view of women's employment chances and argues that even those women who did remain single could do so because of skewed sex ratios rather than through any personal preference. In the towns of Sussex (unlike London), there is no evidence that women were ever formally apprenticed and, even in the late medieval period, female employment was confined to a rather narrow range of low-pay, low-status jobs. In the countryside, women's paid work was often irregular and usually low-paid: on the lords' demesnes, dairy-work was a female preserve but dairy managers were always male. The centralisation of the brewing trade into the hands of a small number of professional brewers who produced on a relatively capital- and labour-intensive basis also meant a reduction in the chances for women to earn money by selling their surplus domestic production. Women's work was vital to the household, but economic centrality did not bring a commensurate social power or legal rights and the ideology of female subordination remained firmly in place. Mate's analysis also challenges the view that late medieval England had passed to a regime of late marriage and low fertility. She invokes the 1379 poll tax returns to question 'whether the "Northwest European" marriage system existed in much of rural Sussex in the late fourteenth century' (p. 29), stressing that it is impossible to say whether the number of female servants increased in the post-Black Death period or whether their working conditions were so much better that it was worth their turning down offers of marriage. As in classical Malthusian theory, Mate suggests that it was the contracting economic opportunities and declining demand of the mid and late fifteenth century that were most likely to produce deferred marriage, rather than the labour shortage that followed the Black Death (p. 48).

Neither, for Mate, did the decline in the male replacement rate and consequent increase in the number of female heirs mean that women enjoyed any more power, since heiresses were particularly likely to marry at an early age, at which point they surrendered most of their property rights for life to their husbands. Widows may even have experienced an actual decline in their rights in this period. For customary land, a widow could, in theory, acquire a third of her husband's land by right of 'free-bench'. However, since this right often applied only to land which her husband had inherited and which he possessed at the time of his death, the existence, at least in the Weald, of an active *inter-vivos* land market meant that many women came to have no legal claim to much of their husband's property. The growing practice of granting land to feoffees could also deprive women of their common-law right of dower, so that even when, as was often the case, a widow was granted a third or more of the family estate, she was now dependent upon her husband's good will for this land rather than acquiring it by legal right. The rights of women who held property on a joint tenure with their husbands were more secure – but only a minority of women acquired land in this way (p. 85).

Mate stresses how economic class influenced every aspect of a woman's life, from her food, clothing and housing to her age of marriage and freedom in choosing a spouse. Such huge differences between women, even between women of the upper and the lower nobilities, meant that there was no possibility for a 'common consciousness' or group identity to emerge amongst women (p. 192). Indeed, even women's common legal subordination to their husbands was experienced in different ways by the women of different classes (p. 197). Nevertheless, objectively, all women 'shared certain experiences in common' (p. 182), from childbirth, childcare and responsibility for running the household to common legal disabilities and inequalities. Mate even claims that, for women, the disabilities and experiences they shared were, at least in the sense that they 'combined to prevent any transformation of women's status', 'more fundamental' than those of class (p. 8).

Covering women from all classes, from the peerage to wage-labourers, exploring both town and country, and stressing both local specificity and general relevance, Mate's study will be welcomed by anyone interested in the history of medieval women. It not only offers much new information and historical interpretation but, in its controversial claims, will itself provoke further research. For example, Mate stresses the tendency for widows to remarry and so criticises the prevailing orthodoxy that widowhood provided 'the best years of a woman's life in the late middle ages'. Escaping the legal subordination of marriage may not have been the priority of most women: 'many widows, whatever their age, might well have preferred to find another partner, rather than enjoying the independence of widowhood' (pp. 131–3). Yet, inevitably in a work of this scope, all readers will find areas of disagreement. For instance, Jane Whittle has already criticised the tendency for the book's pessimism to become rather unrelenting[26] (and occasionally, one might add, unfalsifiable). Thus, life 'could be bleak for widows with limited resources' (p. 115) but, on the other hand, yeomen's wives suffered when their husbands took on too much land (p. 197); wives 'may not always have been able to find as much work as they would have liked' (p. 58) but, when they did, such work was not an unalloyed blessing, since it was carried out 'on top of their regular domestic tasks' (p. 73).

Yet perhaps the biggest problem is one readily acknowledged by Mate herself: the fact that the surviving sources offer so little information with which to answer the kinds of questions in which we as historians are now interested. Thus we frequently encounter sentences such as 'how many Sussex marriages involved a significant disparity in ages between spouses is impossible to say' (p. 35) or the admission that although women of the early sixteenth century may have married at a later age than those of a century before, 'without proof, one cannot say for sure' (p. 75). As a result, the reality of social life in late medieval Sussex is often inferred, frequently by analogy with elsewhere. We are told that 'although there is little direct evidence' about the economic role of women in the town of Lewes, 'there is every reason to believe' that it would have been like that of women in other small towns. Women in Lewes therefore 'probably' worked in low-paid jobs, were 'likely' to have been in domestic service, victualling and textiles, were 'probably', as at York, employed by dyers, 'may' have been employed by alien hatters, were 'unlikely' to have equalled the wages paid to men, 'must have' worked as independent traders and 'may' also have combined such trades with spinning and carding (p. 43). When historical reality can be deduced in this way, Mate's own stress on local specificity tends to be undermined.

Furthermore, if there is little evidence which would allow us even to describe late medieval social conditions, the absence of personal records such as the *Paston Letters* means that any claims about affective relations and subjective experiences become even more conjectural. For example, in a case concerning three orphans, Mate deduces that 'if their paternal grandfather or uncles were still alive, they surely visited and took an interest in the children' (p. 108). Similarly we are told that when young noblewomen married men they scarcely knew, they 'probably' took their own servants with them but 'may' still have been lonely, frightened and glad of the opportunity to visit friends and relatives (pp. 162–3). At times, a rather loaded vocabulary is employed: when widows' rights are challenged, it is a sign that they are being 'harassed' but when widows challenge the rights of others, this is an instance of their 'determination and independence' (p. 112). Finally, we are frequently told what happened to individual women but it is not always clear that such things happened *because* they were women. For instance, a number of peasant women can be shown anecdotally to have concentrated on pastoral husbandry, but it is never really established whether or not they were more likely to be involved in such activities than men were.

In a narrow perspective, medievalists may be divided on whether they find Goldberg and Barron's optimism or Bennett and Mate's pessimism more persuasive as an account of women's position in the century after the Black Death. In a broader perspective, the new generation of archivally based studies which these historians represent is a sign that women's history has now moved firmly into the mainstream of medieval historiography. Mate's monograph is a welcome contribution to this literature and, despite its problems (most of which flow from the paucity of sources available to us rather than from any failing on Mate's own part), *Daughters, Wives and Widows after the Black Death* will be compulsory reading for all medieval social and economic historians.

Notes

1. S. Shahar, *The Fourth Estate: A History of Women in the Middle Ages* (Methuen, London, 1983) is one of the best of such surveys; for an excellent survey of women in England, see H. Leyser, *Medieval Women: A Social History of Women in England 450–1500* (Weidenfeld and Nicolson, London, 1995).

2. P. Abrams, *Historical Sociology* (Open Books, Shepton Mallet, 1982), p. xiii.

3. M. Kowaleski and J. M. Bennett, 'Crafts, Gilds and Women in the Middle Ages: Fifty Years after Marian K. Dale', *Signs*, 14 (1989), p. 488.

4. A. Diamond, 'Chaucer's Women and Women's Chaucer', in *The Authority of Experience: Essays in Feminist Criticism*, ed. A. Diamond and L. R. Edwards (University of Massachusetts Press, Amherst, 1977), p. 61.

5. E. Power, 'The Position of Women', in *The Legacy of the Middle Ages*, ed. C. G. Crump and E. F. Jacob (Clarendon, Oxford, 1926), pp. 428–9; E. Power, *Medieval Women* (Cambridge University Press, Cambridge, 1981), pp. 74–5.

6. J. C. Ward, *English Noblewomen in the Later Middle Ages* (Longman, London, 1992) pp. 164–70; see also P. Payne and C. M. Barron, 'The Letters and Life of Elizabeth Despenser, Lady Zouche (d. 1408)', *Nottingham Medieval Studies*, 41 (1997), p. 142.

7. S. H. Rigby, *Chaucer in Context: Society, Allegory and Gender* (Manchester University Press, Manchester, 1996), pp. 137–51; S. H. Rigby, 'The Wife of Bath and the Medieval Case for Women', *Chaucer Review*, forthcoming.

8. See, for instance, S. Crane, *Gender and Romance in Chaucer's Canterbury Tales* (Princeton University Press, Princeton, 1994), pp. 7, 58–9.

9. M. McIntosh, 'Finding Language for Misconduct: Jurors in Fifteenth-century Local Courts', in *Bodies and Disciplines: Intersections of Literature and History in Fifteenth-Century England*, ed. B. A. Hanawalt and D. Wallace (University of Minnesota Press,

Minneapolis, 1996), pp. 87–8; C. W. Bynum, *Fragmentation and Redemption: Essays on Gender and the Human Body in Medieval Religion* (Zone Books, New York, 1992), p. 152.

10. For the use of social 'exclusion' and 'closure' as a means of understanding gender and other social inequalities, see S. H. Rigby, 'Approaches to Pre-industrial Social Structure', in *Orders and Hierarchies in Late Medieval and Renaissance Europe*, ed. J. H. Denton (Macmillan, Basingstoke, 1999), pp. 6–25.

11. J. Hatcher, *Plague, Population and the English Economy, 1348–1530* (Macmillan, London, 1977).

12. F. R. H. Du Boulay, *An Age of Ambition: English Society in the Late Middle Ages* (Nelson, London, 1970); S. H. Rigby, 'Deference, Ambition and Resistance: English Society in the Later Middle Ages', in *Towards a New Time*, ed. G. Dahlbäck (Stockholm, Sällskapet Runica et Mediaevalia, forthcoming).

13. S. H. Rigby, *English Society in the Later Middle Ages* (Macmillan, Basingstoke, 1995), pp. 80–87, 124–7.

14. R. H. Hilton, *The English Peasantry in the Later Middle Ages* (Clarendon, Oxford, 1979), pp. 109–10; P. J. P. Goldberg, 'Female Labour, Service and Marriage in Northern Towns During the Later Middle Ages', *Northern History*, 22 (1986); P. J. P. Goldberg, 'Mortality and Economic Change in the Diocese of York, 1390–1514', *Northern History*, 24 (1988); P. J. P. Goldberg, 'Women's Work, Women's Role in the Late Medieval North', in *Profit, Piety and the Professions in Later Medieval England*, ed. M. A. Hicks (Sutton, Gloucester, 1990); P. J. P. Goldberg, *Women, Work and Life Cycle in a Medieval Economy: Women in York and Yorkshire, c.1300–1520* (Clarendon, Oxford, 1992).

15. P. J. P. Goldberg, 'Women in Fifteenth-century Town Life', in *Towns and Townspeople in the Fifteenth Century*, ed. J. A. F. Thomson (Sutton, Gloucester, 1988), pp. 121–2.

16. K. L. French, 'To Free Them from Binding: Women in the Late Medieval English Parish', *Journal of Interdisciplinary History*, 27 (1996–7), pp. 411–12.

17. C. M. Barron, 'The "Golden Age" of Women in Medieval London', *Reading Medieval Studies*, 15 (1989), pp. 46–7.

18. J. Hajnal, 'European Marriage Patterns in Perspective', in *Population in History*, ed. D. V. Glass and D. E. C. Eversley (Edward Arnold, London, 1974). Hajnal himself argued that the evidence of the poll taxes of 1377 suggested that late medieval England had a marriage pattern characterised by early marriage and uncontrolled fertility and that this shifted to one of uncontrolled fertility with late marriage by the sixteenth century.

19. R. M. Smith, 'Hypothèses sur la nuptialité en Angleterre aux XIIIe–XIVe siècles', *Annales E.S.C.*, 38 (1983); R. M. Smith, 'Human Resources', in *The Countryside of Medieval England*, ed. G. Astill and A. Grant (Basil Blackwell, Oxford, 1988), pp. 210–11; L. R. Poos, *A Rural Society After the Black Death: Essex 1350–1525* (Cambridge University Press, Cambridge, 1991), p. 129. Whether the northwest European marriage pattern existed in the *pre*-plague period has proved a controversial issue, see L. R. Poos, Z. Razi and R. M. Smith, 'The Population History of Medieval English Villages: A Debate on the Use of Manor Court Records', in *Medieval Society and the Manor Court*, ed. Z. Razi and R. M. Smith (Clarendon, Oxford, 1996), pp. 313–23, 333, 349–53, 363–7.

20. F. Parkin, *Class Inequality and Political Order* (Paladin, St Albans, 1973), pp. 14–15; N. Z. Davis, *Society and Culture in Early Modern France* (Stanford University Press, Stanford, 1975), p. xvii; G. E. Lenski, *Power and Privilege* (McGraw-Hill, New York, 1966), pp. 75, 79, 86–7.

21. M. K. Whyte, *The Status of Women in Preindustrial Societies* (Princeton University Press, Princeton, 1978), pp. 107–16, 168–79.

22. Goldberg, *Women, Work and Life Cycle in a Medieval Economy*, p. 337; Goldberg, 'Women in Fifteenth-century Town Life', p. 122; Barron, 'The "Golden Age" of Women in Medieval London', pp. 47–9.

23. M. Bailey, 'Demographic Decline in Late Medieval England: Some Thoughts on Recent Research', *Economic History Review*, 49 (1996), pp. 1–19.

24. For references, see J. M. Bennett, 'Medieval Women, Modern Women: Across the Great Divide', in *Culture and History, 1350–1600: Essays on English Communities, Identities and Writing*, ed. D. Aers (Harvester Wheatsheaf, New York, 1992), pp. 149–51.

25. Bennett, 'Medieval Women, Modern Women', p. 158; J. M. Bennett, *Ale, Beer and Brewsters in England: Women's Work in a Changing World, 1300–1600* (Oxford University Press, New York, 1996), especially ch. 8.

26. J. Whittle, review of Mate in *Economic History Review*, 52 (1999), p. 146.

13

Nunneries, Communities and the Revaluation of Domesticity

Felicity Riddy

Diane Watt (ed.), *Medieval Women in Their Communities* (University of Wales Press, Cardiff, 1997).

Jeffrey F. Hamburger, *Nuns as Artists: The Visual Culture of a Medieval Convent* (University of California Press, Berkeley, Los Angeles, London, 1997).

Marilyn Oliva, *The Convent and the Community in Late Medieval England: Female Monasteries in the Diocese of Norwich, 1350–1540,* Studies in the History of Religion XII (Boydell Press, Woodbridge, 1998).

All three of these books – a collection of essays and two monographs – seem to demand that we re-evaluate the domestic sphere. Ever since Aristotle, the *domus* has had a bad press. Lampooned in the middle ages by the anti-marriage brigade, it was the place where brats squalled, pots boiled over and wives nagged. Medieval women were not confined to the home, but they defined it: the idea of home had a woman in it. The everyday worlds evoked by preachers' exempla show this clearly: 'Hur husbond come home passand seke & bad hur make hym a cuche þat he myght lig on'; '... onone after þer come a duke & fand þis childe, and he sent it home vnto his wyfe becauce

he had no childe hym selfe'; 'And þis done, onone hur husband come home
fro huntyng & bad hur oppyn hym þe chamber dure, & he wold lay hym
down & slepe a while'.[1] The men go out and come back, knowing that at
home there is a woman waiting, who will make up a couch, receive a child,
or open the bedroom door. As Rosalynn Voaden points out, in the excellent
collection of essays edited and intelligently introduced by Diane Watt:
'Women were – and usually still are – far more likely than men ... to be kept
inside by domestic chores, maternal responsibilities and patriarchal restrictions. As nuns, they were cloistered, not permitted the wandering life of the
friar or the public exposure of the preacher' (p. 83). Although I do not think
we should take women's enclosure too literally (Marilyn Oliva shows that
even nunneries had a good deal of contact with the world outside), nevertheless it makes sense to see the home as associated with the things women
do and know about.

Revaluing the domestic sphere in the light of what these writers are telling
us means seeing it as more than the locale of marriage. 'Home' takes many
forms in these books: the convent, the town house, the anchorhold, the
beguinage, the country manor. There is a strong recuperative drive to much
of what is written here: for both Hamburger and Oliva, as well as for most
of the authors of the essay collection, femininity or femaleness or womanhood represents an alternative but not inferior mode of being or knowing or
doing. It seems to me, though, that what is at issue is not simply femininity
per se, but also the living space in which femininity is played out. For example, Penelope Galloway's exceptionally informative essay on the neglected
northern French beguine communities in the thirteenth and fourteenth centuries presents a picture of the beguine movement as fluid, unstructured and
essentially domestic. The smaller beguinages must often have looked like
the ordinary homes of the poor: the first beguines were the daughters of
bourgeois families who renounced their parents' ambitions for them in order
to embrace lives of poverty, chastity and hard work. They made their livings
by doing the things that no doubt their mothers had taught them: they
wove, spun, sewed and laundered; they cared for the sick and taught school.
They offered up women's household chores to God. The movement – if so
loose, spontaneous and everyday a phenomenon can be called that – seems
to have been extraordinarily successful, attracting aristocratic female patronage as well as humbler bequests from the townspeople among whom the
beguines lived.

In contrast to this, Jane Cartwright produces the surprising fact that
there was hardly any provision in late medieval Wales for women to enter the
religious life (there were only three Welsh nunneries, compared with fifteen
in Scotland, about sixty-four in Ireland and around 150 in England). There
were no informal options, either – no beguinages or hospitals – so Welsh
women's spirituality must have been channelled almost exclusively into chaste

marriages, muddled up within the domestic sphere with the squalling brats and the boiling pots. The spirituality of married women with family responsibilities is an area we need to know more about, and not just for Wales. It is worth recalling that even the autobiographical narrative of the fifteenth-century English townswoman Margery Kempe (the subject of a thorough essay by Janet Wilson), which is so concerned with compulsive travelling, was actually composed, so we are told, back at Lynn in her own chamber. Her life may have been mobile and exotic; writing about it was a domestic activity intertwined, in its first phase at least, with cleaning up after her incontinent elderly husband.

For nuns, writing was a domestic activity too. Marie-Luise Ehrenschwendtner's striking essay in *Medieval Women in Their Communities* addresses the old problem of the relation of women religious to Latin. She argues that the Dominican nuns of southern Germany in the thirteenth and fourteenth centuries used the vernacular by choice everywhere except in chapel. Their vocation was not, like that of the Dominican friars, to preach or exercise pastoral care outside their convents. Their calling was to prayer, and so the study of Latin theology was irrelevant to their strict enclosure. Study for its own sake was anyway never part of the Dominican ideal. Confined in a way the men were not, they spoke – of course – everyone's first language of the home. And so they read translations and wrote original works in the vernacular, developing within their convents a prayer life of intense, mystically influenced spirituality. Ehrenschwendtner contrasts the Dominican sisters with the Latin-learned nuns of Helfta in the late thirteenth century, who belonged to an older and more conservative Cistercian tradition in which training in the liberal arts was held to be a precondition of monastic contemplation. The story of these same Helfta nuns, especially Gertrude the Great and Mechtild of Hackeborne, is picked up in Rosalynn Voaden's fine essay. Their writings are in Latin (though when Gertrude the Great began having visions at twenty-five she gave up Latin learning), but the domestic setting they shared fed into their transformation of the cult of the Sacred Heart 'as a place of shelter, a home for the community of the faithful, a sanctuary where they could be comforted and restored' (p. 74). Their fluid, interconnected writings are infused, Voaden argues, with an awareness of the female body's physicality and with the imagery of enclosure as a place of mutual indwelling. I would add that the indwelling takes remarkably domestic forms: Christ's heart is a house, a kitchen; through its gate runs a flood of cleansing water.

Jeffrey Hamburger devotes a chapter in *Nuns as Artists: The Visual Culture of a Medieval Convent* to the heart as a house. His book is a fascinating and redemptive study of twelve apparently naive little pictures drawn around 1500 by a nun of St Walburg's Abbey, Eichstatt, in Bavaria. They are all devotional images in what Hamburger is able to identify as a conventual style that is used elsewhere as well: the figures all have the cheerful round faces and rosy cheeks of old-fashioned clothes-peg dolls. Hamburger's aim in this book (which contains handsome colour reproductions of ten of the twelve pictures) is to find a way of talking about these images that does not patronise them or assume that the *Malerin*, or convent painter, was trying to do what her male contemporaries were doing, but failing. Insofar as they have been paid any attention to at all, the pictures from St Walburg have been lumped together by scholars with other late-medieval products of German convents as *Nonnenarbeiten* or 'nuns' works' (though, as Hamburger points out, no one dreams of lumping paintings by Fra Angelico and Fra Lippo Lippi together as 'friars' works'). The St Walburg artist was apparently unaware of the techniques of the contemporary high art produced by formally trained guild masters such as Schongauer, Strigel or Holbein the Elder, whose drawings have recently been exhibited at the National Gallery of Art in Washington.[2] Nevertheless, as Hamburger is able to show, some of the twelve pictures from St Walburg are the products of sophisticated ways of thinking about the self in relation to the divine. For example, one of these images, now in Berlin, depicts the house of the heart, in which the heart is both the viewer's and Christ's: it is an image of interiority and divine love. The little picture shows the heart-house from the outside, with steps going up from the flowery garden that surrounds it to a bolted door, while through an open window can be seen the soul, an apple-cheeked golden-haired girl, being embraced by the Trinity. God the Father, with Christ and the Holy Spirit in the form of a dove on his knee, is seated on an altar, on which stands a chalice. Vernacular inscriptions on scrolls support a mystical and eucharistic interpretation of the image. The topos of the heart as the dwelling-place of the soul is, as Hamburger points out, an ancient one; the heart can also signify the monastic cell as a place of contemplative withdrawal: the nun's own home, in fact. He spends a chapter skilfully tracing a web of interconnecting texts and images – the Song of Songs, *Herzklosterallegorien* (in which the heart is allegorised as architecture), Mechtild of Hackeborne's *Liber specialis gratiae*, a drawing in Magdalena of Freiburg's meditations on the Paternoster, an illustration in Suso's *Exemplar* and so on – which show that the apparently naive picture is a creative contribution to a long-standing and fluid meditative tradition.

Cynthia Kraman's fascinating article on 'Communities of Otherness in the *Merchant's Tale*', which is in some ways an oddity in *Medieval Women in Their Communities*, reverberates off Hamburger extremely suggestively. Kraman argues that the Song of Songs, referred to several times in the *Merchant's Tale*, offers an opposing model of marriage to January's 'onanistic fantasy' of possession; 'the confusion of speakers', she comments, 'points to the flowingness and exchange which characterize the *Song*'. In medieval Jewish commentary, which fed into thirteenth-century scholastic commentary, marriage rather than virginity was 'the sacred model', a model not for containment but for reciprocity. Kraman's way of talking about the Song of Songs, with its shifting voices, its attachment of body to landscape, its lovers' exchange of desires, its creation of 'an impossible liminal territory of the word in conjunction with the free imagination' (p. 143), all seems directly relevant to the erotic mysticism based on the Song of Songs that underlies the drawings from St Walburg: 'The Canticle', says Hamburger, 'provides the cues for a passion consummated in the nun's body as well as Christ's, with the heart of each the place where this ecstatic introspection is consummated' (p. 136). No one before Hamburger, so far as I know, has attempted a full-scale study of pictures of this kind in their own terms, locating them in a wide-ranging but largely unregarded female devotional culture.

The other monograph, Marilyn Oliva's *The Convent and the Community in Late Medieval England,* is a systematic study of the personnel, organisation and social functions of the eleven female monasteries in the diocese of Norwich from 1350 to 1540. Five were Benedictine, three Augustinian, one Gilbertine, one Cistercian and one Poor Clares. The book starts from a similar position to Hamburger's: Oliva points out how little has been written about female monasticism since Eileen Power's *Medieval English Nunneries* was published in 1922, and suggests that this is because in general nunneries are perceived as being too poor, too unaristocratic and too local to command the interest that has been paid to male houses. In order to understand the significance of the female monastic life, we need a different set of criteria, or to use the criteria differently. As Roberta Gilchrist and others have pointed out, the poverty of nunneries may not, after all, have been because they failed to attract patronage, as if the aim of all monastic institutions was necessarily to enrich themselves. Poverty may have been embraced by these nuns as an apostolic virtue and a form of penance, as it was by the beguines. And their social origins – Oliva shows that East Anglian nuns were largely from parish gentry families or urban elites – are far from insignificant: they may reflect the greater freedom of daughters of the middling sort to decide whether or not to marry, compared with daughters of the aristocracy. (The same seems to be true of the urban women who flocked into beguinages across the Channel.) Oliva's evidence, which challenges Power's view that late-medieval nunneries were mostly inhabited by aristocratic women, can be put alongside the evidence that Jeremy Goldberg and Shannon McSheffrey have produced about young urbanites choosing their own marriage partners. Whom to marry, and whether to marry at all, look as if they are related choices; aristocratic daughters seem to have been too important to family property strategies to be allowed either. And nunneries require us to shift attention from the national to the local scene, to their role in parish life both as centres of worship (most East Anglian nunneries allowed local people to use their churches) and as sources of neighbourly charitableness. Reading this book alongside Jennifer Ward's essay in *Medieval Women in Their Communities*, on English noblewomen and their more distant relation to their localities, makes clear just how middling the convents were.

Hamburger's work is quite different methodologically from Oliva's, which is not surprising given their different disciplines. Both are exhaustive, but in different ways. In the face of the limitations of his evidence (all he has from St Walburg, apparently, are the pictures, some tapestries, some sculptures and some manuscripts), Hamburger is willing to speculate in order to present a detailed and eclectic context of mystical and paraliturgical writings, images and material objects, going back over several centuries and across geographical boundaries. The problems he faces (and which I do not think he entirely solves) are where to stop and how to explain the *Malerin*'s familiarity with all this: how does she know as much as he knows? He is not concerned to trace the routes by which the kind of spirituality he attributes to St Walburg might have been disseminated: it all seems to proceed by a process of osmosis. It may be that the evidence is not to be found, and I certainly do not want to take Hamburger to task for not having written a different kind of work, when what he has done is so rich.

Oliva's book, by contrast with Hamburger's, is a prosopographical study that carefully marshals detailed empirical evidence about 553 individuals, which she uses as the basis for statistical arguments (she is able to work out, for example, that there must have been roughly one thousand nuns in the Norwich diocese during the period she studies), and slowly builds up a case for the unsensational ordinariness of female monastic living. As she describes it, it was a way of life shaped by prioresses' competent running of their households, and by the unscandalous behaviour of nuns who, though enclosed, were not out of contact with the world outside. Visitors came and went; the poor required succour; children needed to be taught. There are very few wayward nuns here; instead it is a narrative of consistency and decency. The book is pitched at several points explicitly against Eileen Power, who was generally sceptical about nuns' moral and intellectual achievements in the later middle ages. (One can't help feeling, for example, that she might have been pretty sniffy about the St Walburg-artist's picture of the bearded St Kümmernis, otherwise known as Wilgefortis or Uncumber, whose origins lie in a misinterpretation of the *Volto Santo*. Even the generous-minded Hamburger has little to say about this picture.) Nevertheless the argument that Ehrenschwendtner offers about the irrelevance of Latin learning to south German Dominican nuns also applies here: the calling of these English-women was thoroughly domestic; they prayed, they taught school, they conscientiously fed the poor. Oliva is able to show that they did not fiddle their books in relation to alms-giving as several men's houses did.

What is lacking from Oliva's study, because it is lacking in her sources, is a sense of the quality of the nuns' lives (to which she devotes three pages), or how their days were filled. Was the spirituality of German convents around 1500 quite different from that of England, or should we assume that East Anglian nuns too practised passionate and intensely self-aware forms of a religion of the heart? One of the sources Hamburger uses to illuminate the spirituality of St Walburg is a fifteenth-century English manuscript associated with the Carthusian priory of Mountgrace in Yorkshire (London, British Library, Additional 37049), famous for its drawings of blood-spattered Christs and bleeding hearts. Although he does not argue for the relevance of English evidence to a German image, nevertheless the illustrations he uses make their own point, and seem to arise out of a shared world of mystically influenced spirituality. One point of direct contact between St Walburg and the Norwich diocese is Gerhard of Liège's *De doctrina cordis*, a Middle High German version of which was in the library of St Walburg,[3] while an English version, *The doctrine of the herte*, was owned by Margaret Yaxle, a nun of Bruisyard.[4] *De doctrina cordis* is a mystical text which at one point uses the trope of the heart as a house; Hamburger proposes it as a parallel to, though not a source of, the St Walburg picture of the house of the heart. He does not say much about prayer books, especially psalters and books of hours, though these, too, are full of references to the heart. The reader of the psalter – and several of these survive from the nunneries of the Norwich diocese – is offered an interiorised and embodied subjectivity, in which interiority is above all located in the heart as the centre of feeling and understanding. Susannah Mary Chewning's article in *Medieval Women in Their Communities* draws attention to an English mystical and female-oriented tradition in the thirteenth-century texts, known as the 'Wooing Group' (þe *Wohunge of Ure Lauerd, One God Ureison of Ure Lefdi, On Wel Swuðe God Ureison of God Almighti, On Lofsong of Ure Louerde* and *On Lofsong of Ure Lefdi*). They constitute what Chewning calls a 'non-traditional, non-mainstream' and culturally feminine means of expression: 'submissive, fallen, biologically-centred and driven by desire' (p. 128). We do not necessarily have to subscribe to Chewning's now slightly dated-looking roll-call of French feminist theorists (the essay was first read as a paper in 1994) in order to assent to the drift of her arguments, and to see a parallel with Hamburger's use of thirteenth-century German mystical writings to illuminate the spirituality of St Walburg in 1500.

Closer to home, J. A. Tasioulas, in an elegant article in *Medieval Women in Their Communities*, toys with the idea that the Marian plays in the N-town cycle, which is East Anglian in origin, might have been written for nuns – in which case we might even be able to locate their performance within one of Oliva's nunneries. Tasioulas rejects this thought, however, in favour of a wider audience for the 'complicated blend of theology [relating to the Immaculate Conception] and domesticity' (p. 240) that the plays offer. Nuns are daughters before they are sisters, though: Oliva tells us that on average they entered their convents at around fifteen, not as children like the nuns of Helfta. They must have brought with them, and perhaps never lost, their knowledge of the rich devotional traditions of their region, evidenced not only in plays and processions but in the carving, the glass and the wall-paintings of its parish churches. This is the region that produced two women visionary writers in two generations, one of them a theologian: Julian of Norwich and Margery Kempe. The latter was quite a frequent visitor at Denny, the Cambridgeshire house of Poor Clares, while Julian, whoever she was, may even have been a nun in one of the convents of the Norwich diocese, before she became an anchoress at St Julian's, Conesford, in Norwich.[5] In fact the example of Julian of Norwich could be used to suggest that, indeed, passionate and intensely self-aware forms of a religion of the heart were available to devout women in the Norwich diocese in the late middle ages. Julian's commitment to the vernacular – we do not know whether she had Latin, but she does not use it – which nevertheless goes along with a sophisticated knowledge of old and new theological ideas, sounds very like the cultural situation of the south German Dominican nuns that Ehrenschwendtner describes: they read vernacular theology and 'their preachers were trained theologians, who took up a range of learned topics in their sermons; and in the confessional the nuns could discuss religious questions'. And Julian's sense of the divine is, like the St Walburg artist's, domestic: 'homely' is one of the key words in her book of revelations. The sixteenth and last of these revelations begins: 'And then oure good lorde opynnyd my gostely eye and shewde me my soule in the myddys of my hert. ... and by the condicions þat I saw there in I vnderstode þat it is a wurschypfulle cytte, in myddes of that cytte sitts oure lorde Jhesu, very god and very man.' And a little later: 'The place that Jhesu takyth in oure soule he shall nevyr remoue withouten ende, for in vs is his homlyest home and his endlesse dwellyng'.[6] Here, it seems, Norwich and St Walburg meet.

Notes

1. Mary Macleod Banks (ed.), *An Alphabet of Tales*, EETS OS 126, 127 (Kegan Paul, London, 1904, 1905; repr. in 1 vol., Kraus Reprint, Millwood, NY, 1987), pp. 26, 393, 117.
2. See *From Schongauer to Holbein: Master Drawings from Basel and Berlin* (Hatje Cantz Publishers, National Library of Washington, Washington, 1999).
3. See Hamburger, *Nuns as Artists*, pp. 162, 163, 170.
4. See Oliva, *The Convent and the Community*, p. 68.
5. There is some confusion in Oliva's dating of Julian and in the location of the anchorhold. Julian was born in 1342/3 and therefore could not have been at Carrow between 1433 and 1478 (p. 130). St Julian's was not 'adjacent' to Carrow (pp. 155, 173), but was within the city walls while Carrow was outside them.
6. Edmund Colledge, OSA and James Walsh, SJ (eds), *A Book of Showings to the Anchoress Julian of Norwich*, 2 vols (Pontifical Institute of Medieval Studies, Toronto, 1978), vol. 2, pp. 639, 641.

NOTES ON CONTRIBUTORS

Leslie Brubaker is Senior Lecturer in Byzantine Studies at the University of Birmingham. Her most recent books are *Vision and Meaning in Ninth-Century Byzantium* (1999) and, with J. F. Haldon, *Sources in Byzantine Iconoclasm* (2000). An earlier article on gender, 'Memories of Helena', appeared in *Women, Men and Eunuchs*, ed. L. James (1997).

Kate Cooper is Senior Lecturer in Early Christianity and Director of the Centre for Late Antiquity at the University of Manchester. Her publications include *The Virgin and the Bride: Idealized Womanhood in Late Antiquity* (1996), and she is currently finishing a book on early medieval devotional literature for married women.

Katherine J. Lewis is a lecturer in History at the University of Huddersfield. She is the author of *The Cult of St Katherine of Alexandria in Later Medieval England* and co-editor of *Young Medieval Women*. She has also published several articles on aspects of the cults of saints Katherine and Margaret in later medieval England.

Conrad Leyser is Lecturer in Medieval History at the University of Manchester. His publications include *Authority and Asceticism from Augustine to Gregory the Great* (2000), and he is presently at work on a study of family-based patronage in the early middle ages.

Anneke B. Mulder-Bakker is a senior lecturer in Medieval History and Medieval Studies at the Rijksuniversiteit Groningen (Netherlands). She has published on historiographical and hagiographical topics, including *Sanctity and Motherhood* (1995) and is presently working on a book on female anchorites (recluses) in the Low Countries.

Janet L. Nelson is Professor of Medieval History at King's College London. She has written quite widely on women's history, and, more recently, on gender, in the earlier middle ages. She is President-elect of the Royal Historical Society.

Cordula Nolte works at the historical institute of the Ernst-Moritz-Arndt University of Greifswald. Her current research is on the family and kinship networks of princely families of the empire in the fifteenth and early sixteenth. She is the author of *Conversio und Christianitas: Frauen in der Christianisierung vom 5. bis 8. Jahrhundert* (1995).

Felicity Riddy is a professor of English at the University of York. She is writing a book on late medieval domesticity, and is director of a research project on late medieval urban manuscripts.

S. H. Rigby is Reader in History at the University of Manchester. He has published a number of works on social theory and medieval social history, including *English Society in the Later Middle Ages*, *Chaucer in Context* and *Marxism and History*.

Ludwig Schmugge has been Professor of Medieval History at the University of Zurich since 1979. He is editor-in-chief of the *Repertorium Poenitentiariae Germanicum* (German Historical Institute, Rome; 3 vols to date, 3 more in preparation).

Patricia Skinner is a lecturer in Medieval History at the University of Southampton. Her work focuses on the history of southern Italy, and she has published *Family Power in Southern Italy: The Duchy of Gaeta and its Neighbours, 850–1139* (1995), as well as a number of articles on women's status in this region in *Early Medieval Europe, Reading Medieval Studies* and *Women's History Review*. She has just completed a book, *Women in Medieval Italian Society, c.500–1300*, to be published by Longman.

Julia M. H. Smith is Reader in Mediaeval History at the University of St Andrews, where she teaches late antique and early medieval history. She publishes widely on politics, religion and gender in early medieval Europe and is currently co-editing a volume of essays on *Gender and the Transformation of the Roman World*.

Pauline Stafford is Professor of Medieval History at the University of Liverpool and the author of *Queen Emma and Queen Edith: Queenship and Women's Power in Eleventh-century England* (1997) and *Queens, Concubines, and Dowagers: The King's Wife in the Early Middle Ages* (2nd edn, 1998).

Eva M. Synek studied Theology and History in Vienna followed by additional studies in Salzburg of Law. Since 1991 she has been Research Assistant at the Institute for Law and Religion, University of Vienna. In 1999 she gained her habilitation for Patristic Studies, History of the Ancient Church and Early Ecclesiastical Legal History in Eichstätt, Germany.

Helen Tobler received a BA from the University of Birmingham in East Mediterranean History in 1997, with a dissertation on 'Images of Empresses on Byzantine Coins'. She is now working in Switzerland.

Rosalynn Voaden teaches medieval literature in the Department of English at Arizona State University. She is the author of *God's Words, Women's Voices: The Discernment of Spirits in the Writing of Medieval Women Visionaries* and is currently at work on *Household Saints*, a study of holiness and domesticity in the late middle ages.

Stephanie Volf is a PhD student at Arizona State University where she is writing a dissertation that examines non-verbal speech in mystical and hagiographic writings by and about women.

Index